THE EARLY CHILDHOOD DIRECTOR'S GUIDE to SOLVING EVERYDAY CHALLENGES

by Thomasa Bond, EdD

Gryphon House
www.gryphonhouse.com

Copyright

Published by Gryphon House, Inc.
P. O. Box 10, Lewisville, NC 27023
800.638.0928; 877.638.7576 [fax]
Visit us on the web at www.gryphonhouse.com.

Library of Congress Control Number: 2021942820

Bulk Purchase

Gryphon House books are available for special premiums and sales promotions as well as for fund-raising use. Special editions or book excerpts also can be created to specifications. For details, call 800.638.0928.

Disclaimer

Gryphon House, Inc., cannot be held responsible for damage, mishap, or injury incurred during the use of or because of activities in this book. Appropriate and reasonable caution and adult supervision of children involved in activities and corresponding to the age and capability of each child involved are recommended at all times. Do not leave children unattended at any time. Observe safety and caution at all times.

This book is not intended to give legal or financial advice. All financial and legal opinions contained herein are from the personal research and experience of the author and are intended as educational material. Seek the advice of a qualified legal advisor or financial advisor before making legal or financial decisions.

Table of Contents

Acknowledgments iv

Introduction v

Chapter 1: The Many Roles of a Program Director 1

Chapter 2: Meeting and Maintaining Licensing 23

Chapter 3: Building and Equipment Maintenance and Safety 33

Chapter 4: Child Health and Safety 45

Chapter 5: Classroom Arrangement and Management 91

Chapter 6: Caring for Infants and Toddlers 115

Chapter 7: Developmentally Appropriate Classroom Practices and Pedagogy 121

Chapter 8: Challenges with Parents 139

Chapter 9: Challenges with Children's Behavior 157

Chapter 10: Challenges with Staff 169

Chapter 11: Outdoor Play 187

Appendix: Online Resources 197

References and Recommended Reading 201

Index 207

Acknowledgments

First, I would like to thank the Lord for giving me the strength that I never thought I had to complete a task that I did not believe was attainable. I would not have been successful in completing this book without the support of my husband, David P. Bond, Sr. It was his love, patience, support, and encouragement that allowed me the opportunity to complete my second book. I would like to recognize my son, David II (DJ), for his love, encouragement, and endless assistance, and my daughter, Ashley, for her love and support. Mostly, I would like to thank my mother, Lucille Spates, who was with me in spirit. She instilled in me the confidence and tenacity needed to complete this book. I wish to express my sincere gratitude to my extended family, friends, and coworkers for their support and encouragement.

Introduction

Having worked in the early childhood field for more than thirty-five years, I have had the opportunity to work in multiple positions: student assistant; lead teacher for toddlers, preschoolers, and school-age children; program director; and educational coordinator. I earned a doctorate in education with a concentration in organizational leadership, with a minor in early childhood education. Currently, I am employed as a child-care licensing consultant, where I interact daily with a diverse population of early childhood professionals.

I started my career as a student assistant at the university lab school, which is why today I have a great appreciation for observation. The school had a one-way mirror in each classroom, and you never knew when you were being observed. (I'll discuss the importance of direct observation throughout the book.) After graduating, I worked for Head Start as a preschool lead teacher, center director, and education coordinator. Later, I worked as a program director for a chain center. After the birth of my second child, I worked part-time as a before- and after-school teacher for a school district, and then I moved to a position as a full-time toddler lead teacher. Within two years, I became the director of the program; this was my third program-director position. Each position was with a different type of organization that had different policies and required procedures. The only thing that did not change was the state requirements. For this very reason, I understand how important it is to know the licensing rules—with each new position, the licensing rules are one less thing to learn.

I served as a program director for many years before my licensing consultant encouraged me to apply for the open licensing position. I was not sure if I wanted to leave my position as a program director because I was very comfortable and the licensing position would create a substantial change for my family. One of the main reasons I decided to apply for the position was my desire to help child-care centers provide the best care possible for the children and families they serve.

This book is a resource that I wish I had had when I was first promoted to the program director position. At the time, I thought I was fully prepared to handle the new position. I can laugh about that now, because I had no idea what the program director position actually involved. I literally learned on the job and made mistakes along the way. My hope is that this book will help new and current program directors to avoid some of the mistakes that I have made and witnessed.

One of the things I've learned is that organization is crucial. I have been at centers where program directors have the required information, but they cannot locate it and they become frustrated. For years, I've blogged and presented at conferences on preparing for licensing inspections by reviewing the required postings, policies, procedures, and other inspection information. Being prepared and maintaining compliance will create a level of confidence between the program director and staff members. An organized program director can provide staff with the knowledge and support needed to be comfortable and confident within their positions, which will transfer to their interactions with the children and parents.

This book is designed to provide current and future early childhood program directors a solid foundation for managing staff and successfully operating a center. You will learn organizational tips and tools needed to help you become a productive and successful leader. This book examines common issues that directors and staff have experienced at real child-care centers. There are times when child-care professionals may feel like they are alone and they are the only ones who have experienced issues. I offer scenarios of actual situations[1] I've encountered, to show you are not alone in your experiences! And because there are always two sides to a story, whenever possible I offer the perspectives of both the director or staff and parents. This is not a book to place blame or to make anyone feel guilty or ashamed. It is designed to show how to avoid mistakes, oversights, accidents, and incidents as much as possible by developing and implementing policies and procedures and training staff to prevent these scenarios from occurring.

HOW THIS BOOK IS ORGANIZED

In the first chapter, I discuss the program director's qualifications and the role of the position, the importance of being a strong leader, how requirements for education and experience differ from state to state, and the different types of business models for child-care centers.

Each subsequent chapter is organized around an area of particular challenges. We'll explore licensing concerns and ways to reduce the anxiety related to onsite inspections. We'll look at how to maintain the building, and child health and safety. In chapter 5, we'll explore classroom arrangement and management. In chapters 6 and 7, we'll examine practices and pedagogy with infants and toddlers and with preschoolers. In chapters 8, 9, and 10, we will explore ways to successfully navigate challenges

[1] I've changed the names and altered any identifying factors to protect the privacy of those involved.

with parents, with children, and with staff. In chapter 11, we'll wrap things up with outdoor play. For each scenario I include, I describe an event that actually happened and then describe a resolution. In most cases, the resolutions are positive; in some, however, they were opportunities for learning even though they were not necessarily positive. I also offer ways to reduce the risk of an incident occurring and ideas for positive resolution if an incident does occur.

I offer information you can use to create policies and procedures to be *proactive* so that you can reduce the need to be *reactive* when an issue occurs. With sound policies and procedures in place, staff training will reduce mistakes. Through the scenarios outlined in the book, I will provide ways for staff and parents to work together, because when staff and parents support each other the children will flourish.

CHAPTER 1

The Many Roles of a Program Director

A child-care program director must wear many hats and multitask daily. Depending on the type of center, the program director's responsibilities may vary somewhat, but on any given day her duties may include the following:

- Greeting children
- Maintaining an open-door policy for parents, children, and staff
- Meeting with parents
- Recruiting, interviewing, and hiring new staff
- Training staff
- Observing classrooms
- Evaluating staff
- Addressing discipline issues with children
- Collecting tuition
- Conducting tours for prospective parents and enrolling new parents
- Paying the bills
- Reviewing and maintaining staff files
- Reviewing and maintaining children's files
- Scheduling field trips
- Caring for sick children

- Covering classrooms when needed
- Addressing staff concerns
- Maintaining accreditation
- Maintaining compliance with the state licensing requirements
- Creating menus and ordering or shopping for supplies
- Cooking and serving meals
- Overseeing building maintenance and arranging repairs
- Rewarding, reprimanding, or terminating staff
- Reviewing the teachers' lesson plans
- Conducting regular staff meetings
- Marketing the center to increase enrollment
- Managing the budget
- Handling payroll
- Supervising or screening volunteers
- Supervising specialists, such as speech pathologists, social workers, and occupational therapists
- Representing the center in the community

Yes, it is a lot! It is also an incredibly important and rewarding job. Child-care program directors nurture and influence the development of young children every day. In doing so, they help support families and ensure that children have a strong start in life.

QUALITIES OF A STRONG PROGRAM DIRECTOR

A skilled program director has interpersonal abilities beyond the required education and experience and an understanding of the state and program requirements. Let's explore the role of the program director in more detail and discover ways to be successful with the leadership and organizational portion of the position.

In his book *Introduction to Leadership* (2021), Northouse notes that there is no one path to take to become a successful leader because the process is complex. In my opinion, leadership qualities are a way of life, not the position you hold. Leadership is the transformation of yourself and others. Gini and Green (2014) define the role this way: "Leaders help to set the tone, develop the vision, and shape the behavior of all those involved in organizational life." Some leadership skills, such as friendliness, sensitivity, and empathy, are ingrained.

Leaders are confident in their abilities and the decisions that they make. They are also determined to motivate their staff to perform the necessary tasks to the best of their abilities. The program director's success or failure is directly related to the cooperation of the staff. These leaders are charismatic and engaging with their employees, the parents, the children, and the community at large. They maintain an open-door policy that generates two-way communication between themselves and the staff. They provide consistency during their interactions, maintaining their integrity and the integrity of the center. They are articulate and communicate their vision for the center and expectations of the staff without abusing their power.

The program director should have previous experience working with children in a child-care setting. She should be able to articulate how she will perform the required duties in a timely and efficient manner. The program director should continue to learn and improve her skills by staying current on research and issues that are affecting the early childhood field. She should have the capability to change course as necessary and to address situations when they arise. A program director should also be able to acknowledge the areas where she needs growth in her leadership abilities.

The director sets the tone for the center. An effective program director cares for, nurtures, and directs the staff in a way that produces an appropriate atmosphere for the children and families served. In contrast, an ineffective program director is negative and focuses on the staff's mistakes. An effective director is a competent communicator. An ineffective program director lacks people skills. An effective program director explains what is needed and why. An ineffective director gives orders without explanation or a reason. An effective director is well organized and conducts regular staff meetings; an ineffective director is disorganized and does not consistently hold staff meetings. An effective director talks *with* the staff and listens; an ineffective director talks *at* the staff and is unwilling to listen to their concerns. An effective director is committed to the growth of the program and its staff. An ineffective director does not encourage staff to attend early childhood conferences or workshops or to develop their skills.

The best leaders use their power with intellect by placing their priorities on meeting and exceeding the program's goals and objectives. They recognize the staff's strengths and encourage them to develop their skills in that area. They also recognize the staff's weaknesses and provide training and support to improve their skills. They possess excellent conflict-resolution skills. The leader has to be able to both lead and follow.

STRONG INTERPERSONAL SKILLS

People skills are important because it is not what you say but how you say it that makes the difference. Chawla and Renesch (2006) define *people skills* as an individual's ability to communicate in a positive, effective manner with employees. Positive communication is very important in all areas because people want to be respected and treated fairly. Chawla and Renesch point out that individuals with various skills can make it to the top, but interpersonal effectiveness is required to maintain that leadership position. Individuals tend to follow leaders who are more charismatic because they have the ability to create a work environment where employees are empowered to be innovative. According to Sergiovanni (2007), charismatic leaders know and focus on what is important. They care deeply about their work and learn from their successes and failures. These individuals tend to take calculated risks and tend to be trustworthy. They share knowledge and are often leaders within an organization before they gain the official title.

Strong leaders hold the knowledge of the organization's goal and objectives, and they are successful in incorporating the best practices to meet and exceed the organization's objectives. These individuals are not only confident in their abilities and decisions; they are also determined to be the best while motivating the staff to perform to the best of their abilities.

A HANDS-ON ROLE MODEL

Many individuals see the role of the program director as a desk position with minimal classroom interactions. However, the actual role requires overseeing the day-to-day operations and establishing and maintaining the overall philosophy of the center. The program director can lead by empowering the employees within their positions, giving employees the confidence to perform at a higher level, which, in turn, will elevate the program.

I have discovered over the years that the best program directors are hands-on in the classrooms but do not micromanage. They are able to work with many different personalities and bring out the best in their staff while meeting the needs of the families. They influence the staff by modeling the appropriate behavior that sets the tone for the center. If the staff observe the program director behaving poorly or inappropriately, they will get the idea that their poor behavior will be excused, or they will view a correction of their behavior as hypocritical. Program directors must be professional in their actions and proactive rather than reactive when situations arise.

Effective program directors know their staff and recognize their strengths and their weaknesses. They set high expectations, provide the necessary training to develop and grow the staff, and recognize and reward their staff members' individual strengths. Their expectations do not change, and they do not alter their style based on their mood or outside influences. Employees appreciate program directors who provide support, guidance, and correction when needed.

They allow flexibility in the ways their staff fulfill their duties, so long as the tasks are completed. They recognize that there are many ways to provide a developmentally appropriate classroom environment for the children; if that goal is achieved, then parents will be satisfied.

When issues arise, a strong program director is an effective communicator, a good listener, and offers prompt, constructive, and specific feedback. As Cooper, Robertson, and Tinline (2003) point out, "Feedback should be given face to face, not via written communications. The feedback should be linked to a plan of action and feedback should be provided as soon as possible."

Caregiver Hit a Child on the Hand

PROBLEM

Jill, the assistant program director, was standing in the hallway when she saw Senna, a parent, walk out of the toddler classroom with her daughter. Shortly after, Kiki, the toddler teacher, asked Jill to come to her classroom because she needed help. Kiki told her that she had hit a child named Jace on the hand a few times while Senna was in the classroom. Senna asked Kiki if hitting the children was allowed at the center, and Kiki replied that it was not allowed but that Jace was not listening and she was trying to keep him safe.

Jill checked Jace for any bruising. Jace was not crying and had no visible marks on either of his hands. Jill told Kiki to leave the classroom and wait for Lizzy, the program director. Jill called the office to inform Lizzy, who stated that she was speaking with Senna.

Senna informed Lizzy that she had just witnessed Kiki hitting Jace on the hand three or four times. She said she had asked Kiki if hitting is allowed per the center's discipline policy. Senna stated that Kiki admitted to hitting Jace's hand and that hitting was not allowed at the center. Senna reported that Kiki had said that she had asked Jace to stop touching the toys, but he would not listen. Senna was extremely concerned that Kiki was hitting Jace and was obviously not following the center's discipline policy. Senna was so upset by what she had witnessed that she promptly disenrolled her daughter from the center.

Lizzy headed to the toddler classroom and found Kiki standing outside the room. They returned to the director's office where Lizzy asked Kiki about Senna's allegations. Kiki admitted to hitting Jace on the hand. She explained that she had asked Jace to stop touching the toys that had been put away and that he had just looked at her. She said she was trying to get Jace to stop touching the toys because the area was closed and she did not want him to get hurt. She said she only hit him on the hand to get him to listen to her.

RESOLUTION

Lizzy terminated Kiki's employment but not before explaining to her how wrong her actions were and that under no circumstances are any teachers, staff, or volunteers allowed to hit a child. Instead, they are to use redirection and verbal reminders when a child is not listening. Lizzy was upset that one of her employees would hit a child.

When Jace's mother, Rosa, arrived to pick him up, Lizzy informed her that another parent had witnessed a caregiver hitting Jace on the hand. Lizzy explained that that behavior was not allowed at the center and the staff person had been immediately terminated. Rosa was not happy that a staff person had hit her son, but she appreciated the fact that Lizzy had informed her and that the person was no longer employed at the center. Lizzy also told Rosa that she had scheduled a training at the end of the week to retrain all of the staff on the center's discipline policy. Rosa did not disenroll Jace.

Staff must understand that if they get in a power struggle with a child, they will lose every time. When Jace refused to do as Kiki asked, she should have redirected him to an alternative activity or even considered letting him play in the closed area. To reduce temptation when a center is closed and the teacher wants children to engage in a different activity, she can simply turn the cabinet around or cover the toys. Children are unlikely to try to play with toys they cannot see.

When staff are trained (or retrained), they should sign an acknowledgement that they have received, read, and understand the discipline policy and the ramifications of not following the policy.

SUPPORTIVE

An effective program director creates a supportive atmosphere that shows her commitment to the staff and their professional growth. She holds regular staff meetings and encourages the staff to discuss their concerns and offer ideas for improving the center. This practice will help a director to determine the areas that need to be addressed immediately. She offers the staff positive feedback and validation of their concerns. She outlines goals and objectives for the center and the part that the staff will have in meeting those goals. This approach will allow the staff to connect and function as a team.

They should see that the program director is actively addressing issues in the center. In this way, the staff and program director can create a positive work environment and share a vision for the staff and the center. The keys to developing trust are to be consistent and trustworthy.

A New Program Director

Cassandra has been hired to take over for a program director who was not supportive of her staff. Cassandra knows she will have to demonstrate to the staff that she is not going to operate in the same fashion as her predecessor. To develop trust, she implements an open-door policy, inviting them to come to her when they are struggling with an issue or just want to talk something over. She also schedules regular staff meetings and intentionally listens to staff concerns and suggestions.

PROBLEM

As part of learning about the center, Cassandra visits each classroom to observe, learn about the teachers' techniques, and get to know the children better. After visiting the older three-year-old and the four-year-old classrooms, she realizes that the use of worksheets is widespread in the center. The teachers seem to think that the children need to do worksheets to prepare them for kindergarten. Cassandra knows that children learn best through play, so she considers how to address the problem.

RESOLUTION

Cassandra reaches out to the center owner, and she gets the okay to have a professional- development trainer work with the staff. She hires a trainer to do an all-day session on play-based, developmentally appropriate practice. While this does require that the center be closed for a day, she believes the benefit to the children in the long run is worth it. The owner agrees and is impressed with Cassandra's commitment to helping her staff develop their skills and knowledge.

Not only will a strong program director be responsive to the needs of the staff as a whole, she will also help her staff understand that it is okay for individual staff members to ask for help when they are having problems with children in the classroom. If a staff member finds herself frustrated, she should ask for assistance and know that she will receive the support she needs.

That said, the director must draw a firm line between her responsibilities and those of her staff. A program director should not have lead-teacher responsibilities on top of her director duties; these are two separate positions and should not be overlapped. The program director can and should help in the classrooms when needed, but that should not be part of her main duties.

Too Many Hats

Alice, who has a bachelor's degree in early childhood education, is the program director at a center with five classrooms for children ranging in age from six months to five years. The center is open each weekday from 6:30 a.m. to 6:00 p.m., and Alice is scheduled to work from 8:00 a.m. to 4:00 p.m. Alice is also the preschool lead and is required to work in the classroom from 8:30 a.m. to 2:30 p.m. This schedule leaves Alice with a half hour in the morning and one-and-a-half hours in the afternoon to perform her program-director duties. She must work longer hours at the center to complete billing and payroll and to address parent concerns.

PROBLEM

When Alice is in the classroom, she cannot address staff concerns, maintain staff and children's files, observe, and evaluate the staff in the classroom, communicate regularly with staff or parents, or update the center's policies if needed. Without a full-time program director completing the duties, the center does not function properly, and the situation results in parent and staff complaints.

RESOLUTION

Alice met with the center owner to discuss the situation. She emphasized the importance of positive parent reviews of the center in encouraging new families to enroll. The center owner realized that Alice needed another lead teacher for the preschool children. She agreed to add that position and authorized Alice to start seeking applicants.

OPEN TO GROWTH AND CHANGE

In his book *Building the Learning Organization* (2011), Marquardt points out, "Being a learning organization[2] is not a static condition. Change is constant, and the need for learning is never finished." For program directors to transform their centers into learning organizations, they must take incremental steps. "Organizations committed to quality take continuous improvement seriously because one question is always uppermost in everyone's mind: "How can we do this better?" says Marquardt. The objective is to continually look for new ways to improve the center.

To become a child-care center functioning as a learning organization, the program director—with the support of the center owner, executive director, or regional or district managers—must create a process for embracing change. Program directors of learning organizations look at the larger picture for the direction of the company. They have a desire to learn and reinvent themselves, their staff, and their centers through training and education. Having the capability to change course when necessary is essential and can produce a competitive advantage. Where to start? I suggest the following:

- **Begin with assessment:** Conduct a survey of the staff and the parents to determine what changes are needed.
- **Categorize the information:** Review the survey feedback. Categorize the list of items that need to be addressed and the time frames needed for each section.
- **Weigh the benefits and costs of implementing change:** All change will take time and money. Outline the pros and cons related to the change, then define each goal.

---

2 Clarification: Marquardt's use of the term *learning organization* refers to any organization—not just an educational program—that intentionally pursues learning as a route to improvement and growth.

- **Identify the application:** Outline the objectives for each goal and the tools needed to make the necessary changes. For example, what training will be required? How will the training be implemented?
- **Apply the ideas from gained knowledge:** Once you have determined the who, what, why, when and how of the change, implement the change based on the knowledge gained.

When a director takes the time to seek information, develop a timeline, and outline the change that will be implemented based on the information, she will be able to articulate the goals and the vision because she has included all parties in the process from start to finish.

Operating as a learning organization, child-care centers will encourage ideas to flow in both directions between the program director and the center staff. All parties will work together, displaying their mutual respect for the center's philosophy and vision. The program director will incorporate new ideas and different ways of thinking to improve the center's operation for the betterment of the program for the children, families, and staff.

The director should survey the staff to determine what type of training they would like and need, then provide multiple opportunities for the staff to obtain training, whether onsite, virtual, or in-person offsite. Offering various ways for the staff to obtain training is beneficial for different learning styles and time schedules.

AN OVERVIEW OF THE BUSINESS OF OPERATING A CHILD-CARE CENTER

In the following section, we will take a quick look at the business of operating a child-care center and the program director's role in each type of center. There are many types of child-care centers: family home care, child-care chains, corporate centers, privately owned centers, government-funded centers, and franchises. They differ in setup, design, and curriculum, but all are required to follow the laws and rules of their states.

CHAIN CENTERS

Chains are branded centers that have multiple locations with the same owner. Decker and Decker (2005) explain that "a chain is ownership of several facilities by the same proprietorship, partnership, or corporation. These facilities are administered by a central organization." Chains may exist within one state or in multiple states. They typically have screening, hiring, and termination policies that directors and staff must follow. They also have recruiters who work hard to find new employees for the centers, so the program director does not have to spend time on recruiting, which can save many hours of work. They have a human resources (HR) department located in the state where the corporate office is located, and all staff are screened and officially offered a position after being vetted by the HR department. Chain centers will often provide monetary support to the individual centers for advertising and marketing. Like corporate centers and franchises, chains will often use the same building design and classroom design across all of their centers. The educational staff, executive director, or board of directors often design and distribute the curriculum. Because the curriculum is mandated by the corporation, there is little to no opportunity for the teaching staff to create individual lesson plans for the children. This can cause a problem for teachers who have students who need additional or even different activities to promote their development. We will dig deeper into developmentally appropriate teaching practices in chapter 7.

FRANCHISE CENTERS

A franchise is a business in which the owners lease the business name, business plan, operating practices, and sometimes the buildings to franchisees. Essentially the franchise is the owner, and the franchisee is the renter. They have staff hiring and firing guidelines and processes. The franchise owners handle marketing and advertising for their franchisees. Each building will have the same layout and classroom setup, so if a parent leaves one center and goes to the same franchise in another city or state, the layout would be identical. Like corporate centers and chains, the educational staff, executive director, or board of directors often design and distribute the curriculum for the franchise. Because the franchisor provides the curriculum that the centers will use, there is often little to no opportunity for the teaching staff to create individual lesson plans for the children. This can cause a problem for teachers who have children that need additional or even different activities to promote their development.

CORPORATE CENTERS

Corporate child-care centers support or operate a center for the use of the corporation's employees on-site or within close proximity to the work site. These centers provide their employees the opportunity to work while having their child(ren) close enough to check on frequently during the workday. This approach supports a positive work-life balance.

They may recruit and hire independently or utilize the corporation's HR department to hire the staff. If the center is physically located on-site, it is typically for the exclusive use of the employees of the corporation. If the center is located off-site, it will generally accept families that are not associated with the corporation. Smaller corporations will often choose an off-site location to help reduce the cost of child care for their employees; they supplement by accepting additional families who do not work for the corporation.

The corporation protects individual center employees "from certain liabilities by creating a decision-making and accountable board of directors. Although the board may delegate decision-making power to a director, [the board] is still responsible" (Decker and Decker, 2005). Like chains and franchises, the educational staff, executive director, or board of directors often design and distribute the curriculum for corporate centers.

PRIVATELY OWNED CENTERS

In this model, the center is owned and operated by a private entity. The owner will either purchase or lease the property where the center is located. These centers are typically located within standalone buildings, churches, strip malls, or public or private schools. Privately owned centers can be for profit or nonprofit, depending on the program. They handle their own recruiting and hiring, as well as advertising and marketing efforts. The owner or program director chooses classroom designs and curriculum.

GOVERNMENT-FUNDED CHILD CARE

The U.S. Department of Education provides funding to states for a range of early childhood programs, including the following:

- Initiatives to support high-quality preschool services and expand preschool to all four-year-olds from low- and moderate-income families
- Coordinated early learning and development systems and programs for children from birth through age five
- Programs and services for children with disabilities and their families
- Community learning centers to provide academic-enrichment opportunities during nonschool hours for young children, particularly students who attend high-poverty and low-performing schools
- Programs to support school readiness

Government-funded programs such as Head Start have specific requirements that are often higher than the minimum state requirements. In hiring program directors, for example, if the federal government requires program directors to have a bachelor's degree and the state requires program directors to have an associate's degree, the federally funded program must hire program directors who have a bachelor's degree. These programs can pay the program director a higher salary because they receive their funds from the federal government; unlike other centers, they are not reliant on the parents for income to operate the center. The local governing body will determine the curriculum that the center will use. They will provide an opportunity for the teaching staff to create individual lesson plans to meet the needs of the children.

STATE REQUIREMENTS FOR PROGRAM DIRECTORS

Regardless of the type of center, the program director is responsible for supervising the implementation of all policies, requirements, and procedures for the program. Without a strong program director leading the center, the program will suffer. Program directors can be successful by continually learning and sharing their knowledge with their staff.

All states have program director or administrator requirements related to education and experience, but the requirements vary from state to state. In addition, owners, executive directors, and district or regional directors of chains, corporations, franchises, and privately owned centers can set requirements for their individual program directors. They follow a sliding scale for education and child-care experience required by the state licensing department, so they may have program directors at different locations with different qualifications.

In this book, I outline and compare the program-director licensing requirements for Michigan, Mississippi, Arizona, Montana, Washington, and Alaska. If you would like additional information on other state licensing requirements, visit the National Database of Child-Care Licensing Regulations at https://childcareta.acf.hhs.gov/licensing

For most states, program directors must be either a minimum of eighteen or twenty-one years of age. Michigan, Mississippi, Arizona, and Alaska require the program directors to be at least twenty-one years old; Montana and Washington require them to be at least eighteen.

Education requirements vary from state to state, ranging from having completed state-approved training to having earned a bachelor's degree or higher in early childhood education. A program director's qualifications must be approved by the state licensing department before the person can be appointed to the position. (Note: The information listed here is not comprehensive. Please refer to your state's official licensing rules and procedures.)

In Michigan, early childhood program directors must have one of the following:

- a bachelor's degree or higher in early childhood education or child development;
- a bachelor's degree or higher in a child-related field, with eighteen semester hours in early childhood education or child development and 480 hours of experience;
- a Montessori credential, with eighteen semester hours in early childhood education or child development and 480 hours of experience;
- an associate's degree in early childhood education or child development, with eighteen semester hours in early childhood education or child development and 480 hours of experience;
- a valid Child Development Associate (CDA) credential, with eighteen semester hours in early childhood education or child development and 960 hours of experience; or
- sixty semester hours, with eighteen semester hours in early childhood education or child development and 1920 hours of experience.

In Mississippi, child-care directors must have:

- a bachelor's degree in early childhood education, child development, elementary education, child care, special education, psychology (with emphasis on child psychology), or family and consumer sciences (with emphasis on child development), or equivalent degree from another child-related field or course of study; or
- a two-year associate's degree in child-development technology, which must include a minimum of 480 hours of practical training supervised by college instructors in a college-operated child-care learning laboratory; or
- a two-year associate's degree in child-development technology or child care and two years paid experience in a licensed child-care facility; or
- two years of paid experience as a caregiver in a licensed child-care facility and a current child-development associate (CDA) credential from the Council for Early Childhood Professional Recognition, a Mississippi Department of Human Services (MDHS) Division of Early Childhood Care and Development child-care director's credential, a MDHS Office of Children and Youth child care director's credential, or twenty-four semester hours credit with a grade of "C" or better from an accredited college or university in courses specific to early childhood.

The state of Washington requires program directors to have an early childhood education (ECE) state certificate or equivalent as approved and verified in the electronic workforce registry by the department. As of August 11, 2021, a center director must complete an ECE state certificate or equivalent by August 1, 2026. A center director hired or promoted must complete an ECE state certificate or equivalent within five years of the time of hire and have two years of experience as a teacher of children in any age group enrolled in the early learning program, as well as at least six months of experience in administration or management.

In Arizona the program director has to have at least twenty-four months of child-care experience, a high-school or high-school-equivalency diploma, and:

- six credit hours or more in early childhood, child development, or a closely related field from an accredited college or university; or
- at least sixty actual hours of instruction, provided in conferences, seminars, lectures, or workshops in early childhood, child development, or a closely related field, and an additional twelve hours of instruction, provided in conferences, seminars, lectures, or workshops in the area of program administration, planning, development, or management.

Program directors may also have three months of child-care experience and a bachelor's degree from an accredited college or university in early childhood, child development, or a closely related field.

Alaska refers to program directors as administrators. The administrator of a child-care center must have at least twelve semester hours of college credit in early childhood development, child development, child psychology, or the equivalent, or must hold either a current CDA credential from the Council for Early Childhood Professional Recognition or a Montessori certificate issued by a program accredited by the Montessori Accreditation Commission for teacher education. College credit in management may substitute for three of the twelve required hours.

Montana requires approved program directors to complete the program-management essentials course within sixty days of becoming a director or to complete an approved new-director orientation such as program essentials.

Michigan requires approved program directors to have at least two semester hours or 3.0 continuing education units (CEUs) in child-care administration or to have an administrative credential approved by the department.

Montana and Michigan require centers to have a substitute director if the director will be absent from the center for more than thirty continuous days. The licensing department has to be provided with a written notice of the substitute because that individual must be approved.

The program director establishes and supervises the implementation of policies, requirements, and procedures for the program, so it is important to hire a qualified person. If a center is located in a state that has a range in program-director qualifications, from minimal to highly qualified, whenever possible the center should hire the program director with the highest qualifications and experience. A candidate with a low level of qualifications will not have the same productivity as an individual with the highest qualifications and experience. This does not mean that the individual with low qualifications cannot perform the duties of the position, but she will often require more guidance to perform them successfully. This is especially true when the owner does not have an early childhood background. If an individual with the minimum required education is hired, then it is important that she has extensive experience as a program director—I would recommend at least three years' experience as an active program director or assistant director.

HIRING AND TRAINING STAFF

Once the program director is hired, she will screen potential staff and volunteers according to the center's screening policy, which defines all the requirements for employees who work at the center. The screening policy, at a minimum, should include a criminal background check along with a child-abuse-and-neglect clearance; most child-care centers have more comprehensive screening policies. (See my book *Build Your Dream Team: How to Recruit, Train, and Retain Early Childhood Staff* for more in-depth information on the recruiting and hiring process.)

At a minimum, the screening and hiring policy should include the following steps:

- Review the résumés and/or applications.
- Conduct phone interviews.
- Conduct face-to-face interviews.
- Complete background checks on each candidate.
- Check the candidates' references.

Budgeting is a big part of all centers, with staffing being the highest expense in the budget. Decker and Decker (2005) state, "For-profit programs operate almost exclusively on tuition and fees and are usually the most expensive." When working for a chain and corporate center, a program director must implement the policies and procedures as outlined in the manual or guidelines provided by the corporation, including meeting the enrollment goals and ensuring that the parents are paying their tuition. The pay scales and schedules for raises are defined by the corporation.

In a franchised center, the franchisor has staff who will work with the program director if the director needs support in operating the center. However, the franchisor will not take any ownership and will offer only guidance. The pay scale for staff is defined by the number of children attending the center and the revenue that the parents have provided.

Program directors for privately owned centers create the design and classroom setup. They determine the curriculum that will be implemented and are responsible for meeting the licensing requirements. They maintain the budget for the center (which is usually tight). Decker and Decker point out that "although child care is costly, for-profit independent centers do not make substantial profits." Program directors will often arrange fundraisers to supplement income for the center.

Government-funded programs have set pay scales for the staff, and the parents are not required to pay tuition. The federal government provides guidelines related to the materials and instruction that should be provided for the children.

BENEFITS AND INCENTIVES

Centers will often offer benefits and incentives to encourage education professionals to develop their skills or meet certain requirements or to recognize effort or years of service. For example, chain and corporate centers, in some cases, provide monetary incentives for program directors who increase enrollment, meet their enrollment quota, obtain National Association for the Education of Young Children (NAEYC) or other accreditation, have low staff turnover, or have reduced or few licensing issues. Centers often have a connection with an online institution so staff can obtain their child development associate (CDA) certification or continuing education units (CEUs) to meet the requirements for a lead-caregiver position and to complete yearly training. Staff may be recognized for years of service with a certificate of appreciation. Some centers assign a parking place for the employee of the month. Most chain and corporate centers provide a 401(k) with a company match, health insurance, and employee discounts on tuition for continuing education and for employees' children who attend the centers. They offer signing bonuses and referral compensation for staff and parents who refer new parents or new employee applicants who are ultimately hired. At a chain center, if a staff person is not working well with the program director and she is a good employee, the staff person may ask for a transfer to another center, which will allow her to maintain her employment and retain her seniority.

For franchise centers, franchisors may offer incentives, such as yearly trips and paid attendance at conferences, to the owners and program directors. They often offer employee discounts on tuition for employees' children who attend the center. They may have a referral program for staff who recommend new employees for the center.

Privately owned centers must be more creative when it comes to incentives; their incentives are usually not as large as those offered by chains or corporate centers. They will offer health care but, due to the high cost, most employees will opt not to pay for the benefits. Privately owned centers cannot afford signing bonuses. They can provide their staff with days off to attend trainings, and in some cases, they will pay for the staff to attend a local conference. They offer referral compensation for staff and parents who refer new parents or new employee applicants who are ultimately hired. They often offer discounts for employees' children to attend the center.

TRAINING

Chains and corporate centers typically provide yearly training. Some have corporate retreats and conferences specific to their program directors. They also have center-wide training days during which the center is closed and the center staff attend an all-day or two-day training. They have a set number of training hours and a timeline defining when the trainings are to be completed. They often have their own training institutes that are set up for their staff, and staff can obtain their CDA credentials through these institutes.

Government centers have educational coordinators who schedule and provide for the program director and the staff.

A franchisor will offer training for franchisees on how to operate the center based on the franchisor's specifications. This training is specific to the franchise, leaving the franchisee and program director responsible for incorporating the state and local requirements on their own without support from the franchisor. The franchise will provide coaching to support the center with training manuals for hiring and training their employees.

Privately owned centers will have a training schedule for staff and will provide trainings during staff meetings. They may have a small budget, so they may purchase resources that can be used by the whole staff. The owner will often pay for a program director to attend trainings; the director is then expected to train the staff on the information that they have learned. This type of training does not allow for addressing specific areas with the staff because everyone is being trained on the same information. See the appendix for resources for trainings and professional development.

GROUNDS FOR TERMINATION

Training, communication, and support can go a long way toward developing the skills the staff need to care for young children appropriately. There are, however, reasons for which a staff member's employment should be immediately terminated:

- Any form of sexual abuse
- Abusive, threatening, bullying, or inappropriate treatment of children, parents, management, or coworkers
- Being insubordinate to the program director
- Lying or distorting the truth for any reason
- Creating a hostile work environment
- Refusal to perform the duties of the position or additional job-related duties as asked by the immediate supervisor
- Placing or having the child place any substances in their mouth such as soap, dirt, or hot sauce
- Restricting a child's movement by binding, tying, or holding down. (Most states will approve restraining children only to prevent them from harming themselves or others.)
- Deliberate destruction of or unauthorized removal of property
- Threatening or depriving a child of rest, such as telling the child that they cannot go to sleep because they were not following directions
- Threatening or depriving a child of necessary toilet use
- Threatening to exclude or excluding a child from any activity as a form of punishment
- Confining a child in an enclosed area, such as a closet, bathroom, or locked room. (While this practice is legal in some states, in others it is prohibited.)
- Attempting to obtain or obtaining confidential parent, child, or staff information
- Sharing confidential information with others inside or outside of the center, including any form of social media
- Threatening or depriving a child of meals or snacks as punishment

The circumstances under which a staff member would be immediately terminated should be clearly spelled out in the staff handbook.

POLICIES AND PROCEDURES

According to Decker and Decker, "Policies are written as comprehensive statements of decisions, principles, or courses of action that achieve goals. Policies directly answer the question: "What is to be done, and by whom?" The policies should be followed consistently (Decker and Decker, 2005). When exceptions are necessary, they should be stated and outlined in the center's written policies and procedures.

All child-care programs are similar in that they provide care and services for families and children; for many child-care centers, that is where the similarities end. Written policies and procedures must address what each individual center offers and requires for their program.

Program directors who work for a chain or corporate child-care centers have parent and staff handbooks, policies, and procedures provided by the company that are not specific to any one center, state, or region. If there are additional state licensing requirements needed to maintain compliance, the program director, in conjunction with the regional or district manager, will have to create an addendum to address these requirements. For franchised centers, a program director or franchisee may have to purchase generic parent handbooks or staff handbooks approved by the franchisor. They would also have to create an addendum to address any state requirements.

Program directors at privately owned centers have the responsibility to create and maintain staff handbooks, policies, and procedures, particularly when the owner is not familiar with early childhood or how to operate a center. The procedures are written specifically for the individual center.

Government-funded programs have to write their policies and procedures. They have educational coordinators who help the centers maintain the required policies and procedures. They are required to have the state requirements and the federal guidelines in the handbook, as well. If the program has more than one location, they would have written policies and procedures for the whole program. And sometimes the individual program directors would be responsible for making sure that the handbooks' policies and procedures are specific for their individual locations.

Regardless of the type of center, the staff handbook should define the policies and procedures for staff, including the following:

- Staff code of conduct and accountability
- Job descriptions of each staff role
- Center organizational chart and chain of command
- Process and criteria for performance reviews
- Raise criteria
- Promotion criteria
- Benefits
- Conflict of interest: working for parents outside of the center
- Termination conditions: voluntary and involuntary
- Vacation, sick-time, and holiday policies
- Training and professional-development requirements for staff
- Conferences: local, state, and national
- Disciplinary actions for the staff/consequences for not following the policies
- Grievance procedures
- Employees' children attending the center
- Discipline policy for the children
- Administering medication
- Accidents/incident and illness reporting policy for children, staff, and volunteers

- Illness policy for children, staff, and volunteers
- Confidentiality
- Mandated reporting of suspected child abuse or neglect
- Unapproved areas for child-care use: kitchens, office space, lobbies, and any other area that is not approved by the state
- State licensing requirements
- Curriculum used by the center
- Communication within the staff
- Communication with parents
- Policy on media interaction, including interactions with the press and on social media
- Policies and procedures for parents
- Policies and procedures for volunteers

The written information relevant to families should also be provided to the parents, so that they are aware of the center's expectations and requirements. This way, the parents and staff will have ample time to review, understand, and comply with the center's expectations.

There may be additional policies that your employees should be aware of. The program director should evaluate the center's policies and procedures frequently to make sure that they are meeting the current needs of the employees at the center. The policies should be preventive and not reactive. These policies should be given great consideration because the outcome has the potential to affect all aspects of the center. Provide the employees with the center's policies and procedures that outline not only the expectations but the consequences of not adhering to them.

During your center orientation with new employees, go over the policies and procedures so that new hires are aware of them before they start to work with the children.

VOLUNTEERS

Parents and community members often want to participate in the activities with the children in a child-care center. Their help is invaluable. There are two types of volunteers: supervised and unsupervised. Volunteers are not employees, and they should not be left alone with the children unless they have a cleared background and criminal check for child abuse and neglect and criminal offences and have been deemed eligible to work with children. *Supervised volunteers* are those who have not been cleared; *unsupervised volunteers* have been cleared and can be alone with the children. For example, a supervised volunteer cannot take children to the bathroom without a cleared adult accompanying them. Once, I was at a center where they had a volunteer who had not been cleared to be alone with children. She was taking the children to the bathroom. When I asked why the volunteer was alone with the children, the response I got was, "She's only taking them to the bathroom." They had completely missed the point of "supervised at all times." Parents who have not been cleared and are helping in the classroom or on field trips can take their own child to the bathroom or outside alone, but they cannot be alone with other children. Gymnastic, dance, music, and karate employees who are paid by parents, as well as therapists, speech pathologists, and social workers, must be supervised if they are working with the children at the center and have not been cleared.

PARENT HANDBOOK

The parent handbook is a contract between the parents and the center, in which the center outlines the services that it will provide. The handbook creates and defines the working relationship between the center and the family. Reno, Stutzman, and Zimmerman (2008) stress that the parent handbook should be written in a positive tone directly in line with the center's philosophy and mission statement. At a minimum, the parent handbook should include the following:

- The services to be provided by the center
- The center's philosophy
- Hours of operation, the holiday schedule, and any additional days that the center is scheduled to be closed
- Drop-off and pickup procedures
- Admissions and withdrawal policies
- The discipline policy—have a written policy to be followed by the staff
- A description of food service outlining what meals are served and whether the center or parents will be expected to provide the food
- Parent involvement expectations, including field trips, birthday celebrations, and volunteering in the classroom
- Intoxicated parent policy
- Tuition schedule, including when tuition is due, how tuition will be collected, under what circumstances a refund will be provided, and late fees

Include in the parent handbook a statement that explains there may be circumstances that will require an update to the written handbook before the scheduled review and updated edition. This statement should explain how the parents will be notified of the amended policy or procedure. Review the parent handbook annually to determine whether the policies and procedures are current and still appropriate for the center. The following is a scenario of what can happen when the parent handbook does not fully address center policies and procedures.

Treatment of Children with Special Needs

Wafiya, the program director, called a meeting with Queeni, the preschool lead caregiver, and four-year-old Zayan's mother, Yochana. Zayan, a child with autism spectrum disorder (ASD), had been suspended for three days the prior week. Because his behavior had not changed since the suspension, Wafiya and Queeni decided that the center was not a good place for Zayan. They informed Yochana that Zayan was being disenrolled from the center.

Wafiya told Yochana that the center was not an appropriate setting for Zayan because the caregivers were not trained to handle children with ASD. Wafiya pointed out that Zayan's speech had not developed and that he did not talk at the center. Therefore, when he could not communicate with the children or caregivers, he would become upset, hit other children and his caregivers, and throw toys. Wafiya said that Zayan was a good child but he had a hard time keeping himself under control.

Queeni informed Yochana that she had talked with Zayan about hitting and keeping his hands to himself and had explained that he could not hit anyone. Zayan would sit on the floor and scream sometimes. She would redirect Zayan, and sometimes this approach would work and he would calm down. Queeni said that Zayan was a nice child and his behavior was only a problem when he got upset. There was not a plan to address his autism.

Wafiya explained that the center has a three-strikes rule for children who are not following the rules and that rule had been extended to accommodate Zayan's special needs. She said that Zayan was disenrolled because she and Queeni had informed Yochana on several occasions about Zayan's behavior in the classroom and the behavior had not improved. Yochana was given the following incident report that addressed Zayan's behavior:

1st: Zayan hit and kicked another child.
2nd: Zayan hit assistant caregiver Queeni on the leg.
3rd: Zayan hit Vedhika, the preschool assistant caregiver, and another child.
4th: Yochana was given a warning letter informing her of a possible three-day suspension and detailing what would happen if Zayan continued hitting Vedhika and the other children. The letter stated that hitting was not allowed at the center.
5th: Zayan hit Queeni.
6th: Zayan threw a toy and hit another child.
7th: Zayan was suspended for three days because of his continued hitting and throwing toys.

Wafiya and Queeni suggested that Yochana have Zayan evaluated through the local school district so that he could receive services that the center was not able to provide.

PROBLEM

The center had accepted a child with ASD, but they had not provided the staff with the training needed to work with him. If staff are not equipped to handle children with special needs and the center accepts a child with special needs, the program director must make sure that the staff is trained and able to meet the child's needs. Without the correct training and equipment, the staff will not be successful. Having staff working without proper training will be detrimental to the child and frustrating for the staff and the family. When staff are frustrated, one of two things will happen: They will quit, or they will do something inappropriate or hurt the child out of frustration. In this case, Zayan's family was forced to look for appropriate care for Zayan. Yochana had to take time from work to care for her son, risking her employment. When she did find a center that could care for Zayan, the four-year-old had to become accustomed to new teachers and classmates and a new school.

RESOLUTION

Child-care centers should have a policy stating that they are willing to work with all children but making it clear that if the child requires more attention than they are able to provide, then the situation will be discussed with the parents. It is important to help the parents to find the best care for the child. The written policy should address the circumstances, other than lack of payment of fees, under which a child would be disenrolled from the center.

A good leader engages in open communication, is willing to compromise for the betterment of the program, is open to change, and is willing to listen. A strong program director will address mistakes and issues quickly and directly. The center will benefit from a director who uses her power in a productive and positive fashion that empowers the staff.

CHAPTER 2

Meeting and Maintaining Licensing

All child-care centers must be licensed by the states in which they operate. Program directors and managers are responsible for keeping a center in compliance with the state licensing rules and laws as well as with the policies and procedures required by a chain or corporate child-care office (if they work for one). In this chapter, we will explore what is typically needed to maintain compliance and prepare for inspections.

AN OVERVIEW OF TYPICAL STATE POLICY REQUIREMENTS

No two states' licensing requirements are the same, but they do have strong similarities. It is important to know the legal rights and responsibilities of your state. Are you feeling anxious about your next licensing inspection? Is it because you do not feel prepared? Is this your first licensing inspection? Are you new to the center? Are you a new program director? Read on for an overview of what to expect.

The best way to prepare for your licensing inspection is to maintain compliance daily. You should not have to do anything special to prepare for your inspection; it should simply be the way that the center is operated on a daily basis.

DOCUMENTATION

Keep your paperwork up to date and organized. Few program directors go into the early childhood field or take on the program director position because they have a desire to maintain files and complete paperwork. They go into the field because they have a desire to work with children and make a positive impact in their lives. But, when you are a director, keeping up with paperwork is essential, so learn how to work smarter—not harder. Organize your work in a way that is systematic and functional. This will allow more time for your true passion and create less stress during inspection or observation.

For our examples, we refer to the requirements for child-care centers established by the State of Michigan, Bureau of Community and Health Systems, Child Care Licensing Division, Licensing and Regulatory Affairs (2019), the Arizona Department of Health Services, Bureau of Child Care Facilities Licensing (2019), and the State of Alaska Department of Health and Social Services, Division of Public Assistance, Child Care Program Office (2020). (Note: The information listed here is not comprehensive. Please refer to your state's official licensing rules and procedures.) The current license for the center must be displayed, and a licensing notebook must be kept on the premises and accessible to parents and prospective parents. The notebook should contain all licensing inspection and special investigative reports and related corrective action plans for the previous five years.

In Michigan, a licensee must have a written policy regarding screening and supervision of staff and volunteers, including volunteers who are parents of a child in care. The policy must include a statement that any individual registered on the public sex-offender registry is prohibited from having contact with any child in care.

A written policy must be developed and implemented regarding the age-appropriate, non-severe discipline of children. The policy must be provided to staff and parents.

A center shall have a written policy detailing when children, staff, and volunteers will be excluded from the center due to illness.

The following policies have to be provided to each parent enrolled in the program:

- Fee policy
- Discipline policy
- Food-service policy
- Transportation policy, if applicable
- Medication policy
- Exclusion policy for child illnesses
- Required inspections completed

Keep up-to-date files and documentation on the following:

- Fire-safety inspection records
- Environmental health inspection records
- Playground safety inspection records
- Lead hazard risk assessment records
- Boiler, furnace, and/or water-heater inspection records, as applicable
- Program director qualifications: transcripts to verify the semester hours of credit from an accredited college or university and/or verification of hours of experience working with children
- Staffing files:
    - Accurate daily attendance, with first and last names along with arrival and departure times
    - Number and ages of children enrolled in the program
    - Number of staff/volunteers present throughout the day: early morning, nap time, lunchtime, afternoon, and so on
    - Location of classrooms approved to be used for child care
    - Documentation that staff are free of tuberculosis; are physically capable of meeting the duties required; meet the criminal and children's protective services history requirements; have signed the child abuse/neglect statement; and have obtained CPR, first aid, and blood-borne pathogen training
    - Staff training plan
- Program plan:
    - Planned daily activities for each age group
    - A sample daily schedule with a description of activities that meet children's social, emotional, physical, and intellectual needs
    - A plan for rest and outdoor play
- Equipment list: A detailed listing of age-appropriate equipment in each of the following subcategories for each age group to be served:
    - Large and small muscle groups
    - Sensory exploration
    - Social interaction and dramatic play
    - Discovery and exploration
    - Early math and science experiences
    - Language and literacy experiences
    - Creative experiences through art, music, and literature

- Nutrition and food service program plan
- A sketch of the child-use spaces:
    - Indoor activity space, including all dimensions of all child use areas, with labeled hallways, bathrooms, kitchen, and storage areas
    - Outdoor activity space, including location and denoting names of streets, adjacent parks, and so on
- Policies and procedures:
    - Admission and withdrawal criteria
    - Procedures for screening staff/volunteers for prior criminal convictions and substantiated abuse or neglect of children
    - Fee policy, including when and how payment is due, payment policies for holidays, child illness or absence, or when the center is closed due to inclement weather or other reasons
    - Discipline policy indicating the child management techniques which will be used in the center, as well as those that are prohibited
- Emergency and Evacuation Plans: Crisis management for fire, tornado, and other natural or man-made disasters, as well as serious accidents, illness, or injury. The emergency procedures must include all of the following:
    - A plan for evacuation
    - A plan for safely moving children to a relocation site
    - A plan for shelter-in-place
    - A plan for lockdown
    - A plan for contacting parents and reuniting families
    - A plan for how each child with special needs will be accommodated during each type of emergency
    - A plan for how infants and toddlers will be accommodated during each type of emergency
    - A plan for how children with chronic medical conditions will be accommodated during each type of emergency

Arizona requires the following information to be maintained in children's files:

- The child's name, home address, city, state, zip code, home telephone number, sex, and date of birth
- The date of the child's enrollment
- The name, home address, city, state, zip code, and contact telephone number of each parent of the child
- The name and contact telephone number of at least two individuals authorized by the child's parent to collect the child from the facility in case of emergency or if the child's parent cannot be contacted

- The name and contact telephone number of the child's health-care provider
- The written authorization for emergency medical care of the enrolled child when the parent cannot be contacted at the time of the emergency
- The name of the individual to be contacted in case of injury or sudden illness of the child
- The written instructions of a child's parent or health-care provider for nutritional and dietary needs of the child including, if applicable
- A written record completed by the child's parent or health-care provider noting the child's susceptibility to illness, physical conditions of which a staff member should be aware, and any individual requirements for health maintenance

The licensee must maintain a current emergency, information, and immunization record card for each enrolled child on facility premises in a place readily accessible by a staff member in event of an emergency at, or evacuation of, the facility. Each enrolled child's written immunization record or exemption affidavit must be attached to the child's emergency, information, and immunization record card. When a child is disenrolled from a facility, the licensee must record the date of disenrollment on the child's emergency, information, and immunization record card. Children's records must be maintained for twelve months after the date of disenrollment on facility premises in a place separate from the current emergency, information, and immunization record cards.

POLICIES AND PRACTICES

States vary in their requirements, but most mandate practices such as the following:

- Minimum orientation required for volunteers
- Pets that may be kept at the facility, including their immunization records, written procedures for their care and maintenance, and rules for children's exposure to pets
- Posted no smoking or vaping notices on site
- Posted certificate of building occupancy

Michigan and other states require that emergency phone numbers, including 911, fire, police, and the poison control center, and the facility's physical address and two main cross streets, must be conspicuously posted in a place visible to staff. Guidelines for handwashing must be posted in food preparation areas, in toilet rooms, and by all hand-washing sinks. Guidelines for diapering must be posted in diapering areas. The current list of unsafe, recalled children's products must be conspicuously posted in the center. A typical daily routine must be posted in a place visible to parents. Menus must be planned in advance, dated, and posted in a place visible to parents. Food substitutions must be noted on the menus the day the substitution occurs.

Many states regulate discipline and behavior-guidance policies. Arizona, for example, requires the following:

- Plan for helping children develop age-appropriate patterns of behavior that foster constructive relationships and increasing ability to deal with everyday life
- Positive reinforcement, redirection, and the setting of realistic expectations and clear and consistent limits
- No discipline or a behavior management technique that is cruel, humiliating, or otherwise damaging to the child, such as the following:
    - Discipline in association with food or rest
    - Punishment for bedwetting or actions in regard to toileting or toilet training
    - Discipline administered by another child
    - Verbal abuse, derogatory remarks about the child or members of the child's family, or threats to expel the child from the child-care facility
    - Placement in a locked room
    - Physically restrained, except when necessary to protect a young child from accident, to protect persons on the premises from physical injury, or to protect property from serious damage, and then only passive physical restraint may be used
    - Mechanically restrained, except for a protective device such as a seatbelt
    - Chemically restrained, except on the order of a physician and subject to the provisions of state law
    - Corporal punishment, including infliction of bodily pain as a penalty for a disapproved behavior, shaking, spanking, delivering a blow with a part of the body or an object, slapping, punching, pulling, and any other action that seeks to induce pain

Arizona allows:

- A staff member to separate a child from the other children for unacceptable, age-appropriate behavior
- The separation period must not be longer than three minutes after the child has regained control or composure
- A child may be removed from the other children for more than ten minutes but cannot be separated for longer than ten minutes without staff interacting with the child

Obviously, I cannot include all the policies for every state. Familiarize yourself with your state's requirements, work with your licensing consultant, and maintain an organized records system. If you provide care in a facility that is maintained to ensure children's safety at all times, if you are respectful of children and their families, if you follow all state guidelines and rules, and if you daily offer a quality learning experience for the children, you will be well-prepared for a licensing inspection.

STATE POLICY CHANGES

If a state mandates policies and procedures beyond those required by the chain or corporation, the program director must either contact the corporate office for an addendum to the company policies or must write the policy or procedure and get it approved by the company before adding it to the information provided to parents and staff. Then, the corporation should disseminate the information to all centers within the state. It is important for the centers to work together to ensure that compliance is maintained across the state. Chains and franchise-owned and -operated centers that do not have a process for implementing and disseminating state changes often have a difficult time maintaining compliance, because they are not sure if they are required to create the written procedures themselves or wait for their corporate office to provide them. State requirements do change, so program directors must stay up to date and be proactive rather than reactive. (We discuss building maintenance and safety in chapter 3 and child health and safety in chapter 4.)

Addressing State Policy Changes

In Michigan, the rules changed to require centers to have emergency procedures that address responding to natural and manmade disasters and specify how children with special needs and infants and toddlers will be cared for during an emergency.

PROBLEM

As corporate executive directors and franchise owners worked to create updated emergency procedures, program directors could not train their staff because they did not know how the new rules would be addressed. Consequently, the centers received unnecessary violations.

RESOLUTION

This problem can be resolved by corporations and franchise owners empowering program directors at local centers or district or regional managers to make changes to procedures. The companies can then distribute those changes to the other centers in the state. As a stopgap measure, I suggested that the program directors write their own emergency policies while they waited for the formal changes from their companies.

Center over Capacity during Licensing Inspection

On the day of a center's onsite inspection, Florence, the licensing consultant, observed fifty-nine children in the school-age classroom. The capacity that had been approved for the room was fifty children, but there were nine additional school-age children present. Florence informed Jayla, the program director, that the center was over capacity, but Jayla was unaware that there were fifty-nine children present. She stated that normally there are between forty-two and fifty children present at the center on a daily basis. This week she had several school-age parents request for their children to attend the center because school was closed, and she had approved their requests without realizing that she would exceed capacity for the classroom. Jayla said she would not allow the additional children to attend the center for the remainder of the week.

PROBLEM

Program directors have to create and oversee the staff work schedules. They must review three aspects when approving a schedule change or enrolling new children at the center:

- Will there be enough staff working at the center to maintain the required adult-child ratio for the additional child(ren)?
- What is the capacity for the classroom, and will the additional child(ren) exceed the capacity?
- What is the overall capacity for the center, and will the additional child(ren) exceed the overall capacity for the center?

These details are especially important for centers with capacities that are less than one hundred children. The program director can enroll more children but cannot have more than the maximum capacity at the center at one time.

RESOLUTION

Two days later, Florence completed a follow-up inspection to confirm the correct capacity was being maintained; there were forty-nine children present.

A Disqualifying Background Check

Antoinette, the program director, received notification that a new assistant caregiver's background check showed information disqualifying her from working with children. Antoinette allowed Betsy, the assistant caregiver, to continue to work at the center, thinking that it would be acceptable as long as Betsy was supervised at all times.

During the licensing inspection, Antoinette was cited for having Betsy working with children, and Betsy had to be immediately fired and removed from the center.

PROBLEM

When a staff person is deemed ineligible, that employee is prohibited from being at the center and having any contact with the children at the center until he is deemed eligible. If a child were to be harmed or injured by the ineligible staff person, the center would receive additional violations and possibly be forced to close their doors.

RESOLUTION

Ensure that all staff who are working with children have been properly screened and cleared.

Stay prepared for your licensing inspection by maintaining compliance daily. Know your state's criteria. Then, create a schedule to remind yourself to inspect the building and playground, observe in classrooms, and keep up with paperwork. If you do these tasks on an ongoing basis, the licensing inspection will be much easier.

In the next chapter, we discuss building maintenance and look at scenarios that demonstrate the importance of ensuring the building and grounds are in good repair at all times.

CHAPTER 3

Building and Equipment Maintenance and Safety

The program director has to make sure that the building is in good condition and provides an environment that is safe for the staff and children. When a child-care building is not in good repair, the children's and staff's safety is in jeopardy. The ramifications of not maintaining the building could be injury to a child or staff member, resulting in parents disenrolling their children, staff resigning, or complaints made to the state licensing department. In this chapter, we will look at things that can happen when the building and grounds are not checked regularly.

To keep up with the details of maintenance and safety checks, the center should have a checklist that teachers use each day and share with the program director. Not only will this practice help the program director to have needed repairs made in a timely manner, but it will also instill in the staff the expectation that everyone is responsible for maintaining a safe environment at the center. The following is a sample list of items to check each day. Check with your state to learn the safety and maintenance items required for your center.

- Electrical outlets are covered
- No hot items within reach of the children

- No choking hazards, such as beads, marbles, staples, and push pins
- No flaking paint where the children have access
- Toys are not broken, chipped, or cracked and have no exposed sharp or pointy areas
- All doors are properly secured and sealed to prevent rodents or insects from gaining access
- There are no leaks in the ceiling, walls, or floors
- All cleaning supplies are out of the reach of the children
- Area rugs are secured to the floor to prevent a trip hazard
- All knives, adult scissors, and staplers are out of the reach of the children
- All exits are clear with no objects obstructing them
- All sinks are working properly with warm water not higher than 120 degrees Fahrenheit
- Faucets and toilets are not leaking
- The outdoor equipment is not broken
- There is no standing water outside of the building that could create a bug infestation
- The furnace and/or air conditioner is working
- The building is at the proper temperature
- The refrigerator is working and maintaining the proper temperature
- The smoke and carbon-monoxide detectors are working
- The locks on the gates are working
- The fire extinguisher is properly charged and mounted

Safety comes first—always. For example, having a qualified and reputable fire inspector is important for the safety of everyone at the center as well as for the integrity of the building. When I was a new program director, I had a fire inspector complete an inspection, but he did not note in his report multiple things that I knew to be fire violations: fire doors that did not close; exits blocked by furniture and baby swings; a fire door bolted shut, preventing its use in an emergency; fire extinguishers that were not charged; and flammable materials in the room where the furnace and hot-water tank were located. In fact, his report stated that there were *no* violations at the center. Because I knew there were violations, I called in a different fire inspector who found and cited all of the things that I had discovered.

The owner of the center was not happy that I had requested another inspection, especially since the first inspection report stated that the center was in compliance. But I could not look the other way; I wanted the violations corrected for the safety of everyone at the center. After the second inspection, the center had to make costly corrections. I knew that the children's safety had to come first, and I was more than willing to defend my decision. Unfortunately, the owner refused to understand that the cost for the repairs was minimal compared to what he could lose if a child were injured in a fire or if a fire damaged or destroyed the building.

The second fire inspector reported the first inspector to their supervisor, and the first inspector was suspended for providing an inaccurate report. At that point, the owner and the first inspector were furious with me, to the point that the owner wanted to write me up for having a second inspection. I refused to sign the write-up and explained that my responsibility was to make sure that everyone attending or working at the center was safe. After that conversation, I realized that the owner and I were not going to see eye to eye when it came to the safety and well-being of the children and staff, and I started looking for a new job. Sometimes you have to do what's right, even if others are upset with you.

ADDRESSING ISSUES AT A CENTER

When issues are discovered, the program director should address them quickly. If the center owner also owns the building, it is a good idea to have the building inspected yearly to ensure that the structure is sound. Any needed repairs can be completed before they interrupt the care of the children. If the facility is rented, the building owner is responsible for the repairs. Maintenance must be completed on a timely schedule to ensure that the children's care is not disrupted. The following are examples of common issues in building maintenance and safety.

Leaking Roof in the Toddler and Infant Classrooms

When Abhiramnew was dropping off his fifteen-month-old son, Wriddhish, in the toddler room, he was shocked to see water dripping from the ceiling inside the classroom. Two of the four walls were wet, and five ceiling tiles were missing where the water was dripping. The remaining ceiling tiles were stained and broken, and pieces of ceiling tiles littered the floor. The window ledge was wet, and water pooled on the floor. The classroom smelled of mildew. There were no other children in the classroom, and Abhiramnew was not going to leave Wriddhish there. Abhiramnew had not been informed that the classroom was not being used. Ekaja, the program director, had not been at the front desk when he arrived, and there was not a sign on the door saying that the classroom was closed.

As Abhiramnew was exiting with Wriddhish, he met Gautami, the toddler lead caregiver, in the hallway. She informed him that the toddler class had been moved to the preschool classroom. As he walked past the infant classroom on his way to the preschool room, he observed more leaks and a child-size wading pool in the middle of the floor collecting water from the leaking roof. At that point, Abhiramnew decided to leave the center with Wriddhish because he felt uncomfortable leaving his child in that environment.

On his way out, he asked Ekaja what was being done about the leaks in the classrooms. Ekaja informed him that the roof in the toddler classroom had started with a small leak five days earlier, and the leak in the infant room had started leaking three days earlier. Both leaks had worsened because of rain the previous night. She told him that the building maintenance man had been working on the roof to locate and repair the leak. He had put fans in the toddler classroom to dry up the water and was using a wet/dry vacuum to remove standing water. Ekaja believed that the mildew smell was coming from the wet carpet in the classroom, which was why she had instructed the staff to keep the classroom door closed so that the odor would not seep into the rest of the center. She assured him that the children from the infant and toddler classrooms had been removed from the classrooms when the leaks occurred.

PROBLEM

Abhiramnew did not like the fact that he had not received any notice prior to his arrival about the leaks or the closed classrooms even though the roof had been leaking for days. Abhiramnew also expressed concern about the children becoming ill from the mildew smell in the classrooms; Ekaja stated that she was not aware of any children or caregivers becoming ill as a result of the smell. He did not feel that Ekaja was taking the situation seriously and found her lack of communication and her explanation of what was being done to correct the leaking ceiling unacceptable. He disenrolled Wriddhish from the center.

RESOLUTION

When there are maintenance issues that affect the classrooms or care that the children will be receiving, the parents must be informed promptly. Parents should receive an explanation of the center's plan of action that outlines what will happen, when the repair will be completed, and how the children will be affected by the maintenance. In this case, the director should also consider the classroom capacity of the preschool room. The center must maintain the state-required adult-to-child ratio.

Clean running water is a necessity at a child-care center. Children brush their teeth and wash their hands with soap and water after diapering and toileting, when their hands get dirty from playing, and before and after handling food or bottles. Lack of access to water can place the children and staff at risk of exposure to germs that can cause disease.

Water not Working at the Center

Lisa, the program director, was having new sinks installed in two infant and toddler classrooms. The installer started working on the sinks on Friday after the center closed; the project was scheduled to be completed over the weekend before the center reopened on Monday morning.

When the center reopened on Monday, Lisa found that the sinks were leaking under the cabinets. The plumber had to turn off the water on the infant and toddler side of the building while he made repairs. He thought the leak was fixed, but when the caregivers used the sinks, they would start leaking again. The plumber took three days to completely fix the leaking sinks. In the meantime, the five preschool classrooms on the opposite side of the building had water. Lisa instructed the infant and toddler caregivers to take the children to the other side of the building to wash their hands after diapering, before and after eating, and when their hands were dirty from play.

PROBLEM

Vera, fifteen-month-old Ekon's mother, found out that the water was not working when she dropped her son off in the toddler classroom with Amy, the lead toddler caregiver. The infant and toddler side had not had running water for three days, but Vera had not been informed. She was even more upset when Amy told her that she was taking the children to the kitchen to wash their hands. Vera went to Lisa to express her concern; Vera felt that the center should have closed. Lisa explained the situation, telling Vera that she had instructed the infant and toddler teachers to take the children to the other side of the building to wash their hands. She was surprised to learn that Amy had been taking the children to the kitchen. She was not sure why Amy was doing this.

After Lisa talked with Vera, she called Amy into her office and asked her about taking the children to the kitchen to wash their hands. Amy explained that she changed the children's diapers in the classroom and would then take them to wash their hands together in the kitchen after all of the diapers were changed. She would not wash their hands after each diaper change, and she would not wash her hands after each diaper change. Instead, Amy would clean her hands and the children's hands with a diaper wipe after each diaper change. Lisa asked Amy why she did not utilize the preschool bathrooms as instructed, and Amy stated that there was a line at the preschool bathroom, so she found another sink to use. Lisa gave Amy a write up for taking the children into the kitchen, which is not a safe place for them.

RESOLUTION

The kitchen is not an approved space for children; therefore, they should not have been taken there under any circumstances. The children especially should not have been washing their hands after diapering or brushing their teeth in the kitchen, because they could potentially cross-contaminate the food areas.

It is important to inform the parents when there is something that will directly affect the care that their children will receive at the center. Parents have a right to know and then make a decision based on the information that has been provided. If parents do not like the solution that the center has put in place, they have the option to find alternative care. The center should provide parents with that option without asking them to pay for the time that the center does not have water. Most parents are willing to accept an alternative plan so long as they are aware of it. They can also hold the staff accountable when they do anything that differs from the stated plan.

No Heat at the Center

Nyla, a toddler parent, was dropping off her seventeen-month-old son, Jackson, at the center at 8:00 a.m. She did not recognize that the center was cold indoors because she was wearing a coat. As she was taking Jackson's coat off in his classroom, Anaya, the program director, stepped into the room and informed her that when she had arrived at the center she had discovered that the furnace was not working. She had contacted the heating company, and they had sent someone out to repair the furnace. She told Nyla to leave Jackson's coat on until they could get the furnace repaired. But, when Nyla looked around the classroom, she noticed that there were three space heaters running in an attempt to heat the classroom. The temperature in the classroom was in the forties, which was too cold for the children. Anaya stated that the repairman was currently at the center working on the furnace, and it should be repaired soon but she did not know when.

When Nyla asked Anaya why she had not been informed about the lack of heat, Anaya said that she had posted the information on the center's portal and their social-media site to inform the parents and to let them know that they had the choice of whether to bring their children in. Nyla felt that she should have been notified by another method, such as a phone call, that the center did not have heat before she arrived that morning. Nyla did not want to leave Jackson at the center, but she had to get to work, so she had Grayson, Jackson's father, pick him up from the center until the heat was fixed. Anaya called Grayson just before lunch, and he returned Jackson to the center. When Nyla picked Jackson up at the end of the day, she expressed her concern to Anaya. When situations occur, she said she wanted Anaya to communicate with her in a way that is appropriate.

PROBLEM

Nyla was new to the center, and she had not received certain information when she enrolled Jackson, so she was not aware of the center's social media site. She was aware of the portal, but she did not usually check the center's portal until later in the day after Jackson was at the center for a while. If Nyla had known, she would have made different arrangements for Jackson.

The center's written policy that was provided to her when she enrolled Jackson stated that parents would be informed with a phone call or email in the event of an emergency. Nyla felt that the fact that Anaya used any form of social media to inform the parents was a major misstep because she was not following the center's written policy.

Another issue to consider: Space heaters are not allowed at child-care centers. They are not safe to use around young children.

RESOLUTION

The center should have closed until the heat was repaired. If it was going to be fixed in the morning, Anaya could have told the parents to bring the children in the afternoon. Centers are often fearful of closing because parents need the centers and because the directors do not want to have a reason to prorate payments. However, parents have the right to be informed and to voice their concerns when they are taking their child to a center and expecting a certain level of care. Not communicating with parents is always a misstep. Centers could send a mass text message or email to quickly notify parents of an emergency (no heat at a center would constitute an emergency). When new parents enroll, they should be informed of the center's communication procedures in the event of an emergency. Once a center has created communication policies and procedures, the staff should adhere to them at all times.

Health and safety do not just apply to the indoor parts of a child-care center; the outdoor areas are equally important. The play areas should be free of sharp objects, broken outdoor toys and climbing equipment, wire protruding from fences, poisonous plants, and trash. If a potentially dangerous animal wanders onto a playground, the children should be kept indoors until the animal can be safely removed.

Rodents on the Playground

Indali, an assistant caregiver, called Baghyawati, a center owner, after she resigned from the center. Indali had worked there for six months, and she resigned because the center had a rodent problem outside on the playground that the children use every day. She told Baghyawati that she would find dead rodents outside on the playground. She had informed Hemangini, the program director, so she was aware of the problem, but Indali said the director did nothing to address the issue. Other caregivers have also observed the rodents on the playground. Indali told Baghyawati that the children are not safe from the rodents outside, and she could not work in those conditions.

Baghyawati went to the center and spoke to Hemangini about the rodent problem. Hemangini stated that the center had had a rodent problem the previous month, but the children were not on the playground when the rodents were observed. Hemangini said that she had hired an exterminator, who placed traps outside of the fenced area away from the children's play area. He had told her that the rodents were coming from the dumpster at the apartment complex next door. Hemangini said that she had contacted the city to have them address the problem as well. Since the exterminator was at the center, they have not had a problem with the rodents, nor have they ever seen rodents in the building.

Baghyawati asked Hemangini why she had not informed her about the rodents on the playground and why the staff were not aware of how the situation was being addressed. Hemangini stated that the staff were made aware when the exterminator put down the traps. Baghyawati spoke with the lead caregivers to confirm what Hemangini had reported. They were aware that

Hemangini had had an extermination company put out traps for the rodents on the outside of the fence away from the children. Since the traps were put down, they have not observed any rodents on the playground. The children were not on the playground when the rats were observed.

PROBLEM

The owner was not informed of the rodent problem. While the lead teachers were told of the measures to address the issue, the rest of the staff was not.

RESOLUTION

The program director should communicate with the owner when there is a problem at the center, even if the director is resolving the problem. The owner should be involved and updated with progress reports. The staff should also be informed when there is an issue at the center that will affect the children or staff. They should know how the issue is being addressed. They should also be empowered to let the program director know whenever there is an issue at the center that needs to be addressed.

Playground Injury

Four-year-old Max was playing outside on the playground in an area where tire swings had been removed. The area was bordered with wooden planks and was filled with wood chips. Max was running when he tripped and fell on a nail sticking out of one of the boards. He received a gash from his knee down his leg, resulting in fifteen stitches.

Lina, the lead teacher, contacted her program director, telling her that Max had fallen outside on the playground, hitting his leg and knee on a nail that was sticking out of a board near where the play equipment had been removed. Lina also called Max's parents, and his father picked Max up and transported him to the hospital. Bram, the maintenance person, inspected the boards that Max tripped on and determined that there were numerous exposed nails, so he roped the area off.

The next day, Max's father, James, went to the center and spoke with Hailey, the program director. He informed her that Lina had called Max's mother, Ella, and had told her that Max had tripped on wood chips and hurt his knee. Lina stated that Ella should come to the center when she could. Ella had contacted her husband and informed him that she had received a call from the center. He called the center and spoke with Lina, and he could hear Max crying in the background. He knew that Max was in pain from the type of cry he heard. He said Max was still crying when he arrived at the center about an hour after Max was injured. Lina had not stressed the urgency of Max's injury to either of his parents when she had spoken to them. When James arrived, Max's leg and knee were wrapped with gauze, and Max told him that he had cut his leg and knee on a flat part of a nail on the playground. Lina had informed Max's dad that Bram had pounded the nail back into the board. Max's dad had transported Max to the hospital. When the doctor at the hospital unwrapped Max's leg and knee, he informed James that Max may need surgery. But after further examination, it was determined that Max needed fifteen stitches from his knee down the front of his leg.

Hailey told James that the tire swings had been removed from the mulched area about a month and a half prior to the accident and that was why there were nails in the area. James walked the area with her, and they found several more exposed nails. Hailey told James that she would have Bram remove the nails or pound them back into the boards for the children's safety.

James decided that Max would not be returning to the center because the area had not been secured immediately after the swings had been removed. He did not feel that the center was a safe place for Max or any other children. He also did not feel that the center had taken Max's injuries as seriously as they should have.

Hailey had not been present at the center when the accident occurred. She spoke with Lina and the assistant caregivers to find out more about what had happened to Max. On the day of the incident, Lina said that they had instructed the children to stay away from the area. After the accident, she had informed Bram, and he had pounded the nail that injured Max back into the boards. He saw several more nails sticking out of the boards, so he removed them or pounded them into the boards. He told Lina that the area was now safe for children. Lina said that she routinely walks the playground before the children go outside and that she has never noticed the nails because they were hidden by grass. She said she had noticed the boards were splitting, and she asked the children not to walk on the boards.

Lina said that Max was injured ten to fifteen minutes after the class went outside to the playground. Max stated that he had tripped and hit his leg and knee on a nail. They utilized a wagon to transport Max back inside the center because he could not walk. Lina cleaned Max's cut with water, dried the area, and wrapped it with gauze. She said she had called Ella and informed her that Max had fallen on a nail outside on the playground and had a gash on his leg and knee. She said that she had told Ella that Max would need medical attention, to which Ella had replied that she understood but that she was over an hour away from the center. Lina asked Ella if she would like her to call the ambulance or put ice on the wrapped leg and knee. Ella did not want Lina to call the ambulance. Ella stated that she or James would get to the center when they could.

Lina stated that James called the center, and she informed him of what had happened to Max. James stated that he was an hour away and he would be there as soon as possible. She had Max do some deep-breathing exercises, and he stopped crying for about thirty minutes; Max started crying again five to ten minutes before James arrived. Based on the severity of Max's injury, she admitted that she should have called 911 immediately.

Assistant teacher Isa stated that she was standing by a tree, and another child told her that Max had gotten hurt. Max was crying. They transported Max inside the building on a wagon because he was not able to walk. Lina called Max's parents. They had Max keep his leg elevated to stop the area from splitting more, and they placed ice on his leg to stop the bleeding. She gave Max books to keep him occupied until James arrived. Max stopped crying after his leg was cleaned and bandaged. He started crying again just before James arrived.

Assistant teacher Julie stated that she was the first to see Max after she heard him scream. She tried to keep him calm. She provided the wagon so that they could transport Max into the building because she knew that he would not be able to walk with his injury. She said Max was screaming and crying all the way into the building. She did not go inside with Max; she stayed outside on the playground with the other children.

Hailey told Lina that if there is ever a question about a child's injury, 911 should be called immediately. Hailey stated that she would retrain the staff so that this mistake would not happen again. Hailey instructed the caregivers to inspect the playground daily before taking the children outside.

PROBLEM

The staff checked the area but did not check the wooden planks that were on the ground. The area was clearly not safe for children. The accident was compounded when the parents were not provided with a clear picture of their child's injury.

RESOLUTION

The injury was definitely a fluke accident but a preventable one. Staff should check the play areas daily. Staff should also be trained in how to handle a child injury. Parents should be made fully aware of any injury to their child. If the parents are not close to the center, or if the injury may be severe, staff should get the child emergency medical attention by calling 911.

TRANSPORTATION

If the center uses a bus or van to transport children to and from the center, the driver should be trained on the requirements of driving the vehicle and be familiar with the children. The driver should always check the vehicle before exiting to ensure that every child has exited the vehicle.

The center should maintain a transportation file, kept in the office, containing the following information:

- Insurance for the vehicle
- Registration for the vehicle
- Record that the tags are renewed yearly
- Annual vehicle inspection completed by a licensed mechanic
- Copy of the current driver's license
- Record showing that the driver has no points on his driving record

Provide a written checklist for the driver to use before transporting children. The checklist should include, at a minimum, the following items for the driver to verify each time before departure:

- Child information card for each child, with the child's name, photo, and parent contact information
- Permission slips for each child
- Seat belts that are functioning properly
- First aid kit with replenished contents
- Fire extinguisher within date
- Gas gauge showing the tank is full (fill up if needed)
- Bidirectional reflective triangles and flares stored properly
- Headlights and taillights functioning properly
- Turn signals and hazard lights functioning properly
- Mirrors adjusted
- Horn functioning properly
- Tires inflated to the proper pressure
- Brakes functioning properly
- Windshield wipers functioning properly
- Fluids at appropriate levels
- Windshield and windows are clean and unbroken
- No loose items on the bus

Once the items have been checked, the information should be recorded to ensure that the vehicle is properly equipped and functional. Anything that is missing or not working should be reported to the program director immediately.

Having a checklist will reduce the chance of something going wrong or the vehicle breaking down with the children inside. Once, a bus ran out of gas because the driver did not check the gas gauge. The driver had to call the center to have the program director bring gas to the bus. The children had to wait on the bus for forty-five minutes until the program director arrived. Thankfully, the weather was mild, so the children did not freeze or overheat while sitting on the bus that was not running. The bus driver was able to park in a parking lot rather than on the side of the road. The driver acknowledged that this was a preventable situation and resolved to pay better attention to the vehicle in the future.

The goal of this chapter was to help prepare you for maintenance and safety situations that could occur and how they should be managed to protect the children and staff. Plans for how these situations will be managed should be outlined in the parent and staff handbooks so that everyone is aware of the policies and procedures.

The next chapter addresses ways to maintain child health and safety within the child-care environment. Importantly, we will explore issues such as suspected child abuse or neglect as well as the importance of mandated reporting.

CHAPTER 4

Child Health and Safety

In this chapter, we delve into ways that the staff can help keep the children safe and healthy—and what can happen if they don't. Decker and Decker (2005) define the wide scope of child health and safety as covering nutrition and food handling, provision for rest or sleep, health and safety education, the care or exclusion of ill children, medication administration, health services (including screening and immunizations), management of injuries and emergencies, and surveillance of environmental problems. Decker and Decker acknowledge, "Child safety includes planning environmental safety, preparing for emergencies, providing child protection, and promoting safety consciousness and education."

Training is important to reduce safety issues. Staff have to be trained to report issues when they are observed, and program directors have to make sure that they have a clear policy for regulating and maintaining a safe and healthy environment for the children and staff.

CHILD ABUSE AND NEGLECT

As part of their training, staff should learn the signs of child abuse and neglect. It is not a staff member's responsibility to determine whether a child is actually being abused or neglected; it is, however, their responsibility to report *suspected* abuse or neglect to child protective services (CPS). According to the Centers for Disease Control and Prevention (2021a), child abuse and neglect are "any act or series of acts of commission or omission by a parent, caregiver, or another person in [a] custodial role that results in harm, potential for harm, or threat of harm to a child."

The Michigan Department of Health and Human Services (2021) describes physical abuse as harm or threatened harm to a child's health or safety by a person responsible for the child's health and safety. This includes parents and child-care staff. Physical abuse is a non-accidental injury (the injury was inflicted on purpose) to a child that may include, but is not limited to:

- Fractures
- Burns
- Immersion burns (a body part is burned by contact with a hot liquid)
- Cuts, scratches, gashes, and other marks on the skin
- Bruises
- Bald spots or missing clumps of hair
- Swollen lips
- Chipped teeth
- Bite marks
- Puncture wounds

Sexual abuse is any intentional touching/contact that can be reasonably construed as being for the purpose of sexual arousal, gratification, or any other improper purpose. Sexual abuse indicators may include but are not limited to:

- Pain or itching in the genital area
- Bruising in the genital area
- Blood in the child's underwear
- Sexually transmitted disease
- Sexual behavior that is mature for the child's age

Neglect includes, but is not limited to, failure to provide or attempt to provide a child with food, clothing, or shelter necessary to sustain the life or health of the child. *Failure to protect* is a form of neglect when someone allows another person to abuse or neglect a child without taking appropriate measures to stop it. This applies in situations in which a person knows or should know of the occurrence. *Improper supervision* is when parents or a caregiver leave a child alone without providing direct, proper supervision, placing the child at risk for harm. *Abandonment* is a situation in which the legal parent or guardian leaves a child either at home alone or in the care of a noncustodial adult and does not return or call to inquire about the child.

If a staff person is suspected of child abuse or neglect, the employee should also be reported to CPS or the state's licensing department. Several states have a separate department that handles cases involving suspected child abuse and neglect when a staff person is involved. Therefore, it is important for all staff members to be properly trained on the state's child-abuse and neglect reporting procedures.

The reporting department name and numbers should also be provided to staff and parents to ensure that everyone has the correct reporting information.

The person who has the knowledge or suspicion should be the one who makes the report. If the person feels that the child is in danger of imminent harm, he should make the call immediately and not wait until the end of the day. In the United States, the National Child Abuse Hotline is 1-800-422-4453 (https://www.childhelp.org). Every state has its own toll-free number and website as well. There could be numerous reasons for a child's behavior, but if you are concerned, make the call.

When it comes to protecting children, you should never be afraid of speaking up.

MANDATED REPORTER RESPONSIBILITY

A *mandated reporter* is anyone who works with children in any capacity. Mandated reporters are required to report all forms of suspected child abuse and neglect. There are civil and criminal penalties if a mandated reporter does not make a report when he suspects or observes child abuse and neglect. You do not have to have any documented evidence or verification of any find before making the report. A mandated reporter is not expected to investigate the situation. There is immunity from civil and criminal penalties for anyone making a report in good faith. *Good faith* means that a person is making the report because he believes a child is actually being abused or neglected and not because of any other reasons, such as not liking the parent or staff member or wanting to seek revenge.

Program directors are mandated reporters. If a staff member comes to you about suspected child abuse or neglect, support that person in filing a report with CPS. If you have reason to suspect abuse or neglect, you must also file a report with CPS, even if the situation involves staff working at your center. If a child discloses information related to child abuse or neglect, try to avoid showing any signs of shock or disapproval, and avoid asking leading questions. If there is a need to ask a question for clarity, ask an open-ended question such as, "What happened?" instead of "Who did that to you?" The function of the CPS department is to serve and protect children by investigating complaints of child abuse and neglect. As a mandated reporter, it is not the responsibility of the program director or child-care staff to interview the child or the parents. The circumstances should not be discussed with coworkers. Some programs have written child- abuse and neglect policies that require the staff to inform the program director or management before contacting CPS. The program director or manager will then approve or dismiss the allegations and determine whether CPS should be contacted. However, by law the staff person is not under any legal obligation to inform the program director or manager. If staff are questioned during a CPS investigation, it is their responsibility to be honest and not withhold any information.

A mandated reporter should not inform the suspected abuser, as this may place the child in danger. I encountered a situation once in which a child told his teacher that he was being hit at home by his parent. The teacher informed the program director, and the program director instructed the teacher not to call CPS. When the parent arrived to pick up the child that evening, the program director informed the parent that her child had said that he was being hit at home. The parent did not return the child to the center. The teacher and program director had failed to protect the child.

The potential for the parents to remove the child from the center is one of the main reasons why they should not be contacted or informed. The program director stated that she informed the parent because she did not believe the child. She said the parent was always friendly when she was at the center, so she did not believe that the parent would ever hit her own child. The program director also stated that she had never reported a parent to CPS because a child said that something happened to him at home. She did not believe that she should take the word of a child over that of a parent, instead saying that the only way she would believe a child was if a parent displayed abusive behavior at the center. This program director had to be retrained on the mandated-reporter requirements and the importance of protecting children by listening to them.

For some of you, just determining when to report situations of suspected child abuse or neglect may be difficult. Many people wonder, "What if I'm wrong?" or "What if I get fired?" or think, "But the parents are professionals with good jobs," or "They'll know I was the one who reported them." Legally, you cannot be fired or penalized for reporting your suspicions related to a child being abused or neglected or for cooperating with an investigation. When it comes to protecting children, you should never be afraid of speaking up.

I still remember the first time I had to call CPS for a child. The child had multiple bruises that were in various stages of healing. Several were fresh and red, and others had started healing with scabs. When I made the first call, the CPS worker went to the child's home and, after speaking with the mother, determined that the child was not in any danger. The child was not removed from the home. I was not convinced that the child was not being abused, so I contacted CPS again. The worker I spoke with stated that CPS had closed the case. I explained that the visible injuries on the child were not normal marks that a four-year-old child would have. The CPS staffer had me give details of the markings that I had observed. Because I was insisting that something had happened to the child at home, the case was reopened. After the investigation, the child was removed from the home. A relative of the child later told me that the mother had abused her older children, and they too had been removed from the home.

NUTRITION AND FOOD HANDLING

Young children, like all people, need nutritious food every day. Physicians (Mayo Clinic, 2021) recommend proteins, such as lean meat and poultry, eggs, beans, peas, and soy products; fruits (but limit the fruit juice); vegetables, including dark green, red and orange varieties, and bean and peas; whole grains, such as whole-wheat bread, oatmeal, and brown rice; and dairy, such as fat-free or low-fat milk, yogurt, and cheese or fortified soy products. When preparing or handling food, always wash your hands with soap and water and dry them with a clean paper towel before beginning. Closely follow your state and center regulations for safe food handling. If your center doesn't have written procedures on this topic, reach out to your local child-care consultant or your child-care resource and referral (CCR&R) for help in developing safe procedures.

In the state of Washington, child-care centers are required to ensure proper nutrition for children in care by complying with the following child-nutrition requirements:

- Meals, snack foods, and beverages provided to the children must comply with the most current edition of the US Department of Agriculture's (USDA's) Child and Adult Care Food Program (CACFP) nutrition standards for meals and snacks (2013), or the USDA National School Lunch and School Breakfast Program standards (2021).
  - An early learning provider must supply dated menus.
  - Food and beverage substitutions to a scheduled menu must be of equal nutritional value.
  - An early learning provider must serve only water, unflavored milk, or 100 percent fruit or vegetable juice.
  - An early learning provider must limit the consumption of 100 percent fruit juice to no more than four to six ounces per day for children between one and six years old, and eight to twelve ounces per day for children seven through twelve years old.
- An early learning provider must serve a fruit or vegetable during at least one snack per day. The fruit and vegetable serving may count as one of the two required snack components or as a third snack component.

The Wrong Bottle of Breast Milk

Aria, the lead caregiver, is four-month-old Jabari's primary caregiver at the center. When she went to the refrigerator to retrieve his bottle of breast milk, she noticed that he had only one bottle when he should have had two. Aria asked two of the assistant caregivers, Halia and Nalani, about it, but they said they had not seen Jabari's bottle. Aria checked the counter and found Jabari's empty bottle. She then checked the infants' feeding logs to see which child had had an extra bottle and found that Omari had. She then informed Halia, Omari's primary caregiver, that he had been fed Jabari's bottle of breast milk. Aria also informed Carolina, the program director, that Omari had received Jabari's bottle. The center policy was for a caregiver feeding a child to have another caregiver verify the name on the bottle before feeding; each of the two caregivers must sign the infant's daily feeding log.

Carolina spoke to Halia, Lolana, and Nalani, the assistant caregivers, to determine what had happened. Halia said that she was on break when the bottle was given to Omari. She said that Omari's daily log showed that Lolana had given him the bottle, and Nalani had verified on the log that the correct bottle was given. Halia had no idea how such a mistake could have happened. She was upset because she was his primary caregiver, and the situation would not have happened if she had been in the classroom.

Lolana said that she had gotten the bottle from the refrigerator without checking the last name because she did not know Omari's last name; she was covering breaks in the infant classroom. Omari was crying, and she was in a hurry to feed him. When she removed the bottle from the warmer, she held the bottle up and asked Nalani to make sure that she had the correct bottle. Nalani, who was across the room, said yes, and Lolana fed the bottle to Omari. She did not walk over to show Nalani the bottle, and Nalani did not look at the name on the bottle when she verified that the bottle was correct. Lolana was not aware of the feeding procedure until Carolina asked why the policy was not followed.

When Carolina spoke with Nalani, Nalani said that she had verified the bottle without looking at the name, but she was sure that it was Omari's bottle. Omari and Jabari have the same type of bottles that look alike. Nalani and Lolana had added their names to the log without verifying Omari's name on the bottle. Nalani admitted that she did not follow the bottle policy.

PROBLEM

If a child is to be fed breast milk, he must receive only the breast milk provided by the family. The CDC warns that feeding the wrong breast milk risks exposing the infant to diseases such as HIV and hepatitis B and C as well as to medications (2021b). Center policies are intended to prevent such mix ups.

RESOLUTION

A policy is only as good as the individuals who are implementing it. All staff must be trained if they are to care for children. Carolina wrote up Lolana and Nalani and suspended them for two days for not following the center's procedures put in place to prevent children from receiving the incorrect bottles. Carolina informed Jabari and Omari's mothers, and they were both understanding and did not disenroll their children from the center. When Lolana and Nalani returned to the center, they were each retrained on the center's feeding procedures.

The Wrong Bottle of Formula

Andrea, a floater who worked with preschoolers, was in the infant classroom covering breaks. As she was holding and feeding Amede, nine-month-old Jazmin started to get fussy. Andrea walked over to the fridge, grabbed a bottle that she thought was Jazmin's, and placed it in the bottle warmer. By the time the bottle warmer beeped, she had finished feeding Amede and placed him on the floor. She grabbed the bottle from the warmer and began feeding it to Jazmin. Halfway through the feeding, she realized that the bottle actually belonged to three-month-old Irina. Once she realized this, she immediately stopped feeding Jazmin and told Fiorella, the lead teacher. Fiorella called the office and informed Denise, the program director. Andrea stated that she was a little overwhelmed with trying to feed Amede and prepare Jazmin's bottle at the same time. She realized that she should have known the difference between the bottles because Jazmin's bottles were 8 ounces and Irina's bottles were 4 ounces. Irina's bottle that was fed to Jazmin was discarded. Andrea realized that she needed additional training for working with infants because she was not used to checking the names on bottles before she fed a child.

Denise came down to the classroom and spoke with Andrea. She determined that Andrea had not followed the center's feeding policy that requires the staff to check the name on the bottle and make sure that the name matches the child who is being fed. Denise reprimanded Andrea and scheduled an updated infant-feeding training. She saw no need to change the feeding policy, because it worked when it was implemented.

After her conversation with Andrea, Denise called Irina's mother, Ophelia, to inform her that Irina's bottle had been given to another child and to find out what was in Irina's bottle. Ophelia told her the name of the brand of formula. Denise then called Jazmin's mother, Chira, and informed her that Jazmin had been given the wrong bottle by mistake. Chira was provided the name of the formula that Jazmin had consumed. Neither mother was upset about the mix-up.

PROBLEM

A child must receive only the formula provided by the family. Some children have allergies to the proteins in cow's milk or soy, which can cause excessive crying or fussiness, more gas than normal, loose stools or diarrhea, or vomiting, among other symptoms.

RESOLUTION

A policy without training is an accident waiting to happen. Make sure that the bottles are labeled with each child's first and last names. The actual bottle must be labeled, not just the cap. Once the cap is removed from the bottle, there is no identifying information associated with the bottle, which will make it easier for a mistake to be made.

Have a two-step verification: Before feeding a child, one staff member retrieves the bottle from the refrigerator and takes the child and the bottle to another caregiver, who double checks that the bottle is for the correct child.

Keeping Food from Toddlers

The toddlers were seated at the lunch table to celebrate Santiago's birthday with the pizza and cupcakes laid out in front of the children. The children kept getting out of their seats, and for more than ten minutes, their caregiver, Zuri, repeatedly told them to sit down and be quiet. Whenever the children got up, Zuri would take them by their arms and move them back to their seats at the table. Zuri would yell at the children when they got up from their chairs. She told the children that they could not have any pizza or cupcakes or go outside to play if they did not sit quietly in their seats. When her threat did not keep the children in their seats, she threatened to call their parents. She refused to feed the children because they would not remain quiet or seated.

PROBLEM

Toddlers are almost always on the move exploring and investigating their environment. Expecting them to sit for more than a few minutes or to be quiet is not developmentally appropriate. No child should be threatened, humiliated, or deprived of food under any circumstances. If a toddler does not want to sit at a table, the reason might just be that they are not hungry or that they would rather be playing. This is why it is okay to let toddlers eat on demand.

RESOLUTION

Her program director met with Zuri and talked with her about developmentally appropriate practices with toddlers. She also had Zuri participate in training on the topic. She warned Zuri that she would be written up if this situation occurred again.

Sanitary Issues in the Toddler Room

Jamilah was volunteering in the toddler classroom when she observed nineteen-month-old Issa eating food off of the floor and walking around the room with food during lunchtime. He also drank from another child's sippy cup at a different table. Jamilah informed Annabelle, the lead caregiver, and Ivory, the assistant, because they were not addressing the situation.

Jamilah observed Annabelle drop twenty-month-old Chike's sippy cup on the floor and pick it up and give it back to the child without cleaning the cup. When the sippy cup fell on the floor, milk spilled out and Annabelle cleaned the milk from the floor with a dish cloth. She then placed the dish cloth on the table where the children were still eating lunch. Annabelle did not wash her hands. Because the dish cloth was on the table, Ivory—who had not seen Annabelle use it on the floor—wiped down the table with it after lunch. After lunch, Annabelle was changing diapers, Ivory was cleaning the tables, and the children were on the other side of the classroom running around pushing and pulling each other.

Later, Jamilah went to the office and spoke with Melissa, the program director, about what she had observed. Melissa stated that she was not sure why Issa had been allowed to eat off of the floor or why Annabelle would give a child anything from the floor. She said she would speak with Annabelle and Ivory about reusing the dish cloth to clean the table and the other concerns that Jamilah had brought to her attention.

Annabelle told Melissa that she did not remember Chike dropping her cup on the floor during lunch because the children drop their cups on the floor frequently. She said she knows that the cup should be cleaned if it hits the floor before giving it back to the child, and she tries to do so, but she admitted that sometimes she forgets because she is in a hurry or another child needs her attention.

Annabelle agreed that she had made a mistake by leaving the dirty dish cloth on the table; she should have put it in the dirty hamper to be washed. She said that particular day was unusual because Issa had just started in her class and needed additional attention. He was taking the other children's food, but she could not remember if he was eating their food. She did not recall him eating from the floor because she said she would have stopped him. She and Ivory were working on having Issa sit at the table during lunch.

PROBLEM

The program director was not regularly observing in the classroom. If she had been, she would have recognized what was going on with the new child and would have assigned an additional staff member to assist during lunch.

The lead caregiver was not seeing a problem, so she had not informed the program director that additional help was needed. Regular communication between the lead caregiver and program director is crucial.

RESOLUTION

Melissa explained that they should not let a child walk around with food or eat the other children's food. She offered to have the floater help in the classroom during lunch until Issa had adjusted. Melissa helped Annabelle to develop a plan to help Issa in the classroom, including having Ivory sitting with him during lunch. Melissa then explained that dish towels should be used one time and removed from the area so another staff member does not reuse them before they are cleaned. The tables can be washed and sanitized after the children are on their cots for nap time. The caregivers should not be cleaning the table instead of supervising the children.

If you have staff who are not noticing behaviors such as a child eating off of the floor or drinking from another child's sippy cup, they have to be trained to observe the children carefully. Staff have to be trained to not get so busy with other things that they are not aware of what the children are doing. This happens frequently during lunch because the staff are changing diapers, washing hands, cleaning the tables and chairs, and putting out cots. The tables and floors can be cleaned once the children are down for nap time so as not to distract the staff from providing appropriate care and supervision. Directors also cannot assume that staff are aware of procedures for keeping the classroom sanitary.

SLEEP

Infants and toddlers should sleep on demand because they are growing and developing at a phenomenal rate. Each child grows at his own pace and may need a nap outside of a scheduled nap time to regain their strength. Rather than schedule naps for children this age, give them the opportunity to sleep when they are tired. When they are not provided the opportunity to rest, they may be out of sorts and crying or upset.

Allowing the children to sleep on demand also helps with the rhythm of the classroom. When infants and toddlers sleep on their own schedules, some will be sleeping while others are awake. That means that caregivers can be feeding, changing, or playing with the children who are awake. When the sleeping little ones wake up, caregivers can work with them while the other children are likely ready for a nap. Sometimes, caregivers think that having all of the infants go down for a nap at the same time will give them an opportunity for a break. Unfortunately, the price of that approach is that they will be working harder when all the children wake up at the same time. Staff can make mistakes when they are overwhelmed working with the infants who are hungry and crying all at once.

Children older than one year and toddlers should sleep in a crib or on a cot. At this age, a light blanket and small stuffed toy or "lovey" is acceptable (Nemours KidsHealth, 2019). Toddlers will sleep anywhere when they are tired. I had a parent call me once to tell me that he had observed his fourteen-month-old toddler sleeping outside on the playground. What troubled the father was that his child was sleeping while leaning against the caregiver. The caregiver was just standing there, not making any attempt to take the child inside to sleep on a cot. When he asked the teacher why his child was sleeping on the playground, she just stated that he was tired, and she did not want to take him into the center because she knew that he would be picked up soon. The father was furious, and rightly so. Her explanation was not a reason to have a child sleeping on the playground.

Each infant (up to one year of age) should sleep alone in a crib. If an infant falls asleep in or on an unapproved sleeping area such as the floor, a bouncer, a pillow, swing, high chair, infant seat, or anything other than a crib, they should be immediately removed and placed in a crib. I have witnessed many infants sleeping in an unapproved area, device, or on the floor of the classroom. The classroom teacher always says the same thing: "The child just fell asleep." The only word in that sentence that is important is *asleep* and the child should have been moved. When each infant has an assigned primary caregiver, that person will be aware of the child's sleep patterns and can place him in a crib when the child is getting sleepy. This will remove the chances of the child falling asleep outside of the crib.

Place the child on her back, without any objects such as blankets, stuffed animals, or soft toys in the crib. When parents want their infant to sleep with a blanket, explain to them the risk of suffocation. Additionally, parents will often say that their child will not go to sleep without a bottle. This is not appropriate because the child could choke.

Each crib should have a firm mattress with a tight-fitting sheet. *Tight-fitting* means that the sheet does not loosen or bunch up, which could cause infant suffocation. The mattress must be waterproof with no cracks, rips, or tears. If the mattress is not waterproof, and a child has a leaky diaper, the cracked or torn mattress will absorb the bodily fluids and create an area that cannot be cleaned or sanitized. (See the appendix for links to information on safe sleep.)

Toddler Falls Asleep before Lunch

Jagrati, the program director, was observing the toddler classroom from the hallway window when she saw fifteen-month-old Abeer fall asleep at the lunch table. Lakshmi, the lead caregiver, set him on his feet and had Abeer walk around the classroom to wake up. She walked him over to the bathroom door so she could retrieve wipes from Kashika, the assistant caregiver, who was with another child. When Lakshmi let go of Abeer's arm, Abeer fell face first onto the floor because he was asleep. Abeer received a bruise on his cheek. Jagrati had Lakshmi complete an incident report, and she called Abeer's father, Zain, and informed him that Abeer had fallen and hit his cheek.

PROBLEM

Zain was not happy when he picked up Abeer and Lakshmi told him that Abeer falls asleep at the lunch table every day.

RESOLUTION

Lakshmi assured him that, going forward, she would allow Abeer to go sleep on a cot. She apologized for Abeer being injured. Jagrati assured Zain that the toddler caregivers would be retrained. Jagrati suspended Lakshmi for three days and informed her that if she forced the toddlers to stay awake when they were sleepy again, she would be terminated.

Child Held Down on His Cot

Two-year-old Zeke did not want to go to sleep. His caregiver, Skyler, placed her leg over Zeke's back while he was on the cot to hold him down. Zeke's father, Conner, was standing outside the toddler classroom, having arrived to pick Zeke up early, and observed Skyler with her leg across Zeke's back and Zeke trying to get up from under her leg. Conner immediately went into the classroom and confronted Skyler, who stated that she was just holding him down until he settled down on his cot. Conner expressed his frustration and took Zeke out of the classroom. As he was exiting, he informed Natalie, the program director, that Zeke would not be returning to the center and described what he had seen.

After Conner left the center, Natalie went to the toddler classroom and spoke with Skyler. Skyler admitted that she had placed her leg on Zeke's back to hold him down and to keep him on his cot. She said she did so just for a second or two until he calmed down.

PROBLEM

Children who do not wish to sleep should be provided with quiet activities and not forced to stay on their cots.

RESOLUTION

Natalie terminated Skyler's employment for placing her leg on Zeke's back during nap time, which was against the center's nap time and discipline policies.

Child Sleeping in a Swing

Zenia was concerned when she saw her seven-month-old child sleeping in a swing when she arrived. She complained to Yashodhara, the program director. Yashodhara was new to the center, and after receiving the complaint, she scheduled time the following day to observe Watika, the lead caregiver, and Tamanna, the assistant caregiver, in the infant classroom.

Yashodhara observed the classroom for two hours, during which time she saw several infants in confining equipment, such as infant seats, swings, and bouncers, almost exclusively for her entire observation. Rather than using cribs, when the children fell asleep the caregivers allowed them to sleep in the infant seats, swings, and bouncers. The infants were rarely held by Watika or Tamanna; they were only picked up to be changed or moved from one piece of equipment to another. Infants were also placed in high chairs for no apparent reason. They were not eating and had nothing on their trays for fifteen to twenty minutes.

PROBLEM

At best, this approach is mere custodial care and is not developmentally appropriate. Infants need time to lay on their tummies, be held, lay on their backs and kick, discover their hands, try to pick things up, and attempt to roll over or sit up. Caregivers should talk, read, and sing to infants to support the development of their social, emotional, and language skills.

RESOLUTION

After Yashodhara concluded her observation, she explained the risks of infant death to Watika and Tamanna, and she had them move the children who had fallen asleep in infant seats, swings, and bouncers to cribs. She provided Watika and Tamanna with the center's safe-sleep policy that explained the risks associated with unsafe sleep. She also scheduled a time to retrain them on developmentally appropriate practices for infants because the children were spending most of their time in confining equipment with little interaction.

HYGIENE

Proper hygiene is an important part of keeping the children safe and healthy at the center. All toys that the children place in their mouths or that are dirty should be removed and washed, rinsed, and sanitized before children have access to them again. The classroom tables used for meals have to be washed, rinsed, and sanitized before each use. The classroom should be cleaned weekly as well as immediately after the staff learn that a child has tested positive for a communicable disease. This will help to reduce the spread within the classroom and center. If the identified child has a sibling attending the center in a different classroom, that classroom should also be cleaned and sanitized. This is often a step that is missed because the focus is only on the child who is diagnosed.

The staff's and children's hands should be washed when soiled. Regular and proper washing will reduce the spread of germs within the classroom. Handwashing after diapering should take place in a designated sink. The diapering sink should not be used for any other handwashing reasons. This will reduce the chances of cross contamination and the potential of spreading germs. If the staff wear gloves to change the children's diapers, they should wash their hands and change their gloves after each diaper. Once, I was asked by a caregiver if she could wear three pairs of gloves during diaper changes, remove a pair of gloves after each diaper change, then wash her hands after changing the last child's diaper. The answer to that question is no. The staff and children's hands have to be washed after *each* diaper change.

Potty Accident in the Toddler Room

Two-year-old Caleb had a bowel movement on himself. Neither Audrey, the program director, nor Caleb's teacher, Eve, helped clean him up. After they discovered that Caleb had had an accident, Audrey asked Eve to take Caleb to the bathroom. Eve had him take off his clothes and put them in a bag, without assistance. Caleb, of course, smeared feces down the backs of his legs. Two-year-olds need assistance and do not know how to completely clean themselves. Even after realizing that Caleb was not able to clean himself, Eve only gave Caleb a wet paper towel to clean himself rather than helping him. She then gave Caleb his clean clothes to put on without being properly cleaned, leaving Caleb covered in dry feces. The center had just started enrolling toddlers and had not had any children have an accident since they had opened the toddler classroom.

Audrey called Jasmine, Caleb's mother, and informed her that Caleb had had a potty accident at school. She did not inform her that Caleb had not been cleaned afterward. Jasmine arrived during nap time to pick Caleb up to find him asleep on his cot and smelling strongly of feces. She woke him and realized that he had dry feces on his clothes. When she took Caleb to the bathroom, she discovered feces on the backs of his legs and in his pants and underwear. She realized that Caleb had not been cleaned before he put on the clean clothes. Jasmine had to clean Caleb before they could leave the center.

She asked Audrey why Caleb had not been cleaned, and Audrey told her that they were not allowed to clean children, that it was the center's policy that children must be able to clean themselves. Jasmine did not accept that explanation and decided that Caleb would not be returning to the center after the incident. However, she did not inform Audrey of her decision to disenroll her son.

A week later, Audrey sent a bill for the week that Caleb had not attended the center. The center policy states that the parents are required to give a two-week notice when disenrolling their children. Jasmine complained to the center owner about how Caleb had been treated and said she had been willing to leave the center without filing a formal complaint and just put the incident behind them, but she was angered by the center's disregard for Caleb and subsequent request for money after she had removed him from the center.

PROBLEM

The center was wrong in their actions on multiple levels. First, Caleb's caregivers did not clean him after he had an accident. The toddler caregivers should have been trained in how to handle accidents with children this age before the children actually arrived at the center. In this case, accepting toddlers without training the staff on appropriate care for children this age caused issues for the center.

Second, the center sent a bill to the parent after the child was disenrolled. Program directors and managers should not expect parents to pay additional tuition when they have removed their child because of an issue that occurred at the center. When the center asks for payment in these circumstances, they should expect a complaint to be filed against the center.

RESOLUTION

The program director reviewed the center's toddler-care policies and discussed them with other early childhood professionals. She revised the policies and set up training for the toddler caregivers, so they would know how to handle potty accidents with little ones.

The center owner agreed that Jasmine should not have to pay the bill for the time after Caleb had been disenrolled.

SUPERVISION OF CHILDREN

Child Left in the Center's Lobby

Sam, a five-year-old preschooler, was left in the lobby of the center after returning from a walk outside. Beatrice, the teacher, had seven children with her, and after they finished their walk, the children walked inside to look at the center's fish tank. The lobby has two doors: one that leads to the classrooms and one that leads to the outside. Stopping and looking at the fish tank was part of the preschoolers' routine after their walk. This time, Beatrice did not complete the required name-to-face check before or after returning to the classroom. She had the children line up and did not see Sam standing around the corner when they headed to the classroom area.

Selena, another teacher, walked into the lobby and saw Sam. She could tell there was something wrong because Sam was alone and looked scared. When she spoke to the child, Sam started crying and said that her teacher had left her, and she did not know where her class went. Selena returned Sam to her classroom; Beatrice did not know that Sam had not returned with the rest of the children. Selena informed Martha, the program director, that she had found Sam in the lobby unsupervised and that the child's teacher had been unaware that Sam was missing.

In the classroom, Sam said that she wanted her mother. When Beatrice could not calm her down, she tried to call Sam's mother, Carla, but the phone number had been changed. Beatrice called Martha and explained what had happened and asked her if she could contact Carla so that Sam could speak to her.

Martha received the same message when she called Carla. She then called the next number listed on the information card, the contact information for Sam's grandmother. The grandmother provided Carla's new phone number. Martha explained to Carla that Sam had been left in the lobby of the center and was upset and wanted to talk to her. She also told Carla that the phone number that they had on file was not working and reminded her that it was important that they always have the correct phone number in the event of an emergency. Carla spoke with Sam in the classroom, and she calmed down.

Martha spoke to Beatrice, who explained that she did not know that Sam was not with the class when they returned from the walk. She admitted that she had not completed the name-to-face check once they returned from their walk.

PROBLEM

There are two problems in this scenario: first, Beatrice did not provide appropriate supervision of the children, and second, Carla changed her phone number and did not inform the center.

RESOLUTION

Beatrice was written up and retrained on the importance of always providing appropriate supervision of the children. Martha reminded the entire staff to use the required name-to-face sheets to account for all of the children and to make sure there are no blind spots where children can hide during transition periods. A *blind spot* is any area in the classroom where the adults are unable to see the children from every vantage point.

Martha also sent out a reminder to all parents to review and update their children's information records to ensure that the correct information is on file in case of an emergency.

The center should have a written policy that addresses how staff will handle a lost or misplaced child. There should be a code that alerts the staff and means that all available caregivers should begin looking for the child. All exits should be secured, and the surrounding areas should be checked in case the child exited the center. By having a process in place, the center will be prepared to handle the situation and to locate the missing child quickly. Discuss possible scenarios and practice responses with the staff.

Transitions are especially tricky times. Most of the time, children are misplaced because a staff person is distracted, does not know the names of the children in their care, has a new child in the class, did not accurately count the children, or does not have a good transition routine. Teachers, caregivers, and other staff must be especially vigilant to ensure that each child is accounted for. Rather than simply counting heads, teachers should have the children line up and participate in a song or fingerplay while the teacher counts the children with a name-to-face check. The *name-to-face check* means that a staff person actually looks at the child's face and matches it to the name on the daily attendance sheet to recognize that the child is present. Of course, the name-to-face sheets will only work if they are accurate. If the attendance sheets or computer attendance are not accurate, the chances of a child being left behind or misplaced will increase.

As the children move to another room or outside, one staff member should be at the front of the line and the other should be at the end of the line to ensure that no child is left behind. Once the class reaches its destination, a second name-to-face should be completed before entering the new space. Send each child through the door as you complete the name-to-face. The first teacher should stand in the door to be able to see the children in the hallway and the second teacher can enter the gym or outside on the playground to supervise the children.

If there is only one staff person assigned to the classroom, then the name-to-face should be completed before entering the classroom and the children should be given an activity so that when all of the children are in the classroom, they can be counted again to ensure no mistake was made and all of the children are present and accounted for. Whenever possible, when a staff member is working alone, have a floater or managerial staff member available to assist with the transition from one place to another to reduce the chance of a child leaving the group or being left behind. This will ensure that all the children are accounted for before they leave an area and will reduce the chances that a child will be unsupervised by mistake. (We explore more ideas for transitions in chapter 5.)

For older children, give them place cards as they exit the classroom. As they enter the next location, they can return the cards and you can check them against the class list, thereby ensuring that all children are accounted for. For younger children, you can utilize lanyards. The teacher keeps the lanyards on the same clipboard as the daily attendance (name-to-face) sheets. When each child arrives to the classroom, he receives a lanyard with his name, which he places around his neck. When children leave the classroom to go to the next location, such as the playground or gym, they provide that teacher with the lanyard as they enter, and the teacher checks it against the class list. If a lanyard is missing, the teacher will know immediately that they do not have all of the children and, more importantly, which child is not with the group. This is just another layer of documentation to account for the children.

To test the process, the program director could randomly remove a child from a group of children without the teachers knowing and then see how long it takes them to realize that the child is missing. If you remove a child from a group, make sure that the child is provided with an activity and either taken outside to the playground or to the multipurpose classroom so that he has an opportunity to continue to play. The goal is not to cause the child any distress. While doing this to teachers may sound harsh, this exercise is important because most staff have never lost or misplaced a child and can't imagine how anyone could do so. This exercise will show all staff how one mistake can result in a misplaced child and why it is important to always know the name of the children in care and the number of children present in the classroom.

Child Left Unsupervised during New COVID-19 Drop-Off Procedures

Luisa, the program director, was not at the center when three-year-old Bianca was left unattended in the preschool classroom. Eleonora, the office manager, told Luisa that Giovanna, the school-age caregiver, found Bianca in the preschool classroom alone after preschool teacher Elisa had left her in the empty classroom. Luisa reviewed the center's video, which showed Bianca entering the preschool classroom, removing her jacket, and hanging it on a hook. She put her backpack in her cubby and stood there looking around the classroom. After a few minutes, she started to suck her thumb but did not move. Bianca was alone in the classroom for about twelve minutes until Giovanna discovered her.

During the COVID-19 pandemic, parents were required to drop their children off at the center's front door. Eleonora and Elisa were responsible for receiving the children, checking their temperatures, and asking their parents the required questions about possible exposure to the virus. Each child's name had to be highlighted after she entered the building. The child was then taken to her classroom, where the classroom teacher was required to document the child's arrival time. Elisa was also taking care of the breakfast in the kitchen. Eleonora said that they were taking turns greeting the children and taking them to their classrooms. During this time, the maintenance person arrived to fix a sink that was leaking, and Eleonora had to show him where to go, leaving Elisa in the front to greet the parents.

Eleonora heard Giovanna yelling that Bianca had been left alone in the preschool classroom. Eleonora went to the classroom and found Bianca standing alone in the empty room. Giovanna explained to Eleonora that she had found Bianca standing inside the preschool classroom, peeking out of the glass panel in the closed door. Eleonora stated that she was about to take Bianca to the pre-K classroom when the preschool lead teacher, Padina, arrived. Padina had been in the pre-K classroom where the children were combined in the morning. Once the pre-K teacher arrived, Padina brought her class to the preschool classroom. Padina did not know that Bianca was in the preschool classroom alone. Once Bianca was safely with Padina, Eleonora called Luisa and informed her of the incident.

Giovanna confirmed Eleonora's story and added that Bianca had looked scared. Giovanna had gone to the pre-K classroom and looked through the window; Padina was still in there, which meant that the preschool children were still combined with the pre-K class. Giovanna realized that Bianca was alone in the classroom. She immediately called out to Eleonora to come and take care of Bianca.

Elisa said it was a busy morning. She was the opener and was receiving children at the door and taking them to their classrooms, as well as screening parents. She said that Eleonora was busy with the maintenance person, and she was alone to receive the children and to make the pancakes for breakfast in the kitchen. When Bianca was dropped off, Elisa walked her to the preschool classroom. She said that she assumed that the combined room had already split, and all the children were in their respective classrooms. Elisa opened the door of the preschool room and shouted, "Bianca is here." She did not check inside the classroom to make sure that there was a staff member present in the preschool classroom, and she did not hear anyone say anything. Elisa said that she was generally good about making sure that the children are supervised when in her care, but this was her mistake.

Luisa called Bianca's mother, Jade, and informed her that Bianca was left alone in the preschool classroom before Giovanna, her previous caregiver, saw her all alone in the preschool classroom. Jade was not upset and appreciated the phone call.

PROBLEM

The new procedure placed added responsibilities on the staff. Regardless, it is important to make sure that the children are escorted to their classrooms and given to an actual staff member.

RESOLUTION

Jade was not upset and she did not disenroll Bianca from the center. Luisa wrote up Elisa and required that she be retrained on the center's supervision policy. Luisa stressed to Elisa the importance of making sure that a caregiver is present before she leaves a child in a classroom.

Children are frequently lost, misplaced, left behind, or allowed to walk away from the group during transition times. Recognize that mistakes can and do happen, but with training and the proper procedures in place, the chances of a child being left behind during a transition time will be reduced.

Four-Year-Old Left Alone at the Reception Desk

Lila, the program director, completed a tour of the center for a prospective parent and returned to the front desk. Penelope, the cook, told her that one of the toddler teachers had found Liam sitting alone on a wooden bench next to the front desk. Liam was sitting quietly and did not appear upset. When the teacher asked Liam what he was doing there alone, he stated that he was not sure. Penelope happened to walk by and offered to stay with Liam until Lila returned.

Lila went to the preschool classroom and spoke with Madison, the preschool teacher, who stated that she had sent Liam by himself to the front office because he was throwing toys in the classroom. While asking Lila to come remove a child from the classroom was a common practice in this center, Madison had not let Lila know that she was sending Liam.

Lila called Liam's mother to let her know that Liam was found sitting alone at the front desk. The mother was concerned that her son could have walked out the front door because he was unsupervised.

PROBLEM

There are a couple of problems with this scenario. Madison acknowledged that it is normal protocol to either walk a child to the front desk or have Lila come and get the child from the classroom. A center should not have a procedure where children are sent to the office because they are having an issue in the classroom. Also, children should not be sent to the office because it is not an approved space. If a child is injured in the classroom, it would be an accident; if a child is injured in a space that is not approved for children, then it is not viewed in the same fashion because the child should not have been there.

RESOLUTION

Lila revised the staff procedures and retrained the staff on handling challenging child behaviors. Going forward, the teacher would look at the whole situation starting with the classroom setup and the triggers that may be causing a child to behave in challenging ways. Then the teacher would try some developmentally appropriate solutions to change the child's behavior. (We explore ways of handling challenging child behavior in chapter 9.)

Parents need to know that their children are safe at the center. They need to know that situations in which a child is endangered are taken seriously. Mistakes do happen, but parents must be fully informed as soon as possible. Waiting until pickup or calling at the end of the day to inform them of a problem (or worse, not informing them at all) only gives parents the impression that you are hiding something and undermines their trust. If a parent has to ask you about a situation that occurred at the center, you are never going to come out on the winning end of that conversation. Open and honest communication with the parents is crucial.

Child Left Outside Alone in the Parking Lot

I was the program director at the center when the police arrived with three-year-old David. The police officer stated that he had found David walking alone in the center's parking lot. The officer asked if David attended the center, and I said yes. The officer returned David to me and left the center.

I walked down to the preschool classroom with David and informed Jennifer, the teacher, and Ann, the assistant, that a police officer had just returned him. Neither of them had noticed that

David was not in the room. I then had the assistant program director to cover the classroom so that I could speak with each of the teachers separately in my office.

When I asked Jennifer how David had been in the parking lot alone, she stated that they had taken the children on a walk around the building to look at the fall colors on the trees. She thought that all the children were accounted for when they returned to the classroom. I asked her if she had completed a name-to-face check with the children before returning to the building, and she stated that she had. She went on to explain that David was clearly not capable of staying with the group and that maybe he should not be allowed to leave the center. I was genuinely concerned with her logic. I said, "So let me understand. It was David's fault that he was left outside in the parking lot?" Jennifer basically said yes because he had not stayed with the class.

I then spoke with Ann. She stated that she was in the front of the line and Jennifer was in the back, and she did not see David leave the line. She said she did not complete the required name-to-face check with the children when they returned to the building. Ann was very upset and crying about the fact that David had been left outside, and she stated that, going forward, she would always complete the name-to-face check both before and after transitioning from one area to another.

PROBLEM

Policies put in place to keep children safe, such as name-to-face checks, must be followed carefully. It is never a young child's fault when an adult fails to keep them safe. Jennifer did not show any remorse or concern for David's safety and then blamed him for her mistake. This appalling behavior is unbecoming of anyone who works with children. Ann was also negligent in following the center's procedures. However, she recognized the dangers of not counting the children and understood what could have happened to David had he not been found by the police officer and returned to the center.

RESOLUTION

I explained to Jennifer that, because she did not understand the mistake that had placed David in harm's way and because she had not realized that he was missing to begin with, I had no choice but to terminate her employment.

Because Ann showed genuine remorse, I wrote her up and required her to participate in additional training on safely transitioning children to and from the classroom. I also told Ann that if a child in her care were left unattended again for any reason, she would be immediately terminated. Ann again apologized and assured me that this would never happen again, and it did not.

After speaking with Jennifer and Ann, I immediately called David's mother and informed her that he had been returned to the center by a police officer. I explained that David was found alone in the center's parking lot after the class had gone for a walk. I told her that his teacher, Jennifer, was terminated and that the assistant, Ann, had been written up and would receive additional training. She was satisfied with this response.

Child Left Outside on the Playground

Saada, the lead caregiver, told Ashanti, the program director, five-year-old Candis was not in the classroom and was left outside on the playground by assistant caregiver Kagiso. Saada could not look for Candis herself, as she was alone in the classroom with the other children. Ashanti opened the playground door and found Candis standing right outside the door. She asked Candis what had happened, and Candis stated she had gotten in line with the class. Dalmar, her classmate, was holding the door open for them to enter the building, and he had let the door close before she could enter. Although the door was unlocked, Candis did not think to reopen the door to go inside.

Ashanti spoke with Saada and Kagiso. Saada stated that, when the incident happened, she had just come back from her break. Kagiso was coming inside with the children, and he was at the front of the line. He handed the children off to her in the hallway before she entered the classroom. Saada stated she walked the children into the classroom, and they began sitting down and getting ready for the afternoon. Saada stated she knows where all of the children sit, and she saw that Candis's spot was open. Saada thought Candis may have been in the bathroom but then realized that was not the case. Saada called Ashanti to ask her to look for Candis. Saada stated that Candis could not have been outside unsupervised for more than five minutes.

Kagiso stated he was the only staff member outside with the children. He had them line up near the door to come inside, and he completed the required name-to-face check and head count. When he entered the center, he completed another head count in the hallway but must have miscounted. He then gave the children to Saada. He did not know if she completed a name-to-face check or head count once the children were exchanged.

PROBLEM

It is not a good idea to have a child hold the door for the children unless a staff member can see that all of the children have entered the building, gym, or playground before the door is closed. Children should not be exchanged from one caregiver to another without a name-to-face check completed by both staff members. The missing child would have been discovered immediately if each caregiver had completed his own count of the children.

RESOLUTION

Ashanti reminded Saada and Kagiso to always complete a name-to-face check. Ashanti also called Candis's parents to make them aware of the situation. After Candis was left outside on the playground, Saada developed a buddy system for the children. Now when they line up to leave or return to the classroom, each child must stand next to his buddy.

Failure to consistently conduct procedures for keeping track of the children can result in disaster. I include the following scenario as a warning because it actually happened. Spoiler alert: Everyone is fine, and no child was harmed.

Transition Turned Hostage Situation

The preschool class was returning to the center from their nature walk when three-year-old Daniel left the line without being noticed by Alexis, the lead caregiver, and walked back toward the nature walk. There was a professional office located within the same complex that the children walked past daily on their way to the nature trail. Jessica, the receptionist who worked at the professional office, observed Daniel out of the window heading back toward the nature trail without a caregiver. She went outside, and without alerting Alexis, took Daniel by the hand and led him into the professional office. Jessica did not return Daniel to the center because she wanted Alexis and the center to recognize their negligent behavior.

When Alexis realized Daniel was not with her, she asked the assistant program director to watch her class. She retraced her path but was not able to locate Daniel. Alexis knocked on the professional office door, and when she looked inside, she observed Daniel sitting in a chair talking to Jessica. Alexis entered the office and informed Jessica that she needed to take Daniel. Jessica refused to release the child, stating that she did not believe that Alexis was providing proper supervision. She said she would only return Daniel to his parents so that they would know that Alexis had not properly supervised him.

When Jessica would not release Daniel, Alexis did not want to upset him and she did not want to leave him, so she called the center on her cell phone. She informed Kaitlyn, the program director, of the situation, and Kaitlyn asked to speak to Jessica. Jessica again expressed her concerns about Alexis being negligent and refused to release him to anyone other than his parents. Daniel was not upset or crying; he was just sitting in the chair.

Kaitlyn called the police and walked down to the professional office. When the police arrived, the officer informed Jessica that she was essentially holding the child hostage and that she was breaking the law. He told her she had to immediately release the child to the center. Jessica released Daniel.

When they returned to the center, Kaitlyn contacted Taylor, Daniel's mother, and told her what had happened. Taylor was upset because Daniel had left the group without being noticed. She was even more concerned that Jessica had refused to release Daniel and that the police had to be contacted.

After the incident, Kaitlyn learned that Jessica and the staff at the professional office did not like the children walking past the office every day on their way to the nature trail. Kaitlyn decided to look at ways to address their concerns in order to prevent a reoccurrence of what happened with Daniel. Kaitlyn instructed Alexis to walk the children around the back of the building to access the nature trail. Going forward, the teachers were no longer allowed to take the children to the nature trail alone, no matter how many children they had. Two staff members had to accompany the children, one at the front of the line and one at the end of the line, to make sure that the children were accounted for and did not leave the line.

PROBLEM

This situation could have been avoided had Alexis maintained eye contact with the children and ensured that they were all accounted for before they entered the building.

RESOLUTION

Jessica was not employed by the center, so there was nothing that the center could do. Neither Taylor nor the police pressed charges against Jessica.

When children are allowed to leave the classroom without supervision to go to the bathroom, get a sip of water from the drinking fountain, or wash their hands, they could easily leave the area. Depending on what is going on in the classroom, it would be minutes before anyone notices that the child is missing. Children are curious by nature and many things will capture their attention, causing them to stray away from where they were supposed to be and what they were supposed to be doing. Never allow children to leave the classroom alone.

Child Left the Classroom to Wash His Hands and Did Not Return

Preschool teachers Aalia and Trisha allowed the children to wash their hands at the sink in the hallway directly outside of the classroom before and after lunch because there was only one sink in the classroom. Aalia and Trisha felt that it was quicker for half of the children to use the sink in the hallway and half to use the one in the room.

Aalia sent half of the preschoolers into the hallway to wash their hands while she and Trisha set up the tables in the classroom for lunch. Four-year-old Yatan left the classroom, but he did not wash his hands. Instead, he walked down the hallway and out of the center to the main street, where he was picked up by a person who was driving by. The driver was nervous about transporting the child because she was not sure where Yatan belonged. She decided to check with the center first. She walked Yatan to the front door and the secretary recognized him; the driver left him with her.

The secretary walked Yatan to the classroom where Trisha and Aalia were sitting down at different tables having lunch with the children. There was an empty place where Yatan was supposed to be sitting, but neither teacher had noticed that he was not in the classroom. The secretary returned to the office and informed Ucchal, the program director. Ucchal went to the classroom to see what had happened that allowed Yatan to not only leave the classroom but the building as well.

Trisha and Aalia stated that they always send half of the children into the hallway to wash their hands for lunch and the children always return to the classroom. Ucchal asked Trisha who was responsible for supervising the children when they go out to wash their hands. Trisha said that because it is lunch time, the kitchen staff who bring the lunch are responsible for supervising the children that are in the hallway. Ucchal informed them that the kitchen staff would never be responsible for the children; they were just dropping off the lunches. Ucchal asked the teachers when they noticed Yatan was missing. Trisha and Aalia admitted they did not notice that he was missing until the secretary returned him to the classroom. Trisha stated that Yatan did not sit at her table, which was why she had not noticed. Aalia said that, although he typically sat at her table, she just thought that he was sitting at Trisha's table. She was not sure why she thought that because his place setting was still at her table.

PROBLEM

All staff should be trained on supervision and must watch the children and provide direct supervision at all times. Neither Trisha nor Aalia acknowledged their mistake in not noticing Yatan's absence, which allowed him to walk out of the center.

RESOLUTION

Because of their carelessness and their unwillingness to take any responsibility for Yatan leaving the building, Ucchal terminated Trisha and Aalia's employment. She called Yatan's parents, who were alarmed but decided to let Yatan continue to attend the center because the teachers were no longer employed there. Ucchal also retrained the entire staff on correct supervision procedures.

Children Placed in Harm's Way

An ice cream truck parked outside the child-care center's playground while the preschool children were playing. The ice cream man offered the children free ice cream, and the teachers allowed the children to accept it. The children lined up outside the playground to get their ice cream. The free ice cream was not the issue; however, neither the teachers nor the program director knew this vendor.

Makayla, a preschooler's parent, complained to Mateo, the program director, when she realized the teachers had allowed the children to accept the ice cream. Mateo did not understand why Makayla was upset because the ice cream person was just being nice. Once Makayla explained her concerns to Mateo, he realized the teachers had erred in judgment in allowing the children to have the ice cream.

PROBLEM

The saying that warns against taking candy from a stranger also applies to ice cream trucks or any other stranger offering something to the children. The teachers did not have parental permission to give the children ice cream that was not provided by the center. In this case, the vendor's intentions were kind, but what if they hadn't been? What if the ice cream was a malicious attempt to harm the children? No one at the center had any information about the ice cream vendor. Children could have allergies or dietary restrictions that would prevent them from having certain foods. The teachers should have declined the offer.

After the teachers had allowed the children to have the ice cream, Mateo should have informed the parents instead of letting them learn about the incident from their children. This oversight undermined the parents' trust in the center. According to Decker and Decker (2005), "Early childhood professionals must never become complacent about safety.

RESOLUTION

Program directors have to make sure that all staff are aware that the children are not to be provided anything food-related that the parents or center did not provide. Every precaution has to be taken to keep the parents informed and the children safe. The teachers should have respectfully declined the ice cream and suggested that the driver contact the program director if he wished to provide ice cream for the children.

Child Injured while in Unapproved Area

London, the toddler caregiver, had the children sit in the hallway outside the toddler classroom by the kitchen while she went back into the classroom to get the clipboard she had forgotten. The two-year-olds were sitting unattended when the cook opened the kitchen door. Adeline placed her finger in the door jamb, and when the door closed her fingertip was cut off. London did not contact Adeline's mother, Delilah, and transported Adeline to the hospital in her personal car.

Delilah learned of her daughter's injury when London called her from the hospital. She was furious that she had not been called sooner. When Delilah arrived at the hospital, Adeline's finger was bandaged, and the doctor said that it was a clean cut but the fingertip could not be repaired.

The program director, Rhonda, called London into her office after she returned to the center. London said that Delilah had been at work, and London did not want to disturb her because she knew that Delilah had just started her job and was in training. Instead, London had informed

Adeline's aunt, who works at the center. London felt that she had done the right thing because she transported Adeline to the hospital for treatment. She did not call 911 for help because she thought it would take too long for the paramedics to arrive and Adeline needed immediate attention.

PROBLEM

Children were in the hallway unsupervised, close to the kitchen door. A child was injured, but the parent was not notified until after the child had been treated at the hospital. The child was transported without the parent's permission in the teacher's personal vehicle, which was not insured for transporting the children from the center. The children should have been supervised and not left in the hallway near the kitchen door. The parent should have been called immediately, and emergency services should have been contacted for medical attention.

RESOLUTION

Delilah was not pleased with the way that the situation was handled, and she felt that it happened because London was not providing adequate supervision of Adeline. Delilah did not return Adeline to the center. Delilah filed a police report, but the police ruled it an accident and there were no charges filed against London. However, the center had to report the situation to the licensing department because Adeline had received medical attention. The center was cited for not providing appropriate care and supervision.

Rhonda terminated London's employment because of her serious error in judgment. She then retrained the staff on appropriate supervision and the importance of watching children to ensure their safety.

Child Misplaced on a Field Trip

On a trip to the local zoo, a group of children and two caregivers, Sally and Molly, were leaving the enclosed exhibit. Sally was at the beginning of the line and Molly was at the end. Sally did not count the children; she had assigned this duty to Molly. Molly completed a head count, accidently counting one child twice. When she thought that all of the children were accounted for, she gave Sally the okay to proceed to the next exhibit. Unfortunately, four-year-old John had returned to the enclosed exhibit.

When they reached the next exhibit, Molly completed another head count and noticed that John was missing. She did not know when John had left the group because she thought he had been with the group when they left the previous exhibit. They retraced their steps, and when they could not see him, they informed the zoo employees. After about ten minutes, John was quickly located in the previous exhibit. The field trip continued without incident.

Upon their return to the center, Sally told the program director, Jill, about what had happened. Jill called Molly into her office. Molly was a new hire, and she did not feel comfortable supervising the children at the zoo. She had expressed her concern to Sally and Jill, but Jill had informed Molly that going on the field trip was part of her position and she was required to go. Molly did not feel that the program director had provided her with the proper training, and Sally had given her the important responsibility of counting the children when she was not ready for it. Molly stated she was not comfortable going to the zoo because she had never taken children on any field trip before. This job was her first time working with children. She felt confident at the center, but outside of the center she was not.

PROBLEM

Molly had a valid point: all staff must be properly trained. She was not set up for success when her concerns related to supervising children on field trips were ignored. If supervising on field trips was part of the job requirements, Molly should have been made aware of that during the interview process. Jill should have talked with Molly and learned that she was not comfortable or equipped to care for children on field trips. Another candidate should have been hired if Molly was not able to perform the duties.

If Molly was hired despite her misgivings and lack of experience, she should have been thoroughly trained for all the job responsibilities. Sally should also have been aware of Molly's inexperience and should have taken on the main responsibility for keeping up with the children herself.

RESOLUTION

Filling a position is more than just placing an individual in the job. A program director must find the best candidate who possesses the skills and knowledge for the position. The job's requirements, and a candidate's ability to fulfill them, must be clear. Employees should never be forced to perform duties that they are not prepared for or trained to perform.

Jill realized that she and Sally had put too much responsibility on Molly before she was ready. Jill took the time to train Molly more thoroughly, and Sally made it a point to give Molly opportunities to practice her skills before she was allowed to take on more responsibility. Molly flourished under their teaching.

Parents are sometimes late in picking up their children at the end of the day. Extenuating circumstances, such as a storm or a multiple-car accident causing road closures, may cause a parent to be delayed. However, if a parent leaves a child at the center and does not return, that is a cause for concern.

Parent Fails to Pick Up Their Child

XYZ Child Care closes at 6:00 p.m., but three-year-old Raymond's parent had not arrived by 6:30 p.m. Program director Marisol and Raymond's teacher, Susannah, called the parent's cell phone and left messages, but Raymond's father did not answer or return their calls. He had provided an emergency contact, but that person did not answer either. Marisol and Susannah waited until 7:00 p.m. but received no communication from the parent. They contacted the police, stating that the child had been abandoned.

PROBLEM

A child-care center should have clear guidelines around late pickups. The parent handbook should clearly state the procedures that the center will follow when a parent is late. This may include calling emergency contacts, charging late-pickup fees, and calling the police after a certain amount of time with no contact from the parent. In Mississippi, for example, the child-care centers are required to have a policy governing a parent picking up a child after closing hours and the procedures to take if a child is not picked up.

RESOLUTION

The police arrived to gather information at the center. After about ten minutes, the child's father arrived and said that he had purchased a new phone over the weekend, so he had not gotten the center's calls. His ex-wife had let him know that she had an emergency and would not be able to pick up Raymond as scheduled. As soon as he received her message, he went to the center. The father was very apologetic because this was the third time Raymond was picked up late without any communication from either parent.

The center's late policy stated that after three late pickups, a child would be disenrolled. Marisol told Raymond's father that she was sorry, but she had to follow the policy. She told him that his son was sad and upset each time his parents were late picking him up from the center. In addition, she reminded him that it is unfair to the staff to cause them to wait to leave the center and possibly cancel or delay plans that they have with their family or friends after work.

DISCIPLINE

Children should never be threatened to make them behave or follow directions. The staff should be trained on developmentally appropriate expectations and ways to teach children how to problem solve and get along with peers. Staff should sign an acknowledgement statement that they understand the ramifications of not following the center's discipline policy. According to Morrison (2008), "Discipline is not about compliance and control but involves behavior guidance, a process by which all children learn to control and direct their behavior and become independent and self-reliant."

Caregiver Hit a Child on the Hand

Oscar was dropping his son off in the preschool classroom when he heard Amira, the assistant caregiver, raise her voice to four-year-old Jesse because he had hit three-year-old Mick in the face with a block. Mick was crying. Oscar watched as Amira then walked over to Jesse and hit his hand, knocking the block out of his hand. Oscar immediately removed his son from the classroom, went to the office, and reported the incident to Linde, the program director. Oscar refused to leave his son in the classroom until Amira was removed.

Linde walked to the preschool classroom to speak to Amira. Amira stated that she heard Mick cry and asked him why he was crying. He told her that Jesse hit him in the face with a block. Amira stated that she pushed the block out of Jesse's hand, but she did not hit him on the hand; she only hit the block. Linde immediately suspended Amira for the day.

When she returned to the office, she informed Oscar that she had suspended Amira for the day because she had to consult with her regional manager before making a final decision on Amira's employment. Oscar was okay with leaving his son after Amira was removed from the classroom.

Linde contacted Jesse's mother and informed her that a parent had observed a caregiver hit Jesse on the hand. Jesse's mother thanked Linde for informing her and said she just wanted to make sure that Jesse would not be hit again.

After Amira left the center, Linde contacted her regional manager, who instructed her to review the classroom video of the incident. On the video, Linde observed Jesse hitting Mick in the face with a block and Mick crying. She saw Amira turn to Jesse, slap the block out of his hand, grab him by the arm, walk him over to the table, and sit him down in a chair. She did not give Jesse anything when she sat him at the table, but Linde could see that she said something to him. (There was no sound on the video.) Amira then went back to Mick, looked at his face, and gave him a truck to play with; Mick was no longer crying. There was another caregiver in the classroom. Linde saw that her back had been turned to Amira during the incident and she did not observe Amira slap the block out of Jesse's hand. Linde also observed Oscar enter and exit the classroom with his son.

PROBLEM

Hitting a child does not stop unwanted behavior. Young children are impulsive and are learning how to handle feelings such as frustration, anger, and so on. They are also learning language and sometimes struggle to express in words what they feel or need. They need help from the important adults in their lives to learn how to respond when they feel big feelings. According to Morrison (2008), "Talking also helps children think about other ways to solve problems. Children should be involved in the solution of their interpersonal problems and classroom and activity problems."

The video made it clear that Amira had needed a break. If she had taken a time-out from the situation, then returned after a few minutes, she likely would have handled the situation with more patience. She should have empowered Mick to voice how he felt to Jesse. Then, she should have worked with both children to find a peaceful resolution.

RESOLUTION

After reviewing the video, Linde made the decision to terminate Amira's employment.

Amira's refusal to take responsibility for her actions by claiming that she hit the block and not the child's hand did not make the situation better. Teachers are not responsible for solving children's problems, but they are responsible for helping children learn skills for solving their own problems. Because the program director communicated with the parents and took immediate action, they maintained their trust in the center.

Caregiver Aggressive with an Infant

Ana, the assistant program director, was sitting at the front desk when she heard Gerardo crying in the infant classroom. It was his first day at the center, and he had been crying throughout the day. To her knowledge no one had gone into the classroom to assist him or Celeste, the infant lead caregiver. Ana observed the classroom on the video monitor from the front desk. She first observed Celeste place Gerardo on the floor, pat him on the back, turn his head, and force a bottle into his mouth. Moments later, she observed Celeste grab the baby's head, roughly turn his body toward her, and push the bottle into his mouth again in an attempt to make him stop crying. In the past, Celeste had requested that Ana not come into the infant classroom when the children were crying because she said it would make it harder for the children to adjust to the classroom.

Celeste had worked in the infant classroom for years, and Ana did not want to make a rush to judgment.

Ana informed Constanza, the program director, and asked her to watch the video to confirm what she had seen. After reviewing the video, Constanza agreed with Ana's assessment. She and Ana decided to speak with Celeste. They were concerned because clearly Celeste was upset but she did not ask for a break when she became frustrated. Constanza was disappointed because

Celeste has never displayed this behavior with the children. Constanza had Ana remove Celeste from the classroom so that she could speak with her about her behavior. Constanza asked Celeste about being aggressive towards Gerardo and had her review the video. Celeste was not happy, and she was defensive stating that the video was not a fair representation of the situation.

After speaking with Celeste, Constanza called Gerado's mother and informed her that Ana had observed the teacher on the video sharply turning Gerardo's head and body and pushing a bottle into his mouth. Celeste had also placed her hand on Gerardo's back, and he appeared to be struggling to move under her hand.

PROBLEM

When a new infant is introduced to a classroom, an additional staff person should work in the classroom until the child becomes acclimated. This will help the child and the staff during the initial transition period. The assistant program director heard the child crying and did not go into the classroom to help the teacher, who was working alone. This allowed the teacher's frustration to build.

After they observed the incident on the video, the director and assistant director did not go into the classroom to check on the child. No one checked for marks or injuries after the incident.

RESOLUTION

The program director should have gone into the classroom when she observed the staff person being inappropriate with Gerardo. It does not matter how long a staff person has worked at the center or how great she has been with the children; if she is not providing appropriate care the program director has to intervene for the safety of the children. It is not appropriate for any staff member to observe inappropriate behavior and not address it. This is especially true for the program director because she is the example for all of the staff at the center.

After Celeste was observed on the video she should have been removed from the classroom. After reviewing the video, Constanza terminated Celeste's employment. Gerardo's mother did not disenroll her baby because Celeste was terminated. She was not happy with the incident but appreciated everything that the center did to make sure that her son would be safe.

It is crucial that program directors observe their staff members' interactions with the children and complete an evaluation of each teacher's interactions. Before hiring a staff member, the director should interview the candidate to find out her stance on discipline. After being hired on a conditional basis, the new teacher should go through an assessment and observation period to give the program director the opportunity to observe the teacher's discipline procedures. The program director should complete classroom observations of no less than twenty minutes per staff member each month for every person on staff, including those who open or close the center. After the observation, the director should provide feedback to the staff person to help her improve her skills.

When a parent raises a concern about a staff member's treatment of a child, the program director should ask the parent to tell her everything that he observed and heard. Do not tell a parent how great the staff person is and that you have never had any complaints. Take the parent's concerns seriously. Acknowledging parent concerns is important and required to maintain their trust. The director should assure the parent that she will investigate the situation and make sure that any form of physical discipline is stopped. Parents must know that abuse is not allowed or acceptable at the center. The director should then follow through and look into the allegations, then make the decisions necessary based on the information she obtains.

Long-Time Caregiver Hitting Children on Their Legs

Three-year-old Kellan's mother, Chanchal, observed Anushka, the toddler assistant caregiver, walking by the children who were sitting in chairs at the table and hitting them one by one on their legs. As Anushka hit each child, she said, "You were not listening." The children were not crying or upset, which alarmed Chanchal because she felt this meant they were used to Anushka hitting them. Chanchal informed Garima, the program director. Garima stated that Anushka had worked at the center for years without any incidents or complaints from staff or parents.

Nevertheless, Garima called Anushka into her office. Anushka acknowledged that, yes, she had hit the children on their legs. She also stated that she did not hurt the children and that they now know to listen when she tells them to sit down at the table. Garima then realized that she had a problem with Anushka. Anushka always worked alone in the afternoon from 3:00 p.m. to 6:00 p.m., and Garima was off at 4:00 p.m., so Garima had never observed Anushka's interactions with the children in all of the years that she had worked at the center.

PROBLEM

A staff person who hits, kicks, pinch, lays hands on a child, or inflicts any form of physical abuse to a child should be immediately terminated. There is no acceptable level of physical abuse at a child-care center.

RESOLUTION

Chanchal was correct to inform the program director. The program director's initial response to her concern was inappropriate, but Garima did ultimately follow through. Anushka was terminated for hitting the children. Unfortunately, because Garima had not observed her and evaluated her interactions with the children, she did not understand that her actions were wrong and that she should not hit the children to make them listen to her.

Garima decided to create a plan for observing all of her staff on a regular basis.

Young children, especially toddlers, cannot sit still for long periods of time. Very young children should be allowed to wander around and explore the classroom. If, for example, a teacher is reading a story, the children will likely come and go, sometimes sitting nearby to listen for a few minutes and sometimes moving on to another interesting activity. It is not developmentally appropriate to expect a toddler to sit through a whole story or focus on an activity for more than a few minutes at a time.

Caregiver Hit a Child Who Tried to Engage in Another Activity

Tamala, two-year-old Dakarai's, mother, stopped outside his classroom to make a video of him playing in the classroom. As she watched him through the window, she observed his teacher, Eshe, sitting in the reading corner with the children. Dakarai sat on the floor listening to the story for a few seconds, then he lost interest and started playing with the toys on the shelf next to him. Eshe grabbed Dakarai by his arm, pulled him over to her, and forced him to sit next to her. She then tapped him hard on the head. Dakarai was not injured, but Tamala was shocked that Eshe was so aggressive with him. Tamala immediately stopped recording and went into the classroom. Without speaking to Eshe, she picked up Dakarai and left the classroom. She went directly to the office and showed the program director, Hasina, the video and then left the center.

Hasina immediately went to the classroom and removed Eshe. She asked her to explain what had happened with Dakarai. Eshe stated that Dakarai would not sit during story time and, after asking him several times, she pulled him to have him sit down for the story. She saw Tamala filming with her cell phone at the window after she grabbed him, and she immediately regretted grabbing Dakarai.

Hasina also spoke with Bahati, the assistant, who was in the classroom when the incident occurred. Bahati related that she had observed Dakarai moving around and not paying attention to the story Eshe was reading. She observed Eshe grab Dakarai by his arm, but she did not see her tap him on the head. She said he was quiet after Eshe pulled him. When Tamala left the classroom with Dakarai, Eshe told Bahati that Tamala had probably seen her pull Dakarai. Bahati said she had never seen Eshe be physical toward a child before.

PROBLEM

Getting into a power struggle with a child never ends well for the adult. Providing activity options that are acceptable for you and the child works best and reduces the opportunities for a power struggle.

RESOLUTION

Hasina terminated Eshe for being aggressive and grabbing Dakarai. Bahati was written up for not reporting Eshe for grabbing Dakarai before she was questioned by Hasina.

> The next day, Hasina met with Tamala and informed her that Eshe had been terminated even though, to her knowledge, she had never been aggressive with a child before. Because Eshe's employment was terminated, Tamala did not disenroll Dakarai from the center.

MEDICATION ADMINISTRATION AND CARE OF ILL CHILDREN

A child-care center should have clear procedures for handling, storing, and administering medication to children. The information should be provided in the parent and staff handbooks to ensure that everyone is aware of what is expected. The program director could assign two staff members to take on the responsibility of maintaining the medication at the center. Limiting the number of people with access and permission would reduce the likelihood of mistakes. The staff responsible for medication should:

- speak with the parents to understand how the medication should be administered;
- check the expiration dates on all medication;
- make sure that the medication permission slips are completed correctly and filed properly;
- store the medication out of reach of the children in the office or in a locked container;
- ensure that the medication is administered correctly, with two people signing the medication log; and
- return expired medication to the parents or discard it so that it is not administered by mistake.

Parents who are providing medication for their child must complete and sign a medication permission slip giving the center permission to administer the medication. Prescription medication can only be administered to the child for whom the prescription was written. That means that if a parent has multiple children, and a sibling is displaying the same symptoms as the child who has the prescription, the staff cannot give the medication to the second child. The parent will have to take the sibling to the doctor and get a prescription for medication for that child.

Child-care staff should not accept medication from parents unless it is in the original container.

Once I observed a small, unlabeled container that the caregiver identified as being Benadryl. The parent had written the child's name and the expiration date on the container. Whether or not the container actually held Benadryl, we could not tell. I informed the program director that the medication had to be returned to the parents and, for their own protection, the center should not accept any medication that is not in the original container. Dispensing medication is important, and every precaution should be taken to ensure the safety of the children. If the center had administered the contents of the container and the medication was not actually Benadryl, the child's health would have been in jeopardy. The center would be at fault because they would have had no knowledge of what they actually administered to the child.

Staff should check the expiration date on the medication when it is received. Do not accept medication that has expired. Keep a medication log with the month that medications expire, so that staff can notify the parent when the medication is expiring. Then, return the medication to the parent or dispose of the medication. When a child is disenrolled from the center, all medication should be returned to the parents.

I cannot tell you the number of times I have checked medication only for the program director to state that the child no longer attended the center and they have no idea why the medication is still at the center. Classroom staff cannot be responsible for receiving, checking, storing, and administering medication. Having dedicated staff who handle those responsibilities will make the process safer.

Teacher Administers Over-the-Counter Medication to Children without Parent Permission

Preschool teacher Isabelle told her program director, Lelani, that the children were congested and needed medication to sleep during nap time. Lelani allowed Isabelle to purchase a bottle of over-the-counter cold medication for each child.

The parents did not know that their children were being given medication daily until four-year-old Anthony informed his mother, Naomi, that he did not want to take medication at nap time. She was shocked because she had not provided any medication for Anthony to take at the center. Naomi called Lelani and inquired about the medication that Anthony was telling her about. Lelani confirmed that the children had been receiving cold medicine for about a week to help them with their congestion and to help them sleep. Naomi was furious. As a nurse, she was aware of the problems that can occur when children are given medication for symptoms that they do not have. She stressed her concerns to Lelani.

PROBLEM

The children could have had a reaction to the medication, and the provider would have been held liable for any issues that a child had as a result of taking the unauthorized medication. A center should only administer medication prescribed for that child or over-the-counter medication authorized and provided by the parent. If medication is not provided with written permission, then it should not be administered. Lelani was a new program director and did not understand the dangers of administering unauthorized medication to children until Naomi told her.

RESOLUTION

Because Lelani and Isabelle did not obtain written permission to administer the medication to the children, Naomi disenrolled Anthony from the center. Lelani had Isabelle stop giving the children medication before nap time. She also changed the center's policy and trained all the staff on administering only medication provided by the parents with written authorization. The cold medication was discarded.

Incorrect Dosage Administered

Two-year-old Joseph was sleeping when his mother, Liliana, picked him up from the center. She did not think much about him being asleep, but when Joseph could not stay awake when they arrived home, she became alarmed because that was not normal. Joseph was taking an allergy medication, which made him sleepy but not to the point where he could not stay awake. When she called the center to question why Joseph was so sleepy, Gabriella, the program director, said that she would check his primary caregiver, Willow. After speaking with Willow and reviewing the medication log for Joseph, Gabriella discovered that Willow had given Joseph the incorrect amount of medication. Willow is legally blind and needs a magnifying glass to properly read the prescription label and measuring cup. Joseph's prescription called for two teaspoons, and she had given him two tablespoons because she had read the dose requirements incorrectly. Willow had noted the actual amount of medication that she administered on Joseph's medication log, which was how the mistake was discovered. Gabriella immediately informed Liliana, who called Joseph's pediatrician.

PROBLEM

The staff members who administer medication should be properly trained on medication measurements and should be able to properly read the labels. When administering medication, two staff members should verify that the right medication in the correct dose is given to the correct child. Both staff members would sign off on the medication log. There is a saying that construction workers have to help them avoid mistakes: Measure twice, cut once. That logic applies to administering medication: Verify twice, administer once.

The medication should be documented on the child's daily log so that parents can see when and how much medication was administered. This will allow the parents immediate access to the information without having to call the center for the information.

RESOLUTION

Fortunately, Joseph did not require any medical treatment. Two other staff members were trained and authorized to manage administering medication to the children in the future.

Centers should have clear, written policies on how they will handle children who are ill. For example, Montana's health-care requirements say that child-care facilities must have the name and contact information for the physician or health-care facility each parent wishes to have called in case of an emergency with their child. If a child is suspected of being ill, the parent must be notified and must arrange to have the child taken home. If a designated person cannot pick up a child immediately, the child must be isolated from the other children in the center.

A designated staff member must check the daily health status of each child immediately upon that child's entry into the facility. Any child showing symptoms of illness must go home and cannot return until he is:

- without fever of 101° F or greater for 24 hours
- without vomiting and diarrhea for 24 hours

A child diagnosed with any of the following bacterial infections must be treated with antibiotics for 24 hours before he returns:

- strep throat
- scarlet fever
- impetigo
- bacterial conjunctivitis (pinkeye)
- skin infections such as draining burns or infected wounds or hangnails

In addition, Montana has strict requirements on readmitting to the center children who have generalized rashes; chickenpox; jaundice; or symptoms of severe illness, such as uncontrolled coughing, breathing difficulty or wheezing, stiff neck, irritability, poor food or fluid intake, or a seizure. In the case of suspected communicable disease, the center must telephone the local health authority to report it.

Familiarize yourself with your state's requirements around administering medication and handling children who may be ill, and train your staff on these requirements.

MANAGEMENT OF INJURIES AND EMERGENCIES

Accidents happen. Young children love to test what their bodies can do. They will fall, throw things, climb, and otherwise engage in actions that may cause injury to themselves and others. Whenever a child is injured at the center, staff should immediately inform the child's parents according to the center's written policy.

All states have requirements around handling injuries and emergencies. For example, in Mississippi, child-care facilities must have an employee who holds a valid first-aid certificate present during all hours of operation, including the arrival and departure of children. The certificate must be issued by an agent recognized by the licensing authority. If a child is injured, he must be treated by a staff member who holds a valid first-aid certificate. If the injury is serious, the child must be transported to a hospital or medical facility as soon as possible. Child-care providers should be trained and prepared to handle blood and blood-containing body fluids using the principles of universal precautions. Supplies of gloves, disposable towels, and disinfectants should be readily available. Familiarize yourself with your state's requirements, and train the staff on these requirements.

Parents want to receive their child back at the end of the day in the same condition that they dropped him off, and if their child is hurt, they need to know. Keeping parents informed shows that you care about their child's safety and well-being. A child should never be picked up from a center after having an accident or incident without someone from the center contacting the parents or legal guardian. The initial contact with the parent or legal guardian should be followed up with a written accident/incident report, which the staff with knowledge of the accident/incident should complete and sign, the program director should review, and the person who is authorized to pick up the child should sign at pickup. Having a signature from all parties reduces the chances of miscommunication. The parents should receive a copy of the report. The center's incident/accident reporting procedure should be written in the policies included in the staff and parent handbooks. Communication is key.

Child Hits Her Head on a Table

Four-year-old Kaia fell out of her chair in the preschool classroom and hit her head on the table, leaving a large knot on her forehead. Kaia's parents, Sutton and Armand, were not contacted, and the center did not complete an accident report. Kaia hit her head at 9:30 a.m. When Kaia's Aunt Nalani, who was a nurse, picked Kaia up from the center at 5:00 p.m., she noticed the knot on her forehead. She asked Kaia's teacher, Ellie, what had happened. Ellie stated that Kaia had fallen off the chair earlier in the day and hit her head on the table. Ellie said she applied ice to the knot and let Kaia sit for a few minutes.

Nalani was upset because Ellie was not taking the injury seriously and had made no attempt to contact Kaia's parents. Daisy, the program director, said that she did not think to call Armand because she knew that Sutton was out of town. Nalani contacted Armand and suggested that Kaia be seen by a doctor because of the size and length of time that she had had the knot on her forehead. Armand asked Nalani to take Kaia to the doctor and said he would meet her there. The doctor determined that Kaia had a concussion and should have been watched throughout the day.

Armand contacted the center the next day and informed them that Kaia had a concussion and questioned why he was not informed. After Armand complained about the care that had Kaia received, Daisy disenrolled Kaia because she did not like the fact that he complained. This upset Armand even more.

PROBLEM

When a parent makes a complaint, the best way to address it is to listen to their concerns, correct the problem with training, and acknowledge the mistake that was made. Armand had just wanted

Daisy and Ellie to understand the seriousness of Kaia's injuries. Daisy was wrong in her actions because a parent should always be informed when their child is injured, no matter how inconsequential the injury may seem. Ellie should have been retrained on how to respond to an injury in her classroom.

RESOLUTION

The staff should have informed the parents when the child was injured. A child should never be picked up from the center after having an accident or incident without someone from the center contacting the parents or legal guardian. The initial contact with the parent or legal guardian should be followed up with a written accident/incident report, which the staff with knowledge of the incident should complete and sign, the program director should review, and the parents or legal guardians or other authorized release person should sign at pickup. By having a required signature from all parties, it reduces the chances of miscommunication. The parents should receive a copy of the report.

There may be parents who do not want to be informed every time their child is injured because they say their child is accident prone. If you have a parent who does not want a phone call every time, then make sure they sign the accident/incident report at pickup so they cannot say they were not informed. Communication is key on all levels.

Young children are susceptible to a condition called nursemaid's elbow (also called pulled elbow, slipped elbow, and toddler elbow). Stanford Children's Health (2021) describes nursemaid's elbow as a condition resulting from a forearm bone, the radius, slipping out of the ligament that holds it in place. It can happen when a child's arm or hand is suddenly pulled or when a child rolls over, falls, the arm is twisted, or the child is swung by the hand. The condition is common in children younger than age four. Symptoms can include immediate pain in the injured arm, anxiety, and the child's refusal or inability to move the injured arm. The child should be taken to a health-care provider, who can gently move the radius back into place.

Three-Year-Old Has Nursemaid's Elbow

Three-year-olds Amelia and Madelyn were playing a game in the gross motor room. The game involved Amelia and Madelyn "saving" each other by pulling each other by the arm. Their teacher, Lily, warned them that they could get hurt and asked them to stop playing the game. Amelia stopped using her arm right after playing the game. When they left the gross motor room, Lily asked Hannah, the assistant program director, to look at Amelia's arm because she was still holding it against her body and complaining that it hurt. Hannah looked at the arm and had Lily call Evelyn, Amelia's mother, and inform her that Amelia's arm was hurting her after Madelyn had pulled it while they were playing a game. Evelyn was not concerned that Amelia was seriously injured and asked Lily to call her if Amelia's pain worsened.

When Amelia woke up from nap, Lily observed her holding her arm again and crying. Lily asked Amelia if her arm was hurting again, and she said yes. Lily called Evelyn again and told her Amelia's pain appeared to be getting worse and she was continuing to hold her arm. When Evelyn arrived at the center, she said she was going to take Amelia to the emergency room.

PROBLEM

Staff should not allow the children to play games where they pull on each other's arms.

RESOLUTION

The next day Evelyn informed Lily that the doctor had diagnosed Amelia with nursemaid's elbow. She made it clear that Amelia was not allowed to play the game again. She appreciated that Lily contacted her when she did. Amelia recovered and was not disenrolled from the center.

SURVEILLANCE OF ENVIRONMENTAL PROBLEMS

All equipment and classrooms should be inspected daily to ensure that they are clean and safe for the children to use while at the center. If unsafe equipment is not repaired or removed, the center is placing the children in harm's way, and they could be seriously injured. All cleaning supplies and hazardous materials must be kept out of the reach of children. This would include anything that is labeled hazardous to children or adults. For example, shaving cream was used in early childhood classrooms for art and sensory projects for years. The shaving-cream cans specifically state that they should be kept out of the reach of children; shaving cream can irritate children's skin and eyes. Before using something with the children, always double-check the label to ensure that it is safe.

Hot-Glue-Gun Injury

Evi, the program director, was called to the preschool classroom by Lauren, the lead caregiver, because four-year-old Levi had touched a hot-glue gun and burned his finger. Lauren told her that Levi was sitting next to her while she was using the hot-glue gun and had touched the glue. Lauren immediately contacted Levi's mother, Sophie, and informed her about the injury as well. Lauren admitted to Sophie that she should not have been using the hot-glue gun in the classroom, but she said she did tell Levi not to touch it while he was sitting next to her.

Evi did not see the injury because Levi's finger was wrapped with gauze and she did not want to disturb the bandage. She reminded Lauren of the center's policy about hot-glue guns: They are only allowed to be used in the classroom during nap time so that the children do not have access to them.

When Sophie arrived later that evening to pick Levi up, she removed the bandage and was surprised to see that the burn was not what she would consider minor. She was furious because she felt that Lauren had downplayed the injury. Sophie told Evi that the hot-glue gun should have never been accessible to the children and that just telling a four-year-old not to touch something hot is not a way to protect him from burning himself. Sophie informed Evi that she wanted to review the video, then she took Levi to the doctor.

The following day, Sophie told Evi that Levi had received a low-grade second-degree burn. Evi watched the video with Sophie, on which they observed Lauren sitting at a table using the hot- glue gun. Several children appeared to come close to the hot-glue gun as it sat on the table. Lauren did not make any attempt to move the tool out of the reach of the children. Levi walked over and sat down at the table with Lauren; after sitting there for a few minutes, he touched the hot-glue gun. He promptly jumped up, ran to the sink, and ran water on his finger, crying the whole time. Sophie became angry that no one was helping him. Lauren did not go over to check on him. Lauren remained at the table, and Nina was seen walking across the classroom away from Levi. After a minute or so, Levi ran back to Lauren and showed her his finger. Another minute passed before Lauren looked at Levi's injury. After looking at Levi's finger, Nina began caring for the injury, and Lauren called Evi. Nina wrapped Levi's finger. While she was taking care of Levi and speaking with Evi, Lauren left the hot-glue gun on the table where it was accessible to all of the children. Other children could be seen playing at the table near the hot-glue gun.

After reviewing the video, Sophie stated that she could not believe what she had just watched. She disenrolled Levi from the center because she did not believe that Lauren and Nina had provided proper care for Levi, and that Lauren had downplayed the injury when she called her. Evi apologized and ensured Sophie that it would never happen again, but Sophie did not change her mind.

Evi spoke with Lauren and Nina. Lauren said that she was sitting at a table making kites for the children, hot-gluing ribbons onto the strings. All the children were playing on the other side of the classroom. Levi came over to see what she was doing and sat down to the right of her. She turned her body for a second and heard Levi yell and saw him get up and start shaking his finger. Levi ran over to the sink and began running water on his finger. She said Nina helped him at the sink and held his finger under the water for a few minutes. Lauren stated that she called Sophie and notified Evi of the injury. Lauren thought that Levi had put his finger in the hot glue that had dripped from the glue gun and did not think he touched the tool itself. Levi remained in the class for the rest of the day, and he did not complain about his finger.

Nina said the children were having free play and Lauren was sitting at the table making kites for the children. She did not see Levi go over to the table with Lauren or see him touch the hot-glue gun. She heard Levi scream and start crying and saw him run to the sink. She went over to the sink to see what had happened to him; Levi was holding his finger and the skin was burned. Nina had him hold his finger under the water and then she applied a bandage. Levi did not complain about the burn during the day.

PROBLEM

Communication is key on all levels. Staff members should be honest with parents about the severity when a child is injured at the center. If staff are not sure about the severity of an injury or how to inform the parents, it can be helpful to send a photo to the parent to provide additional information that will help them decide whether or not to seek medical attention or pick their child up early.

RESOLUTION

As a result of Levi's injury, Evi implemented a new policy that hot-glue guns are no longer allowed in the classroom when children are present.

Age-Appropriate Playground Equipment

The playground at the school that three-year-old Zoey attended included a play structure intended for five-year-olds and older children. The younger children were supposed to play on structures designed for them. Zoey climbed onto the big structure and was injured when she fell. She told her teacher, Autumn, that her arm was hurting. Autumn did not think that Zoey was injured, so she just sent her back to play and did not inform Zoey's mother, Caroline.

That evening, when Caroline was taking Zoey's clothes off for bed, Zoey could not move her arm because of the pain. The center was closed, and Caroline was not able to reach anyone to find out what had happened. She took Zoey to the emergency room, where they found that Zoey's arm was broken.

The next day, Caroline contacted Ruby, the program director. Ruby had no idea that anything had happened to Zoey at the center. Ruby did say that she would ask Autumn if she knew how Zoey's arm could have been broken.

Autumn told her that she did not see Zoey fall, but Zoey had told her that her arm was hurt after she fell from the big play structure. Autumn did not think that Zoey was hurt because there were no marks or bruises on the arm and it didn't "look broken," so she did not think that she needed to inform anyone or complete an accident/injury report. Autumn said that Zoey had told her again that her arm was hurting after she woke up from nap, but Autumn just thought that maybe she had slept wrong. At that point Autumn did not connect Zoey's arm hurting with her fall outside earlier in the day.

Ruby reiterated the center's accident reporting policy which states that parents are to be informed when an accident occurs. Ruby also informed Autumn that she was not supposed to allow the children to play on the equipment that was not approved for the younger children. Autumn stated that she was not aware that the children could not go on the play structure because all the play equipment looked the same to her. Ruby told her that the play structure has a sticker on it outlining the ages that can utilize the equipment.

PROBLEM

There are a few issues here. The child was on a play structure that was not designed for children under the age of five. The teacher seemed unaware of the policy requiring her to keep the younger children off that play structure. The program director should make sure that the staff are trained on the age-appropriate equipment for each age range, even if the areas are fenced off.

The teacher did not take the child's injury seriously because she did not see her fall. When the child was not moving her arm and told the teacher after lunch that it was still hurting, the teacher did not follow up to make sure that the child was okay. Staff should not attempt to diagnose the severity of an injury. Parents should always be informed if a child falls so that they can have the child evaluated for a possible injury. Even if the staff does not believe that the injury was serious, a note to the parents would be appropriate. Staff should be trained to fill out an accident report each time a child is injured.

RESOLUTION

Caroline did not return Zoey to the center because Autumn did not believe she was hurt, had allowed Zoey to continue to play with a broken arm for several hours, and had not informed anyone of Zoey's fall. Autumn's employment was terminated because of her failure to protect the children by allowing them to play on unapproved equipment and failure to follow the center's policy on reporting an accident. Ruby retrained the entire staff on playground safety and accident reporting.

INTERACTING WITH THE MEDIA

It is never going to be a good day when a center is on the news because something went wrong. If the media reach out to a center for a statement or show up with a news crew, the way in which this situation is handled depends on the type of center.

A privately owned center will typically have a written policy stating that no one at the center, including the program director, is authorized to speak to or correspond with the media without prior permission. Corporate centers usually have written policies instructing the program directors to direct all inquiries to their corporate offices. They are not allowed to provide any additional information and are required to contact their regional or district managers immediately. Corporate centers also have legal departments that provide support when these situations occur. Franchises and government-funded programs will allow the local centers to handle any news or media incidents that occur. Therefore, they have written policies that identify the people or titles of the people responsible for handling media inquiries. Staff must be trained on the procedures to ensure that mistakes are not made, potentially making the situation worse.

Each center should also have clear policies on child privacy and posting photos or content on social media. The policy should state what is and is not allowed, and parents should be provided the policy with the option to remove their children from all social-media platforms. This way, parents and staff will know what is acceptable. Even if a center has a social-media site, parents' permission must be obtained before posting children's pictures on the site.

Staff Member Posts Video of Children Fighting

Aarohi, the preschool assistant caregiver, made a video of two three-year-old children fighting over a toy in the classroom. Rather than stopping the interaction, Aarohi was encouraging the children to fight and laughing at their behavior on the video. Aarohi then posted the video on her social media, and the video was widely shared. Aarohi's friend Bhagyasri viewed the video online. She was disturbed by what saw and reported the incident to Chaaya, the program director. Bhagyasri did not work at the center, but she knew where Aarohi worked. Chaaya did not believe that Aarohi would record the children and especially not encourage them, but she was appalled when she saw the video.

Chaaya called Aarohi into the office and asked her if she had recorded the children fighting and then posted the video on her social media. Aarohi denied recording a video and said that she had no idea what Chaaya was referring to. Chaaya showed her the video that she had received, and Aarohi could no longer deny her actions. Aarohi then said that she had deleted the video from her phone and social-media site.

PROBLEM

The program director must make staff aware of the policy on social-media use. Staff members should always admit when they have made a mistake and should work to correct the situation.

In this case, Aarohi had demonstrated a disregard for the children's safety and privacy.

RESOLUTION

Because of her actions and denial, Aarohi was immediately terminated. Chaaya then informed the parents about the video and assured then that this would never happen again at the center.

FIRE SAFETY

All states have requirements around fire and disaster drills. For example, in Mississippi monthly evacuation drills are required, and a record of each drill must be maintained in the facility records, including the date, time, number of children and staff present, and amount of time required to totally exit the building. During evacuation drills, all staff and children present must exit the building.

In Michigan, a fire drill must be completed quarterly. A tornado drill must be conducted at least two times during the period of March through November. A written log indicating the dates and times of fire and tornado drills must be kept on file at the center. Each child-care staff member must be trained at least twice a year on their duties and responsibilities for all emergency procedures. Familiarize yourself with your state's requirements, and train your staff on what to do.

This chapter has explored the important ways child-care professionals must keep children safe and healthy. In the next chapter, we shift to a focus on classroom management and the classroom environment.

CHAPTER 5

Classroom Arrangement and Management

There are multiple layers to managing an early childhood classroom. The program director has to ensure that the number of children in the classroom does not exceed the approved capacity to maintain the adult-to-child ratio. The teaching staff should create daily schedules that help provide consistency, order, and balance for the children. In addition to these important topics, this chapter addresses implementing successful classroom transitions, maintaining accurate daily attendance and ratios, and creating effective room arrangements. Read on to discover how these elements play crucial parts in providing the children with appropriate care and supervision.

APPROVED CAPACITY AND ADULT-TO-CHILD RATIOS

State regulations define the licensed capacity of children allowed in each center. In addition, each classroom has a maximum number of children allowed. The capacity is the number of children allowed at the center and the number of children allowed in each classroom depending on the square footage of the classroom. For example, in Arizona, a licensee must ensure that the facility meets the following square footage requirements for indoor activity areas based on the child-care services classifications:

- at least 35 square feet of indoor activity space for each infant and one-year-old child
- at least 25 square feet of indoor activity space for each child who is not an infant or one-year-old child
- when one-year-old children are grouped with children older than one year in the same activity area, at least 35 square feet of indoor activity space for each child

In Michigan, the required square footage of indoor space per child must be at least the following:

- 50 square feet for infants and toddlers
- 35 square feet for preschoolers and school-agers

The program director must confirm that the numbers are correct for each classroom and provide those numbers to the owner or corporation. Of course, a center can always have fewer children than allowed but cannot have any more than allowed.

The program director should provide the staff with the licensing rules and review them frequently, especially when there has been a change. All staff should be aware of the adult-to-child ratio for each age group. These ratios are put in place to make sure that the caregivers can provide appropriate care and supervision for the children that they are responsible for. To make both caregivers and teachers aware of the ratio for a classroom, post a visual stating the required adult-to-child ratio, either outside or inside the room by the door. You can also post a sign that has the number of children that are present in the classroom for parents and staff to see. This way everyone, including new staff, floaters, and volunteers, are aware of the requirements for each classroom. If a classroom is used at the beginning or end of the day for a mixed-age group, post an adult-to-child ratio sign for the group of children who will occupy the space.

The *adult-child ratio* is the number of children allowed per adult. States differ in their adult-to-child ratio requirements. For example, see the following chart that show the ratios and group sizes for Arizona, Alaska, Montana, Michigan, Mississippi, and Washington.

STATE	AGE OF CHILDREN	STAFF-TO-CHILD RATIO	MAXIMUM GROUP SIZE
Arizona	Infants	1:5 or 2:11	Not applicable
	One-year-olds	1:6 or 2:13	
	Two-year-olds	1:8	
	Three-year-olds	1:13	
	Four-year-olds	1:15	
	Five-year-olds (not school age)	1:20	
	School-age	1:20	

STATE	AGE OF CHILDREN	STAFF-TO-CHILD RATIO	MAXIMUM GROUP SIZE
Alaska	Through 18 months	1:5	2:10
	19-36 months	1:6	2:12
	Three- and four-year-olds	1:10	2:20
	Five- and six-year-olds	1:14	2:28
	7-12 years	1:18	2:36
Montana	Birth-23 months	1:4	12
	2-3 years	1:8	16
	Four-year-olds	1:10	24
	5 years and older	1:14	32
Michigan	Birth-30 months	1:4	12
	30 months - 3 years	1:8	16
	Three- and four-year-olds	1:10	
	4 years to school age	1:12	
	School-age	1:18	
Mississippi	Birth-11 months	1:5	10
	12-23 months	1:9	10
	Two-year-olds	1:12	14
	Three-year-olds	1:14	14
	Four-year-olds	1:16	20
	5-9 years	1:20	20
Washington	1-11 months	1:4	8
	12-29 months	1:7	14
	30 months-5 years (preschool)	1:10	20
	School age	1:15	30

Sources: State of Alaska Department of Health and Social Services, Division of Public Assistance, Child Care Program Office, 2020; Arizona Department of Health Services, Bureau of Child Care Licensing, 2019; Licensing and Regulatory Affairs for the State of Michigan, 2019; Mississippi State Department of Health, Child Care Facilities Licensure Division, 2019; State of Montana, Department of Public Health and Human Services, 2018; Washington Administrative Code, 2021.

Change in Maximum Group Size

Sally Mae, the program director, was new to the center. The assistant program director, Carolynn, informed her that the preschool classroom was approved for twelve children, so Sally Mae enrolled twelve children. When the licensing consultant observed that classroom, she told Sally Mae that the classroom was only approved for ten children and that she would cite the center for being over capacity.

Sally Mae was upset because she was following the information that she received from Carolynn, who had worked at the center for three years. Carolynn had been informed by the previous program director, which was why she said with confidence that the preschool classroom was approved for twelve children. Neither Sally Mae nor Carolynn had any documentation that supported twelve children in the preschool classroom. However, the licensing consultant referred them to their written report, which outlined ten children as the maximum number allowed.

PROBLEM

Program directors want to trust their staff but must verify any information related to regulations. You always want to know the information for yourself. And in this case, the violation was avoidable. If a director is not provided the correct information about the classroom capacity, she should check with the licensing consultant for additional information that she needs to maintain compliance at the center. This knowledge will help to reduce future violations.

RESOLUTION

Sally Mae verified the capacity and adult-to-child ratio for each classroom and posted that information in each room so that all of the staff working there would be aware of the approved capacities. She added the information to the daily attendance sheets so that the staff working in the classrooms would know the capacity for each classroom.

Arizona, Alaska, Montana, Michigan, Mississippi, and Washington require that when children of different ages are mixed together, the ratio and group size for the youngest child in the group must be maintained. Knowing the capacity and ratio is especially beneficial at the beginning of the day, when the children are arriving and there may be one or two classrooms open, as well as at the end of the day, when classrooms are often combined as children are picked up. Washington only allows children of different age groups to be combined for periods of no more than the first two hours or the last two hours of the day; they cannot exceed two hours in any given day. This means centers have two options: combine for two hours in the morning or two hours in the afternoon, or combine one hour in the morning and one hour in the afternoon each day.

ISSUES RELATED TO ADULT-TO-CHILD RATIOS

When centers are having issues with adult-to-child ratios, especially during morning drop off, it is typically because parents are allowed to drop their children off at any time. This causes a problem for centers because, without overstaffing, it is difficult to maintain the required ratios. When parents do not pick their children up at their scheduled time this causes the center to retain staff past their scheduled time, which is an additional expense for the center.

One way to avoid being out of compliance is to require parents to provide a drop-off and pickup schedule—and to stick to it. For example, what do you do when a parent shows up with her child on Tuesday but the parent only signed up for Monday and Wednesday? The parent should not be allowed to leave the child, because doing so could affect the adult-to-child ratio and cause the center to be out of compliance. The same is true if a parent arrives early and there are not enough staff at the center. The parent should be asked to stay at the center until staff arrives. The center should provide a written policy related to any changes in a child's schedule. The program director plans the staff schedule based on the children's arrivals, departures, and days that they are scheduled to attend, so parents should understand the importance of keeping the schedule they signed up for.

Another way to reduce the potential of ratio issues is to accept full-time students only. For example, have the children start at 8:00 a.m., and offer early care for parents who need it. Parents who need to drop off their children before 8:00 a.m. would be required to sign up and provide a change-of-schedule form the week before so that the staff schedule can be prepared. Late care can be offered as well. Parents who need to pick up their children after the center's end of day would be required to sign up and provide a change-of-schedule form the week before so that the staff schedule can be prepared for the week.

A staff member should never work alone with children. Should the staff person become ill (or simply need a bathroom break) or should a child be ill or injured, there would not be another adult present to help with the situation. Being out of ratio causes a ripple effect throughout the center. For example, if there are not enough staff on hand to prepare meals for the children, staff may take the children into the kitchen, which is not an approved space, while they prepare lunch. If there are not enough staff to answer the door, the caregivers may take the children with them to answer it. I have observed caregivers placing the children in a stroller or having them sit along the wall so that they could answer the door. Of course, staff retention is a serious issue in child-care centers, so much so that I wrote a book about the topic. My book *Build Your Dream Team: How to Recruit, Train, and Retain Early Childhood Staff* offers ways to address and resolve these issues. If you find that your center is out of ratio frequently, you may have to create a waiting list and stop accepting children until the staffing issues have been rectified and there are enough staff working to maintain the appropriate adult-to-child ratios.

Child Left Behind at Pick-Up Time

Saar, the assistant program director, was informed by a floater that four-year-old Julia had been left on the lower level by Nora, the assistant caregiver, the day before. Lotte, the floater, said she had seen Julia crying as she was stepping alone off the elevator on the main level. Lotte said that she told Nora about the child.

Nora and Milou, another caregiver, had been working in the preschool classroom together at the end of the day. Milou had left Nora in the classroom with the children to turn off the hallway lights as part of the closing procedures. The lower-level preschool classrooms were combining at the end of the day to go upstairs for parents to pick up their children. While Milou was at the end of the hallway, Nora led the children out, turned off the lights, and closed the classroom door with Julia still inside. Nora and Milou did not realize that Julia was not with their group until Lotte told them Julia was by the elevator. Neither Nora nor Milou informed Saar or Yara, the program director, about the incident.

Saar contacted Yara about the incident and then spoke to Nora and Milou. She reminded Nora and Milou that they are required to inform the directors when an incident occurs, and she stressed the importance of completing the required name-to-face head counts before and after they leave the classroom. Nora stated that she was in the classroom with three children while Milou turned off the hallway lights before they went upstairs at the end of the day. While Milou was out of the classroom, Nora turned off the lights and closed the door. When Nora left the classroom with the two children, she did not see Julia. Nora acknowledged that there were three children but said that she thought Julia had been picked up. Nora had not seen Julia's mother pick her up, and she did not complete a name-to-face check before exiting the classroom. Neither Nora nor Milou counted the children before they went upstairs or when they arrived upstairs. Nora was not sure why they had not, because normally they do complete a head count before they take the children upstairs. Nora thinks that Julia was alone for five minutes.

Nora was consoling Julia when her father, Lucas, arrived. Nora informed Lucas that Julia had been left alone in the classroom and that the child had taken the elevator upstairs by herself. Nora acknowledged to Saar that it was her actions that resulted in Julia being left alone unsupervised.

Milou stated that she left Nora in the classroom with three children, and she went to the end of the hallway to turn off the lights. After Milou turned off the lights, she observed Nora at the opposite end of the hallway with the children and the caregivers from the other preschool classrooms. They were all heading upstairs, and as Milou walked past the preschool classroom, the door was closed, and the lights were off. Milou thought that Nora had all the children since she had turned off the lights and closed the door. Milou joined Nora and the children and walked upstairs. Milou did not know that Julia had been left on the lower level until Julia arrived upstairs on the elevator. She said that Julia was picked up by her father and that Julia told him that Nora had left her in the classroom. Normally before they head upstairs at the end of the day, they would count the children. Milou was not sure why the head count had not been completed that day.

Yara called Tess, Julia's mother, and found that Tess was not happy that Julia had been left alone and had to find her way upstairs. Yara told Tess that she had taken steps to retrain the caregivers so that the situation would not occur again.

PROBLEM

Because it is so easy for a child to be misplaced or overlooked during a transition, especially when classrooms are combining for pick-up, teachers must be particularly careful to follow the center's procedures for keeping track of the children.

RESOLUTION

Yara designated staff members to serve as "sweepers"—people who go through each classroom to make sure no children have been left behind, before the rooms are closed at the end of the day. Yara and Saar retrained the entire staff on proper drop-off and pickup procedures so that children would not be left unattended.

Of course, the name-to-face sheets will only work if they are accurate. If the attendance sheets or computer attendance are not accurate, the chances of a child being left behind or misplaced will increase.

CLASSROOM DESIGN AND SETUP

An important piece to the classroom-management puzzle is the classroom design and setup. The key is to provide children with the proper learning environment for their growth and development. Classrooms should offer interesting areas for exploration and hands-on activities that support children's developing skills and knowledge and age-appropriate growth and development. The NAEYC position statement on developmentally appropriate practice (2021) recognizes that play "provides an important window for educators to observe children's skills and understandings."

INFANT AND TODDLER CLASSROOM SETUP

Friedman, Wright, and Masterson (2021) point out that teachers must create a "learning environment that reflects the children's interests and provides sustained time and opportunities for children to engage in self-directed play, including individual and small group times."

A developmentally appropriate classroom space for infants and toddlers offers all sorts of intriguing materials for exploration. Children in this age group need objects that are safe to mouth and easy to clean. The design should have ample space for mobile infants to crawl, move around, and safely explore. Make sure that the areas provide a variety of opportunities for children to explore different textures and tactile experiences. Infants and toddlers also require opportunities to climb to develop their gross motor skills. They will explore with all of their senses: sight, sound, taste, smell, and touch. Your center will likely have requirements around what should be set up in an infant or toddler space, such as a diapering area, a feeding and eating area, and a space for napping. Infants and toddlers should have access to age-appropriate climbing equipment, unbreakable mirrors on the wall, tummy-time activities, sensory activities, and a reading/quiet area. Include furnishings such as comfortable adult chairs (rocking or glider), baby gates (if needed), high chairs, a changing table with sides and pad, diaper pail, area rugs, floor mat/cushions, refrigerator, cubbies and bins, cribs (including emergency cribs), child-accessible shelves, bottle warmer, nesting pool, and a one-to-six passenger buggy or strollers. In addition, for toddlers, provide toddler tables, chairs, armchairs, and riding toys. There should be no swings or bouncers; highchairs should be used for feeding only. Children should not be confined to a high chair, car seat, or other restrictive equipment when they are not sleeping or eating. Because infants are mouthing toys, make sure to provide multiple toys so that when a child puts a toy in their mouth it can be removed without limiting the number of toys accessible to the children. Multiple toys are also important as the children age because they are not developmentally ready to share. With multiples of toys, they will not have to compete for time with the one toy in the classroom that multiple children want to play with. If a classroom is multi-age, teachers should set up separate areas for nonmobile infants, crawling infants, and toddlers, so the children are safe from being climbed on, stepped on, or poked by curious older children. Each area should have materials that the children can access and manipulate without adult interaction. Teachers should create a materials list, including the name and quantity of the items, to help them and the program director keep track of everything in the classrooms. Review the list yearly, decide what new materials and equipment are needed, and update the list to reflect the items in the classroom. The equipment list should be maintained on the computer for easy tracking. When new equipment is purchased for the classrooms it can be easily added to the equipment list on the computer.

Infant (Birth to 12 Months) Equipment and Materials List

CENTERS	EQUIPMENT	MATERIALS
Books/Language/Music	· Comfortable chairs · Portable CD player or a device with access to children's music · Musical mobiles	· Infant-safe musical instruments · Cloth/vinyl/board books

CENTERS	EQUIPMENT	MATERIALS
Sensory — Wet	· Fish and aquarium · Individual water bins	· Nature pictures · Bath books · Bubbles · Tub toys
Sensory — Dry	· Baskets	· Items with interesting textures, such as metal cups and soft fabric
Creative Exploration	· Large plastic mess mat · Smocks	· Fingerpaint · Large crayons · Construction paper · Fingerpaint paper
Blocks/Construction	· Large area rug	· Buckets for dumping · Large, soft blocks (foam, cloth, vinyl)
Dramatic Play	· Unbreakable wall mirrors · Telephones · Photos of the children and their families	· Soft puppets · Soft animals · Pots and pans · Washable baby dolls
Gross Motor	· Mats · Tunnel or crawl-through structure · Sturdy items to pull up on · Activity gyms · Crawling ramps · Riding toys without pedals	· Soft balls · Outdoor pad or blanket · Soft mat climber · Push/pull toys
Fine Motor	· Busy boxes · Stacking post and rings · Containers to dump and fill · Books · Mobiles	· Plastic keys · Rattles · Grasping toys · Nesting cupxs · Teething toys · Shape board or cube with attached pieces

Toddler (One to Two-and-a-Half Years) Equipment and Materials List

CENTERS	EQUIPMENT	MATERIALS
Books/Language	• Comfortable chairs • No-climb bookshelf	• Flannel board • Cloth and board books • Play telephone
Music	• Portable CD player or device with access to children's music	• Toddler-safe instruments • Scarves
Sensory — Wet	• Individual water bins or sand-water table	• Treasure-hunt items • Dump trucks and bulldozers • Bubbles • Sand set with bucket, scoop, rake, sieve, trowel, and molds • Dump/fill buckets • Sponges • Dishes • Floating toys • Plastic fish • Fishing rods • Tub toys • Sensory balls
Sensory — Dry	• Baskets	• Items with interesting textures, such as metal cups and soft fabric
Science	• Nontoxic plants • Fish and aquarium • Large Magnets • Magnet wands • Magnifying glasses • Light table	• Flashlights • Plastic color paddles • Nature pictures • Nature and science books • Bubbles • Dinosaur set • Large shells • Pinecones
Blocks/ Construction	• Large area rug • Cloth/vinyl blocks • Interlocking blocks • Snap blocks • Large soft blocks • Wood blocks • Cardboard blocks • Plastic blocks	• Farm and barn set • Toy animals • Large train • Toy people • Large trucks and cars
Manipulatives/ Math	• Large area rug • No-climb shelf • Plastic bins • Child-size table and chairs	• Books with shapes and numbers • Balance scale • Rulers • Shape board or cube with pieces • Geometric shapes

CENTERS	EQUIPMENT	MATERIALS
Creative/Art	· Sponge painting set · Easels · Large plastic mess mat · Smocks · Chalkboard · Paintbrushes · Drying rack	· Construction paper · Easel paper · Drawing paper · Collage materials · Large or jumbo crayons · Watercolor markers · Large pieces of chalk · Block/disc tempera paint · Fingerpaint · Watercolor paint · Liquid paint · Playdough and accessories · Glue · Stickers · Nature items
Dramatic Play	· Unbreakable wall mirrors · Child-size table and chairs · Toy telephones · Pots and pans · Play kitchen · Play food · Housekeeping set with utensils · Doll beds	· Tableware · Toys for various themes: doctor's office, veterinarian's office, tea set, shopping cart, and so on · Washable baby dolls · Soft animals · Soft puppets
Gross Motor	· Tumbling Mats · Small parachute · Play tunnel · Low-wheeled riding toys with and without pedals · Toddler slide · Rocking toys · Climber · Mini basketball hoop · Helmets	· Variety of balls · Push/pull toys
Fine Motor	· Large area rug · No-climb shelf · Busy boxes · Dump/fill containers · Puzzle board · Shadow box · Pounding bench	· Large stringing beads · Nesting toys · Scarves, ribbons · Simple puzzles · Lock boards · Large pegboards · Flannel board · Board and cloth Books · Puzzles with knobs · Stacking rings

At all times, the caregivers should be able to see each child. Make sure that all areas of the room are visible; there should be no blind spots. Check for blind spots by walking around the classroom and observing all areas from different vantage points while standing, sitting on a chair, and sitting on the floor. Remember that children will crawl into small spaces to hide, so look for spaces under furniture, in corners, behind shelves, and anywhere else a child could squeeze into. Anytime a teacher rearranges the developmental areas, she should check again for blind spots created by the new setup. Children have been left unattended in classrooms because the staff could not see them and left the classroom thinking that it was empty.

Child Swallowed a Bead

The infant classroom was used by a preschool teacher for opening at the beginning of the day. Before she left, the preschool teacher was to have cleaned up and removed all toys and materials used by the preschoolers.

Later that day, one-year-old Lola found a set of stringing beads on a toy shelf in the classroom. The preschool caregiver had forgotten the beads when she had taken the preschoolers to their classroom that morning. Lola picked up a bead and put it in her mouth. Her teacher, Livia, did not see Lola put anything in her mouth but noticed the beads and moved them safely out of the toddler's reach. Lola was fine for the rest of the morning.

After nap time, Lola started coughing like she had something caught in her throat, but she then stopped coughing and continued playing. Iris, Lola's mother, arrived a few minutes later, and Livia informed her that Lola had just coughed like she had something caught in her throat but she appeared to be fine.

At home that evening, Lola began wheezing and appeared to be short of breath. Iris took Lola to the emergency room, and they determined that she was not getting enough air. An x-ray revealed that her airway was blocked, but the bead was too small to show up. Doctors performed surgery to find the obstruction and removed the bead. The procedure caused a lot of trauma and swelling in Lola's throat, so she was on a ventilator for two days to keep her airway open.

After the surgery, Iris called Livia and asked if there were any beads in the classroom. Livia said that the preschool class that used the classroom at the beginning of day had a set of stringing beads. At that point, she remembered that Lola was by the beads that were left on the shelf. Livia told Iris about the beads and said that, while playing by the shelf, Lola probably had put the bead in her mouth before the toy was removed.

Livia told her program director, Eline, about what had happened. Livia said that she did not know that Lola had inhaled a bead until Iris had called to tell her about the surgery. Eline and Livia visited Lola at the hospital to make sure she was going to be okay. While they were there,

Iris told them that the entire incident was traumatic and that she just wanted the center to know that it was a serious but preventable mistake. Iris was not happy with the center for leaving beads within reach of the toddlers. Because she felt that the situation was preventable, she disenrolled Lola from the center.

PROBLEM

Older children should not be in the infant classroom, and bringing in toys that are not age-appropriate into the infant classroom is dangerous. If preschool children must gather in the infant classroom in the morning, their equipment can be held in a container and removed when the preschoolers leave the classroom.

RESOLUTION

Eline and Livia decided that the opening process would be changed so that the preschool children are not going into the infant classroom anymore. They also inspected the classroom to make sure that the equipment in the classroom was safe for the infants.

PRESCHOOL CLASSROOM SETUP

Friedman, Wright, and Masterson (2021) affirm that, "the teacher is responsible for ensuring that each child's overall experiences are stimulating, engaging, and developmentally, linguistically, and culturally responsive across all domains of development and learning." The classroom setup plays a major part in meeting this requirement.

Each classroom should be divided into learning centers that are labeled with both words and pictures to assist the children with finding materials and returning them to the correct locations. All toys and materials intended for the children's use should be accessible at the children's level. At a minimum, set up these areas in the classroom: math and manipulatives, gross motor, sensory/sand and water, science, books and literacy, music, art area, blocks/construction, dramatic play, and a large area for circle time. Classroom furnishings should include double-sided bookshelves, a loft system, cots/mats, small play tables, child-sized tables and chairs, area rugs, a refrigerator, a sink, cubbies or bins, room dividers or shelves, and steps for the sink.

Each area should have equipment and materials that the children can access and manipulate without adult interaction. Teachers should create a materials list, including the names and quantities of the items, to help them and the program director keep track of everything in the classrooms. Review the list yearly, decide what new materials and equipment are needed, and update the list to reflect the items in the classroom.

Preschool Equipment and Materials List

CENTERS	EQUIPMENT	MATERIALS
Books/Literacy	• Bookshelf • Portable CD player or device with access to recorded stories • Headphones	• Flannel board and flannel figures • Children's books • Tactile letters • Paper • Writing materials
Music	• Portable CD player or device with access to children's music	• Dance scarves and ribbons • Musical instruments
Sensory/Sand and Water	• Sand and water table or individual sand/water bins • Large plastic bins • Water/sand wheel • Sand set with bucket, scoop, rake, sieve, trowel, and molds • Dinosaur set • Magnetic fishing rods • Dump/fill buckets	• Sand • Water • Bubbles • Treasure-hunt items • Dump trucks and bulldozers • Floating toys • Plastic fish • Sponges • Dishes
Science	• Table • Plastic or metal trays • Nontoxic plants • Fish and aquarium • Nature pictures • Weather charts • Thermometer • Large magnets • Magnet wands • Bin • Soil • Trowels, shovels • Gloves • Watering can • Magnifying glasses • Insect viewer • Balance scales	• Rocks • Toy insects • Large shells • Pinecones • Flashlights • Plastic color paddles • Nature books • Magnetic and nonmagnetic items

CENTERS	EQUIPMENT	MATERIALS
Creative/Art	• Table • Easels • Chalkboard • Drying rack • Large plastic mess mat • Smocks • Paintbrushes • Child scissors • Sponge painting set	• Easel paper • Construction paper • Fingerpaint paper • Card stock • Drawing paper • Wrapping paper • Wallpaper samples • Paint sample cards • Watercolor markers • Thick pencils • Colored pencils • Regular and large crayons • Chalk • Block/disc tempera paint • Fingerpaint • Watercolor paint • Liquid paint • Stickers • Cotton balls and pompoms • Yarn and ribbon • Nature items • Playdough and accessories • Clay • Glue or paste • Tape
Blocks/Construction	• Large area rug • Storage shelves • Plastic bins • Waffle blocks • Snap blocks • Large hollow blocks • Wood blocks • Large soft blocks • Cardboard blocks • Interlocking blocks • Plastic blocks • Unit blocks • Scrap wood • Cardboard boxes • Train set	• Play vehicles • Tunnel/bridge set • Town/street play mat • Large trucks/cars • Toy people • Toy animals • Farm/barn set • Street signs • Tool set • Tool box • Workbench • Safety goggles • Tools/hat/belts

Preschool Equipment and Materials List, cont'd

CENTERS	EQUIPMENT	MATERIALS
Dramatic Play	• Large plastic bins • Storage shelves • Child-size table and chairs • Unbreakable wall mirror • Photos of the children and their families • Washable baby dolls and doll clothes • Large doll house/furniture • Pots and pans • Dishes, cups, utensils • Tea set • Play kitchen • Empty food containers • Dustpan and broom • Cash register and play money • Shopping cart • Strollers • Doll beds	• Props for various • themes: doctor office, veterinarian, and so on • Child-sized furniture • Toy animals • Theater play props • Puppets • Dress-up clothes: hats, vests, shoes, dresses, briefcase, purse, and so on • Play telephone
Gross Motor	• Large plastic bins • Tumbling Mats • Large parachute • Play tunnel • Tricycles • Wheeled ride-on toys • Large wagons • Balance beam • Helmets • Large plastic hoops • Low basketball hoop • Playhouse climber	• Helmets • Balls of various sizes • Ring toss game
Computer (Optional)	• Computer • Computer table • Chairs • Headsets	• Computer games

CENTERS	EQUIPMENT	MATERIALS
Manipulatives/Math	· Table and chairs · Shelves · Plastic bins · Jumbo stacking blocks · Pegboards · Interlocking blocks · Wire mazes · Balance scales · Latch/lock box · Floor puzzles · Geometric shape blocks · 2D geometric shapes	· Rulers · Counting bears · Pattern sequencing cards · Sorting mats · Games · Tactile numbers · Large dice · Lacing buttons/beads · Threading spools

Arrange the exploration and play areas to allow the children to move from space to space freely along clear paths without any bottlenecks. Place clearly defined areas together that complement each other. For example, the dramatic play, music, and block areas provide opportunities for collaborative play. The children may even wish to combine their play in these centers. Position the block area away from high-traffic areas, such as near a door or the gross motor area, so that the children's construction will not be knocked over. The art, sensory, and science centers tend to be messy; position these areas where spills can be easily cleaned up. The book area should be in a quiet area away from the noisier spaces. Children should be able to access toys and materials intended for their use without having to ask the staff for help.

As with infant and toddler classrooms, make sure that all areas of the room are visible; there should be no blind spots. Check for blind spots by walking around the classroom and observing all areas from different vantage points while standing, sitting on a chair, and sitting on the floor. Remember that preschoolers will crawl into small spaces to hide, so look for spaces under furniture, in corners, behind shelves, and anywhere else a child could squeeze into. Anytime a teacher rearranges the developmental areas, she should check again for blind spots created by the new setup. Children have been left unattended in classrooms because the staff could not see them and left the classroom thinking that it was empty.

CLASSROOM SETUP AND DISCIPLINE ISSUES

Proper placement of exploration areas and play spaces within the classroom will reduce discipline issues. Each developmental area should be inviting and contain enough space so that one activity does not interfere with another.

Wide-Open Spaces

Selika, the licensing consultant, walked into a preschool classroom to find a very chaotic space with the children running around and throwing toys. Bailey, the teacher, did not appear to be in control of the classroom. After observing for a few minutes, Selika decided to inform Donetta, the program director, that she was concerned about the children's safety in the preschool classroom. She explained that the classroom setup was not conducive for the children because all the shelving units were placed along the wall, leaving an open path where the children could run and throw toys. As a result, Bailey was spending the majority of her time redirecting the children.

PROBLEM

Wide-open classroom spaces invite children to run, throw things, and otherwise behave in ways that are not acceptable indoors.

RESOLUTION

After Selika spoke with Donetta, Donetta helped Bailey to rearrange the classroom that evening. They moved the shelving units away from the walls and used them to define the developmental areas in the classroom. The next day, Bailey was amazed that the children had stopped running and throwing the toys. Both Bailey and Donetta appreciated Selika's suggestion. Donetta began observing in the other classrooms and helping the teachers to rearrange their classrooms where needed. These changes helped the teachers to provide a better learning environment for the children.

As Bennett, Finn, and Cribb put it: "preschoolers rely . . . on direct experience to gather knowledge. They learn through their bodies by seeing, hearing, touching, tasting, and smelling things that are physically present." Provide enough of the popular toys so that children do not argue over them. Store toys and materials in labeled containers with photos of the items on marked shelves so that the children can find equipment easily as well as return it to its proper place.

DAILY SCHEDULE

Through daily activities and a play-based child lesson plan, the teaching staff will be able to provide an environment that stimulates the children's growth and development. Work with teachers to create consistent daily schedules that incorporate developmentally appropriate activities for the children in each class.

Sample Daily Toddler Schedule

Arrival, greeting children
Open breakfast
Diapering and toileting
Free play: dramatic play, art activities, science and discovery, water-table experiences, sensory table, or activities
Open snack
Diapering and toileting
Small-group activities: story time, music, and movement
Children nap on demand
Gym/Outside: take the children for a walk if there is not a play area
Open lunch
Diapering and toileting
Free play: dramatic play, art activities, science and discovery, water table experiences, sensory table, or activities

Note that the toddler schedule does not include times. Children this age need a flexible schedule. For preschool children, you can add times to the daily schedule.

Sample Daily Preschool Schedule

6:30 a.m.–7:30 a.m. Arrival, greeting children, free-play activities
7:00 a.m.–8:00 a.m. Open breakfast
7:30 a.m.–9:30 a.m. Free-play activities/small-group activities
9:00 a.m.–9:30 a.m. Open snack
9:30 a.m.–10:00 a.m. Cleanup, bathroom, and transition to outside
10:00 a.m.–11:00 a.m. Outdoor activities and exploration
11:00 a.m.–11:15 a.m. Transition from outside back to the classroom
11:15 a.m.–12:00 p.m. Large-group activity/circle time
12:00 p.m.–1:00 p.m. Open lunchtime

1:00 p.m.–3:00 p.m. Nap and quiet activities
2:30 p.m.–3:15 p.m. Bathroom, open snack, free-play activities
3:15 p.m.–3:30 p.m. Cleanup, transition to outside or gym
3:30 p.m.–4:30 p.m. Outside or gym
4:30 p.m.–4:45 p.m. Transition back to the classroom
4:45 p.m.–6:00 p.m. Free play/table activities

Because young children are not able to read yet, teachers can provide visual schedules to help children understand and anticipate the next activity, such as going outside, going to the multipurpose classroom, free play, and circle time. Children can check a visual schedule to see that after they finish snack, they can wash their hands and get a puzzle. When they finish cleaning up from free play, they can get a book.

In his book *The Very Young*, George Maxim (1992) points out, "No one single schedule works for all groups or for all teachers, so it is important to remain flexible and respond to the children's natural rhythms as each day progresses." It is also important to respond to the individual developmental needs of the children, according to NAEYC's *Professional Standards and Competencies for Early Childhood Educators* (2019). Therefore, while you do need to provide a consistent schedule, you do not want to be so rigid that you cannot respond to children's interests. For example, if the children are exploring nature out on the playground and they observe a bird flying into a tree, it would be okay to spend an extra fifteen minutes watching the bird and talking about it with the children rather than rushing them inside to eat lunch. Remember that children are not focused on or aware of time; they are, however, aware of what activities follow each other. Therefore, they will prepare for lunch when you instruct them to, not based on the time. The time on the daily schedule is for the adults, not the children.

As program director, offer training for the staff to ensure that they understand the importance of being flexible in their daily interactions with the children. As you observe staff in their classrooms, make it a point to note how flexible the teaching staff is when interacting with the children and with their daily schedule. "A flexible schedule invites creativity and initiative on the part of the teacher and the children," says Maxim. Through their daily schedule and a play-based, child- and staff-initiated lesson plan, the teaching staff will be able to provide an environment that stimulates growth and development for the children.

TRANSITIONS

Of course, transitions are important pieces of any schedule and can be particularly challenging with young children. Children are not always inclined to do the same thing at the same time as their classmates, particularly when there is a lot going on. If teachers are distracted, it is easy for a child to wander off, head over to a favorite center while the group leaves the room, or leave the classroom while the group stays behind. Add a new child to this equation, or have an injury occur during the transition period, and the chance of a mistake increases. Teachers should have a routine in place for keeping up with the children and moving them from one activity to another. When children understand what they should be doing, fewer problems will occur.

Start by working with teachers to reduce the number of transitions. "Educators should strive to reduce the need for transitions through flexible schedules, strategic use of staff and volunteers, and helping children take responsibility for their own learning," say Friedman, Wright, and Masterson (2021). For example, consider having teachers offer open snack during which the children can eat a snack whenever they would like within a designated block of time. Another alternative is to have open lunch periods. Children can come over during a designated period to eat while other activities are going on elsewhere in the classroom. This works well when it is instituted properly and the children know what to do. Some think that children will go hungry if they are not provided with scheduled mealtimes. On the contrary, children will eat when they are hungry, and not all children are hungry at the same time. Open meals teach children independence and awareness of what their bodies need.

If your program has designated mealtimes, the children should not wash their hands and then engage in an activity unrelated to eating the meal. I have seen teachers have the children wash their hands for lunch and then sit on the floor for story time before lunch arrives. Then, children go straight from the floor to the table without washing their hands again. Instead, have circle time or story time while the meal is being prepared. Once the first table of meals is ready, the first set of children can start washing their hands. The teacher can then set the second table and the children can continue to wash their hands.

If there is more than one sink in the classroom, have the children use both sinks to wash their hands (as long as one is not the diapering sink). This may sound like an easy fix, but I have witnessed long lines at the bathroom with children waiting for several minutes when there is another sink in the classroom that the children could also use. Children who have washed their hands can go ahead and start eating while others are finishing their previous activity. Similarly, children who are finished eating can clean up their spots at the table and go on to the next activity.

If children have to wait for some reason, the teacher and children can sing a song or do a fingerplay or the teacher can read a story to keep the children engaged while they wait.

Work with caregivers to create transition strategies. Whenever a caregiver says to me, "I have such a hard time getting the children to sit down for lunch or to clean up before we go outside," my first question is "What is your transition activity?" When transition times are not defined and organized, teachers and children tend to become frustrated, which is when mistakes can occur. Children are frequently lost, misplaced, left behind, or allowed to walk away from the group during transitions. Having a well-organized transition period will reduce frustration and mistakes, thereby keeping children safe. Work with teachers to identify transition times in the daily schedule and to plan activities that the children will expect.

There are lots of ways to get children to segue from one activity to the next. For example, teachers can give a time limit, such as “Cleanup in five minutes!” and then give warning countdowns before changing activities. Have the children sing a clean-up song, then turn the lights on and off as a five-minute warning, and ring a bell as a three-minute warning. Let the children know what activity will be following cleanup; for example, say that everyone will be cleaning up in three minutes for circle time. Teachers should allow enough time for cleanup so that they are not feeling the need to clean up the area themselves to expedite the process. If there are areas that are more difficult to clean up, teachers can have children begin cleaning up those areas five to six minutes before the rest of the class. This will reduce frustration for the children and the staff. Having a countdown for activities helps children anticipate the transition periods. Some children may need a longer countdown. In that case, teachers may give them five-, three-, and one-minute warnings that do not involve the other children in the classroom.

Have each child sit on the carpet once their area is clean. While they are on the carpet, have them sing a clean-up song, engage in a fingerplay, or do a movement activity. The children could also help their friends to finish cleaning up the other areas. The teacher could start circle time while the other children are finishing up cleaning. Remember that it is okay for children to join an activity after it has begun; not all children have to be finished before another activity can be started. Having children to complete activities in smaller group sizes will provide an easier transition.

When the transition involves moving from one space to another, such as leaving the classroom to go outside, teachers can let the children leave in groups rather than all at once. The first group that has finished cleaning should not have to wait for everyone to clean up. The teacher can have the children who are finished cleaning up go to the bathroom and get ready to go outside or look at a book in the library area. This way the children are doing something and not just standing or sitting around the classroom doing nothing.

An important part of accounting for each child is completing a name-to-face check and counting heads before exiting an area. Complete a second name-to-face check before the classroom door is closed to ensure that all the children are present. It is best to walk behind the children so that you can always see them. If you are alone, request an additional staff person to help you escort the children to the next destination. Having an extra person during transition times will help with issues that may arise such as a child who needs additional attention, a child who walks slowly, a child who is a runner, or a child who is easily distracted and may wander off from the group.

Toddler Left Outside on the Playground

Annette and Tracy, the toddler caregivers, decided to combine their classes because their numbers were low that day. After nap time, Annette and Tracy took the children outside to the playground. When it was time to go back to the classroom, Tracy gathered her four children and went inside, leaving Annette outside with her three. Annette briefly looked around the playground and did not see any children, so she proceeded into the building. She did not complete a name-to-face check or count the children.

Annette was walking the children down the hallway when two-year-old Rocko's grandmother arrived to pick him up. It was at that point that Annette realized Rocko was not with the group; he was still out on the playground. Rocko has a tough time with transitions and has hidden behind the playground play structure before when it was time to go back inside. Annette was well aware of this.

Annette took the children to the room and handed them off to Tracy, then she went back to the playground to find Rocko. She discovered him gleefully playing in the sandbox.

PROBLEM

Children will try to keep doing an activity that they enjoy—this is only natural. Annette knew that little Rocko had a tendency to hide outside on the playground, so she should have been extra careful to ensure that he was with the group as they headed back into the building.

RESOLUTION

Annette told her director, Roberta, about the mistake. Roberta wrote her up and warned her that if she failed to complete the required procedures again, her employment would be terminated for the safety of the children. Roberta later conducted a training for the whole staff on how to properly complete a name-to-face check as well as strategies for moving children safely from place to place. Together, the staff brainstormed ideas for keeping up with the children, especially those who struggle with transitions: holding their hands, assigning each of them a buddy who will walk with them, and counting the children as they enter the building.

Classroom management for program directors requires close observation within classrooms so that issues can be addressed immediately and the children can be provided a quality experience. Reducing the number of transitions and maintaining accurate daily attendance will ensure that all of the children are accounted for at all times. A well-trained staff will reduce and prevent mistakes. In the next chapter, I address developmentally appropriate practices for infants and toddlers, including the crucial part that play has in the growth and development of each child.

CHAPTER 6

Caring for Infants and Toddlers

Infants change quickly in all areas of development: social, emotional, language and communication, cognitive, movement, and physical. Infants learn new skills daily, whereas toddlers are learning and mastering new skills over days and weeks. Within the first two years, children learn to walk, talk, begin toileting, and feeding themselves. Because their needs are evolving and developing, they need caregivers who provide a developmentally appropriate environment that supports their growth and development. This is why the primary caregiver role is vital for infants and toddlers.

PRIMARY CAREGIVERS

All infants, young toddlers, and older toddlers should have a primary caregiver—someone who functions as a surrogate parent while the infant or toddler is in his care. The primary caregiver is responsible for direct care, verbal and physical interactions, most of the responses to the child's physical and emotional needs, and daily interaction with the child's parents regarding the infant's experiences. When a child is tired, hungry, or in need of comfort, the primary caregiver is the one to provide that support and meet those needs. Each infant should be assigned a primary caregiver, and no primary caregiver should be assigned more than three or four infants or toddlers.

The primary caregiver is the first person that the child bonds with at the center. If a child does not have the opportunity to bond, she can develop anxiety and trust issues. When infants and toddlers bond with their primary caregivers, they will develop appropriate attachments within their environment.

Sometimes there is confusion around the role of the primary caregiver. It does not mean that the caregiver only takes care of their assigned children. If a child needs comforting or care, and they are not assigned to the nearest caregiver, it is okay for that adult to meet the child's needs.

Why is it important for infants to have a primary caregiver? The primary caregiver should know a child well and notice when there is a change in the child's behavior. The primary caregiver should recognize when the child reaches a developmental milestone. Parents should know who their child's primary caregiver is so they can collaborate to support the child's growth and development.

I can always tell when the infant or toddler classroom does not have assigned primary caregivers for the children. How? The caregivers are not providing care to a few assigned children. I'll see one person changing all of the children's diapers and another person feeding all of the children. When asked about the primary caregiver system, the caregivers will tell me, "We all take care of the children so there is no need for us to assign primary caregivers."

If you know of infant or toddler caregivers who are confused about the functions of a primary caregiver, tell them the following: Think of a primary caregiver as the relative or friend who would help with their child if the parents were not available. For example, at the family reunion, your sister or brother is outside with your child and your child falls down and is hurt. Your brother or sister would be able to momentarily comfort your child. When you return, your child will only want to be comforted by you as their parent.

This is the role of the primary caregiver for infants and toddlers. The child has one person who will understand and provide for their individual needs and temperament. The primary caregiver provides the children with the emotional and physical bonding that children need to develop. This continuity of care allows children and their primary caregivers to develop a nurturing relationship over time.

DAILY COMMUNICATION WITH PARENTS

Each day, the primary caregiver should fill out a log of each child's activities. Parents should receive a daily log of their child's eating and drinking, sleeping, diaper changes, play, and interactions. The log will help them know what their child was doing during the day, as well as the amount of food and number of bottles their child consumed. The written communication should provide the following information at a minimum:

- Sleep pattern: when and how long
- Temperament and behavior: changes in the child's usual behavior, such as not eating, sleeping a lot or too little, not playing, or crying more than the norm
- Diaper changes: frequency, including bowel movements and any changes such as color, constipation, or diarrhea

- Bottle feeding/food intake with type and amounts in ounces and cups
- Developmental milestones: Do not record that a child has rolled over, walked, or talked for the first time. (Parents hope to experience these milestones themselves.) Instead, write that you *believe* that their child will begin rolling over, walking, or talking *soon*.

The primary caregiver should also communicate verbally with each child's parents each day.

This daily communication provides both the caregiver and the parents with the insight into the infant's or toddler's growth and development. There should never be so many children in the classroom that a staff person cannot greet parents when they arrive at the center. Parents should have the opportunity to discuss with their child's primary caregiver how the child's night and morning were. They should talk about daily behavior, eating patterns, developmental milestones, and any changes in the child's usual behavior. This ongoing flow of information will assure that the children are developing appropriately or, if they are not, will mean that issues are addressed as soon as possible.

The primary caregiver should see the parents at least once a day for this communication to be effective. The last thing that a parent wants to hear at the end of the day is that no one present has any information about how their child's day was. The preferred way would be to rotate the schedule so that the primary caregiver is at the center at the start of the day for several days and then at the end of the day for several days. If more than one primary caregiver is assigned, the child's information must be shared between the primary caregivers. The primary caregiver should have a work schedule that allows him to meet the parents at drop off or pick up each day. If the primary caregiver is not available in the evening at pickup, the child's information should be provided to the caregiver who will be available when the parent arrives at the center.

Primary Caregiver Is Concerned about a Child

Jill, the primary caregiver for a four-month-old, called his parent to say that her child was not being himself, and she suggested that the parent come and pick him up. There was not any particular thing that Jill could state that was wrong with the child. The parent did pick him up from the center, and she also made an appointment with the child's doctor for the next day just to get a check. Unfortunately, that evening, he went to sleep and did not wake up. The child passed away at home from a rare heart disorder.

Even though she could not describe what she was perceiving, Jill simply knew something was not right, and she was correct. She had noticed what no one else had. Because of her connection with the child, the child's mother was able to spend the last moments with her child, and he did not pass away at the center.

EMOTIONAL DEVELOPMENT

Caring for infants and toddlers means more than simply providing *custodial care*: only changing their diapers, putting them down for naps, and feeding them. Children who receive no more than custodial care will have attachment issues because their basic physical needs are met without any regard for their emotional needs. Weiser (1991) describes custodial care as having "disastrous effects." Infants who are only provided custodial care are less likely to grow and develop at the same rate as infants who are provided with developmentally appropriate activities that promote their brain development and enhance their growth and development. Because young children need an atmosphere that is nurturing and safe for exploration, they need to be held, have eye-to-eye contact with their important adults, and be played with, talked to, listened to, read to, and comforted. The work of a primary caregiver is important!

Have each child's primary caregiver feed the children in his care. If that is not always possible, have the primary caregiver double-check that the correct bottle is given to the right child. Hold infants for feeding if they are unable to hold their own bottles. Talk with the child and make eye contact while she is eating. Avoid propping a bottle with something such as a towel, pillow, or blanket. Propping a bottle to keep in a child's mouth increases the likelihood that the child will choke on the contents of the bottle.

Communication Issues

Fourteen-month-old Davu's mother, Belle, informed Athena, the program director, that she was not receiving a written daily report for Davu and she did not know who his primary caregiver was. Athena asked Merissa, the lead teacher, why the primary caregivers were not assigned and why the daily log was not provided to the parents. Merissa said the primary caregivers' list was posted inside a cabinet in the classroom, but Belle could not see the list. When Athena looked at the list, she found it was not correct; a previous caregiver was listed as Davu's primary caregiver. That teacher had left the center three months earlier, and the list had not been updated. Merissa did not know who each child's primary caregiver was.

PROBLEM

Athena was new to the center. She was surprised to learn that Merissa also did not know that each child was required to have a primary caregiver. Merissa had not completed written logs for the children because she did not think a written form was needed for the toddlers.

RESOLUTION

Athena immediately required Merissa to assign primary caregivers for the children in her classroom. She then trained all the infant and toddler caregivers to make sure that they were all aware of the requirements. She did not want to take the chance that the other caregivers were not trained.

She had Merissa contact each parent to tell them who their child's primary caregiver was and to encourage them to connect each day with that person. Belle was relieved to know that Davu's care would be the main responsibility of a particular caregiver and that she would be receiving written updates each day.

PHYSICAL DEVELOPMENT

Each day, infants and toddlers are discovering their bodies and all the amazing things they can do. They need plenty of time to kick, wiggle their fingers, reach for interesting objects, and eventually roll over, sit up, crawl, pull up, walk, and run. Infant and toddler caregivers can support children's physical development by providing safe, interesting spaces where they can learn to use their bodies.

Tummy time should start when infants can hold their heads up, to give them the opportunity to develop the muscles in their necks, legs, hips, and arms. These muscles need to be strong for the child to learn to crawl, to reach for toys and other objects, and to gain control over their environment. Note that tummy time is *not* a time for caregivers to just place the child on the floor for a few minutes while the caregiver changes another child's diaper or some other task. Tummy time is an interaction between the primary caregiver and the infant.

Place the infant on a blanket, towel, or mat on the floor; do not place the infant on anything elevated that he could fall or roll off of. The caregiver should get down on the floor with the infant and smile, sing, or simply comment on what she sees the baby doing. Put one or two objects just outside of the child's reach, and encourage the infant to reach for the toy. Each day the caregiver should move the toy to the right or left of the child to help him learn to move his body in different directions. Offer toys that make a sound when the infant touches them to confirm that the child is making contact and to encourage him to continue to engage with the toy. The time frame depends on the age of the infant and his development. Start off with a few minutes, then advance to a longer period. The child might be resistant to tummy time the first few times it is introduced. However, after it becomes routine, he will enjoy engaging in the activity. Start off a few days a week then advance to a daily activity.

LANGUAGE DEVELOPMENT

Children's language develops by hearing and interacting with the adults in their lives as the adults talk to them. According to Machado (2007), "Language, especially in the area of speech development, is a two-way process; reaction is an important feedback to action." A child's speech can be delayed if he is not encouraged to speak or if others speak for him. Therefore, caregivers should make sure that they are communicating through talking, making eye contact, reading, providing directions, asking open-ended questions, singing, doing fingerplays, and listening to the children. "When interacting with young speakers, an adult must listen closely, watch for nonverbal signs, scan the situation, and use a good deal of guessing to understand the child and respond appropriately," Machado advises.

Infant and toddler development lays the foundation for children. When a center does not implement a primary-care system with lots of personal, individual interaction with children, they are not providing the children with an appropriate bonding environment, which could create a delay in their development.

In the next chapter, we examine developmentally appropriate practice and classroom practices.

CHAPTER 7

Developmentally Appropriate Classroom Practices and Pedagogy

The early childhood field provides many avenues for individuals to make a difference in a child's life. NAEYC defines *developmentally appropriate practices* as "methods that promote each child's optimal development and learning through a strengths-based, play-based approach to joyful, engaged learning," according to Friedman, Wright, and Masterson (2021).

The task of early childhood educators is to focus on the development of the whole child. Friedman, Wright, and Masterson acknowledged that "all young children need daily, sustained opportunities for play, both indoors and outdoors." Educators have to also understand and recognize the importance of the developmental years in a child's life. Numerous studies (*American Journal of Play*, 2020; Pyle, Pyle, Prioletta, and Alaca, 2020; Wah, 2020) confirm the significant role that play has in the growth and development of young children. When age-appropriate play is incorporated into the classroom, each child has opportunities to gain experience and develop at their own pace.

A well-constructed program provides a rich learning environment for young children. "Play helps children develop large-motor and fine-motor physical competence, explore and make sense of their world, interact with others, express and control their emotions, develop symbolic and problem-solving abilities, and practice emerging skills," assert Friedman, Wright, and Masterson. It is through play that young children begin to expand their cognitive skills.

Friedman, Wright, and Masterson point out that children need opportunities to choose the materials, playmates, topics, and approaches they use throughout the day. But, they clarify, "Effective, developmentally appropriate practice does not mean simply letting children play in the absence of a planned learning environment, nor does it mean predominantly offering direct instruction. In the middle of the continuum is guided play."

So what exactly is play? In her book *Planning for Play* (2017), Kemple defines *play* as (among other qualities) enjoyable, spontaneous, participatory, intrinsically motivated, voluntary, symbolic, free of external rules, and meaningful. Trawick-Smith (2020) defines it as "something children choose to do, following their own needs and interests." That rules out worksheets, push-down academics, and expecting preschoolers to read. Bennett, Finn, and Cribb suggest that parents should not rush their children to become scholars before they have a chance to be children. "After all, innocence and youthfulness are treasures that last only so long, and then they're gone." When I was a preschool teacher, it was common for parents to ask why the children were "playing all day and not learning." Ultimately, the best way to eliminate these types of questions is to explain the center's curriculum and philosophy during the enrollment process. Help parents understand the significance of play in a child's development and explain how each child's growth and development is addressed during play. Kemple describes seven types of play:

- **Object play:** child acts on objects to see what they can do
- **Construction play:** child creates something to represent another thing
- **Pretend play:** requires suspension of reality as a child lets an object, idea, person, or action represent something else; solitary pretend play is when a child engages in pretend play alone
- **Sociodramatic play:** pretend play in which two or more children engage in pretense with a shared goal
- **Games with rules:** competition that is regulated either by long-standing rules or temporary agreement
- **Rough-and-tumble play:** characterized by running, chasing, fleeing, wrestling, jumping, play-hitting, smiling, and laughter

THE IMPORTANCE OF PLAY

According to Friedman, Wright, and Masterson (2021), research has shown a link between play and foundational capacities such as memory, self-regulation, oral language abilities, social skills, and school success. Young children are curious about their surroundings, and it is through play that they begin to understand how to navigate and manipulate their environment. Cohen and Waite-Stupiansky recognize that "children are natural experimenters as they try to figure out the workings of the world around them." According to NAEYC's *Professional Standards and Competencies for Early Childhood Educators* (2019):

> Play is a universal, innate, and essential human activity that children engage in for pleasure, enjoyment, and recreation. Play, solitary or social, begins during infancy and develops in increasing complexity through childhood. Play integrates and supports children's development and learning across cognitive, physical, social, and emotional domains and across curriculum content areas. Play can lead to inquiry and discovery and facilitate future learning. . . [and is] essential for young children's development of symbolic and representational thinking, construction and organization of mental concepts, social expression and communication, imagination, and problem solving.

Classroom interactions allow young children the opportunity to engage with their peers and teachers in an age-appropriate fashion. Heidemann and Hewitt (2010) point out that "Piaget thought that children's play does not merely reflect their existing developmental level. Children also use play to integrate new information and grow into a higher level of cognitive understanding." Play provides children with the opportunity to gain experience and develop within the early childhood environment. The desire to explore and learn within their environment is important for children. Play is something that comes naturally to children. "Within play, children are learning the skills that will form a foundation for learning and social interaction in their future lives," say Heidemann and Hewitt. Children will seek out new things that interest them. Educators have to create a safe learning environment that provides opportunities for children to explore and learn at their own pace.

Learning through Play

Play offers so many things a growing child needs to build the foundation of healthy growth and development.

- **Social-emotional skills:** developed through communication skills where children learn negotiating rules, roles, and turn-taking; patience; kindness; peaceful conflict resolution
- **Language and vocabulary:** listening, describing, naming, explaining, negotiating, defining, planning
- **Fine-motor skills:** cutting with scissors, pasting, dressing up, buttoning, zipping, building, molding, exploring art materials, and playing musical instruments

- **Literacy:** "writing" and "reading" menus, rules, signs, and other props in pretend play; letter recognition and sounds; understanding the purposes of reading and writing to communicate; introducing and using books and other print materials; and engaging in conversations
- **Math:** understanding "how many"—people, props, balls, turns, blocks; patterns; sorting and classifying; shapes; comparisons—bigger, smaller, longer, shorter, heavier, lighter, more than, less than; spatial relationships—above, below, near, behind, in front of
- **Creativity and imagination:** roles, costumes and props, building, making, drawing, painting, inventing, exploring, and memory
- **Gross-motor skills:** understanding what the body can do, understanding limits, running, jumping, climbing, rolling, and so on; proprioceptive sense (where the body parts are in space, without having to look); vestibular sense (where the body is and whether or not it is moving; balance)

Parent Concerned That Child Is Playing Too Much

Three-year-old Ayush's mother, Chaitaly, informed Bhanumati, the program director, that she was concerned because she had observed Ayush playing when she arrived to pick him up from the center. She felt that he should be doing more than just playing all day. Before Bhanumati responded, she asked Chaitaly to describe what she had observed Ayush doing. Chaitaly stated that she had observed him over the course of a week playing with playdough at the table, building with blocks on the carpet, and cutting pieces of paper and gluing them onto a blank piece of paper. She said that she did not see where Ayush was learning anything with these activities and was concerned that the teacher was not providing a learning environment.

PROBLEM

Sometimes, parents think that learning must include worksheets and lessons that children complete while sitting at desks. These parents need help understanding developmentally appropriate learning activities for young children and how these activities prepare them for kindergarten and beyond.

RESOLUTION

After listening to Chaitaly, Bhanumati explained that she understood what she was saying and assured her that Ayush was learning through his interactions in the classroom. Bhanumati explained how each area in the classroom is set up to promote children's growth and development through play. Bhanumati also encouraged Chaitaly to discuss with Ayush what he learned each day at the center, because through this daily dialogue she will understand the depth to which the play is contributing to his daily growth. Bhanumati pointed out that this growth and development would assist him when he enters elementary school. Bhanumati consciously mentioned elementary school because she recognized that Chaitaly's ultimate fear was that Ayush would not be prepared for traditional school as a direct result of play at the center. She also encouraged Chaitaly to speak with Ayush's teacher to learn more about how activities support specific skills and understanding. After the conversation, Chaitaly had a clearer understanding of how play relates to Ayush's growth and development, which made her feel better about the play that she was observing.

Notice that Bhanumati acknowledged the parent's concerns, requested specifics from the parent to be sure that she understood her point of view, and did not negate or minimize the parent's concerns. Waite-Stupiansky (2017) suggests that "documenting the children's learning with photos, quotes, and video can communicate the types of learning when words fall short." Remember, educators are the early childhood experts. As a program director, it is your role to educate parents on the best practices for children.

THE ROLE OF THE TEACHER

Where does the educator fit into all this playing? Psychologist Jean Piaget determined that learning for young children was related to their ability to make sense of their environment through play and exploration. The role of the teacher within a play-based environment is to support and guide the children as they explore and learn. Waite-Stupiansky says that "teachers who share this same curiosity about the world engage the child in joint investigations of whatever interests the child."

Friedman, Wright, and Masterson suggest that teachers should incorporate a "mix of self-directed play, guided play, and direct instruction." Therefore, when the program director observes a classroom, she must examine the way in which an idea or exploration is introduced by the teaching staff. Proper play should be hands-on, developmentally appropriate activities that provide opportunities for children to learn and mature. Children will gain socialization and communication skills through their play-based interactions. For example, Machado says children "gain skills in approaching other children and asking if they can play or just nonverbally joining a play group in progress. They begin to understand what attracts others to them, how to imitate another child's actions or words, how to express affection or hostility, how to assume a leadership role, how to negotiate, and how to follow or refuse playmates' requests."

The teachers and assistants interact with the children without completing activities for them. They help the children who need support to understand how to pretend or to engage in play with others. Free-play time is not a teacher's opportunity to relax or take a break. Teachers use this time to observe children, notice which skills the children are working on, step in to support when needed, ask questions, and then let the play continue. The teacher supports and explains when children need information and asks questions to scaffold learning—How will you do that? What makes you think so? How do you know? What will happen if…? The teachers are accessible to the children at all times. If children are playing all day, that is a busy day of learning!

Staff Sleeping and Not Interacting with the Children

When two-year-old Elena's father, Hugo, walked into the toddler classroom to pick up Elena, he saw the caregiver Maria sleeping on the floor. He was in the classroom for about three minutes gathering Elena's belongings before Maria woke up. The children were running around the classroom and playing around Maria while she slept. There was no additional adult in the classroom to supervise or interact with the children.

When Maria woke up, she did not say anything to Hugo, and he just left the classroom with Elena. Elin, the program director, was not at the center, so he did not talk to anyone before leaving. He called Elena's mother, and she called the center and informed Jasmijn, the preschool caregiver, that Hugo had seen Maria sleeping and he was terribly upset that the children were not being supervised. Jasmijn called Elin and told her what had happened. The following morning, Elin spoke with Maria. Maria said she dozed off and was not asleep long.

PROBLEM

Staff who are sleeping in the classroom are not supervising the children. They would be directly responsible if a child were injured because they were sleeping and not watching the children. They are also missing valuable time to observe and support the children's play and skill development.

This is an example of why classroom observations and spot checking are important. A program director would see when a staff member appears to be tired and could offer solutions such as an early break or lunch to give her an opportunity to wake up or have a rest period. Sometimes a fifteen-minute nap is all someone needs to be productive.

RESOLUTION

Elin explained that sleeping at the center was not acceptable and suspended Maria for two weeks. In addition, Maria was not allowed to work in the classroom alone for six months. Elin spoke to Elena's mother and assured her that the staff would not be sleeping in the classroom ever again. The parents were not satisfied and disenrolled Elena from the center.

BEST PRACTICES IN PROGRAMS FOR YOUNG CHILDREN

Teaching staff should provide an age-appropriate learning environment for children in the areas of social and emotional, physical growth, cognitive development, language, and literacy development within a diverse environment. The program director should review the teachers' lesson plans to ensure that they are following the center's curriculum.

What should the program director observe in the classroom? In a well-functioning classroom, all of the children look comfortable in and acclimated to the environment. They know where materials are kept and can remove items from the shelves and return them when finished. They are self-sufficient as they play and explore. Free play is occasionally interspersed with short whole-group instruction. Children are not required to participate in circle time, and the number of group activities is limited. Small groups or individual children engage with the teachers for specific instruction. All activities are optional, and if children choose not to participate, they are offered other activities. If a teacher is changing her approach because of the observer's presence, the children will say things such as, "Why are we going outside? We never go outside," "Why are we washing our hands after eating?" or "Why do we have to wash our hands before we eat?"

The program director should observe how the staff interact with the children within the classroom arrangement. The staff should be observed being play partners and play facilitators, to use Friedman, Wright, and Masterson's terms. A *play partner* is a staff member who interacts with the children during their play activities, such as building a tower in the block area, having a meal in the housekeeping area, or sculpting with playdough in the art area. A *play facilitator* is a staff member who asks open-ended questions to help the child expand his thought processes to take his activities to another level. The play facilitator does not make decisions for the child but helps him reach his own decisions.

It is the program director's responsibility to demonstrate and stress the importance of implementing a hands-on-play approach for young children. During observations, the program director should see the teaching staff engaging with the children in different areas while observing the other areas of the classroom. Teachers should actively assess children's skill development and determine when to offer the children guidance or assistance in trying new skills. Children "may need adult guidance to begin or persist in play or to overcome obstacles they encounter," according to Trawick-Smith (2020). By interacting with the children without completing the task or project for them, teachers allow children the opportunity to grow and mature while developing their confidence and independence at the same time.

If the program director observes any of the following practices, she should address and correct them with the teacher. Most issues can be addressed through retraining.

- The staff are completing projects for the children.
- Staff require the children to create the same product, such as snowmen made of cotton balls glued to paper, in the same way. Children must be allowed to be creative or express their individuality.
- There are no art activities or materials for the children. Children should have access to art materials to use in their own way.
- Teachers provide coloring pages and expect the children to color within the lines. Open-ended art explorations are much more valuable for a child's learning and development.
- Staff does not provide children's books in the classroom.

- Staff provides inappropriate children's books that include derogatory, violent, or frightening content.
- There are no pictures or displays for the children. Classrooms should display children's art explorations, photos of the children and their families, and photos and materials (including children's work) related to what the children are learning.
- The staff only provide the infants with custodial care: changing their diapers, feeding them, and putting them down for sleeping.
- Caregivers allow infants to sleep on the floor, in swings, or in bouncers.
- The staff do not engage in verbal exchanges with infants or toddlers.
- Infants and toddlers are forced to share toys because there is only one of a particular item.
- The staff asks closed-ended, yes-or-no questions rather than open-ended questions that encourage children to use their language skills.
- The staff solve the children's conflicts without allowing the children to gain conflict-resolution skills.
- The staff tell the children no frequently. If no must be the answer, the teacher should follow that with a suggestion for an alternative activity.
- The children are not taken outside daily. Children (and adults) benefit from being outside in fresh air every day.
- The children are not provided music or movement activities.
- The children do not have opportunities to engage in gross-motor activities: running, jumping, climbing, rolling, crawling, hopping, skipping, and so on.
- Infants and toddlers are allowed to watch screens, such as the television or computer. Human interaction with caring adults is what young children need.
- Children are not provided with accessible building blocks.
- Teachers yell at or harshly reprimand children instead of teaching them what to do instead.
- The dramatic play area has a play stove and sink and no additional equipment or materials. The area's theme rarely, if ever, changes.
- The images, materials, books, dolls, and other items in the classroom do not reflect the diversity of the children's families or the community.
- There is no routine or daily schedule, and the children do not know what to expect.
- There are multiple transitions without a process.
- Staff do not work as a team, giving the children mixed messages.
- Children are required to be quiet, sit still for more than a few minutes, and/or not interact with each other.

Licensing Consultant Comes for a Visit

Queanna, the licensing consultant, observed Peyton, the assistant teacher, through the window of the preschool classroom yelling at three-year-old Sebastian as she poked him with her finger and then tapped him with her knuckles on his forehead. When Queanna entered the classroom, Peyton continued hitting Sebastian on the forehead until she noticed Queanna in the classroom. Peyton then told Sebastian to go sit down on the carpet. Queanna informed Peyton that what she had observed was not the way that she should interact with the children. Peyton stated that Sebastian was not listening and that was why she was speaking to him.

Queanna left the classroom and headed to the office, where she told Emery, the program director, what she had observed. She stated that the center would be cited for inappropriate discipline and that Emery must provide an acceptable corrective action plan to Queanna. Emery agreed that what Queanna had observed Peyton doing was unacceptable, but she said she had never observed Peyton being inappropriate with the children and she had not been informed by any of the staff or parents that they had seen her being inappropriate with the children. She did agree to speak with Peyton about the incident.

After speaking with Queanna, Emery went into the classroom and observed Peyton with the children. Emery did not observe Peyton being inappropriate or touching the children to discipline them. Emery asked Peyton what had happened with Sebastian, and Peyton said that Sebastian was kicking another child. She said she fluttered her fingers across his forehead to get his attention because he was not looking at her. Emery informed Peyton that she was not allowed to touch a child's forehead or any part of his body as a form of discipline.

PROBLEM

Touching a child to discipline them is not acceptable. Young children need redirection and instruction, as well as practice, to learn how to behave in acceptable ways with their peers.

RESOLUTION

In her corrective action plan, Emery stated that Peyton's behavior was unacceptable and that she would be reprimanded, retrained, and not allowed to work alone with the children until the discipline training had been completed. If this type of situation happened again, her employment would be terminated.

Emery reviewed the center's discipline policy with the staff and retrained them on how to interact with the children and implement the discipline policy. She reminded them that staff are forbidden from touching the children as a form of discipline. As part of the training, Emery provided various scenarios, and she and staff discussed ways to address the situations appropriately.

She warned the staff that the first violation of the policy would result in a reprimand; on the second violation, their employment would be terminated. Peyton was provided additional training on how to appropriately obtain a child's attention when they are not looking at you without touching them.

Reading an Inappropriate Book to the Children

Four-year-old Violet was having nightmares. When her mother, Eleanor, asked her what was wrong, she told her that she was scared because the tsunami killed the people. Eleanor was concerned because she did not know that Violet even knew what a tsunami was. Violet said that Aaliyah, the preschool teacher, had read a book to the class about a tsunami.

The next day Eleanor spoke to Elizabeth, the program director, about Violet's nightmare and told her that she did not feel a book about death was appropriate for preschool children. Elizabeth said that she would speak to Aaliyah and find out about the book because it was not on the scheduled list of books that were approved for the class.

Aaliyah told Elizabeth that she had checked the book out of the library; it was about the 2004 tsunami that hit in the Indian Ocean. She read the book to the class, but she did not finish the book because the children did not appear to be interested in the story. The children did not seem upset, just not interested. She did not review the book before reading it to the children, and the book was not accessible to the children in the book center. She acknowledged that the book was not part of the approved list of books for the theme of the month nor included in her lesson plan.

PROBLEM

Before any book is read to the children, the staff should read and review it to make sure that it is appropriate for them. If a child appears to be scared or disturbed by anything presented in the class, the parents should be informed so that they can address the issue if it comes up later when they are at home. Once again, communication is key.

RESOLUTION

Aaliyah understood that the book was not appropriate for the children and said that going forward she would review all books before reading them to the children. Elizabeth reminded her that she is required to follow the center's curriculum and use appropriate topics. Aaliyah was written up for reading an inappropriate book to the children without reviewing it first and was retrained on the center's curriculum.

Elizabeth apologized to Eleanor and assured her that Aaliyah would not be reading the book about the tsunami again. The book had been returned to the library. Although she was not happy about Violet having nightmares, Eleanor was pleased with the way that Elizabeth had addressed the situation.

DECIDING WHAT CHILDREN SHOULD LEARN

The children should be actively involved in developing their learning experiences. When toddlers show an interest in an activity or a specific area of the classroom, caregivers can develop learning experiences from that interest. When the children are older, they can and should express their interests and the teaching staff should develop learning experiences that recognize and incorporate their interests and honor their cultures, families, and individual learning styles. Close observation of the children will also provide insight into what they are interested in, how they like to engage with materials, what skills they need to learn, and how they approach and resolve situations.

The teaching staff, with the direction of the program director, should create hands-on learning experiences that generate better understanding for children. It is important to understand and stress to the staff that when children are actively involved, they will learn better than if they are just sitting and watching. Teachers can take advantage of children's curiosity, teachable moments, situations that arise in play and exploration, as well as direct instruction to help children understand concepts. Open-ended questions, rather than questions that have one right answer, give children opportunities to expand upon their critical-thinking skills.

Children learn in different ways. It is important to meet the children where they are and build upon their skills and knowledge so they are not asked to perform tasks that they are not ready to perform. Therefore, as a professional, it is the teacher's responsibility to provide innovative and creative lesson plans that address the individual needs of the children. Teachers can engage with children in cooperative learning groups, through one-on-one instruction, in small groups, as well as paired reading. The overall goal should be to provide experiences for the children that will empower them to learn in their own way in areas that they are interested in.

Very young children move and learn at their own speed. Rather than try to implement a strict curriculum with this age group, provide opportunities for exploration, such as those described in chapter 5. When an infant or toddler classroom is set up to support children's curiosity and teachers actively engage with the children by naming items, colors, animals, emotions, textures, sounds, and so on, the children will learn and develop their skills.

For preschoolers, any curriculum you use should be designed for the ages of the children with whom it will be implemented. If your center franchise does not require a specific curriculum, you have to determine what type of curriculum you want. Will teachers create their own within the guidelines of your state's learning standards? Will it be a published curriculum that the entire center will follow? Will the learning experiences follow a particular philosophy, such as the Reggio Emilia approach or Montessori? Will you use a blended approach, using sections of curricula that best meet the needs of the children and families? Whichever curriculum you use, the staff must be trained on how to implement it. Of course, this would be an important part of new-hire orientation.

The curriculum should address both child-directed and teacher-led activities. This will allow the children the opportunity to learn new concepts and then gain experience through exploring their environment and practicing the new learning. It is important to continually evaluate the effectiveness of any curriculum to ensure that the developmental needs of the children are being addressed and that the children are provided opportunities for growth and development.

In 2019, Michigan maintained child-care-center licensing rules that specify the daily activities must be planned and instituted so that each child in care has the opportunity to practice social- interaction skills, use materials and take part in activities that encourage creativity, learn new ideas and skills while participating in imaginative play, participate in developmentally appropriate language and literacy experiences, participate in early math and science experiences, and be physically active. These activities provide children with the opportunity to feel successful and to feel good about themselves while developing their independence.

OPEN-ENDED PRODUCTS TO SHOW CHILDREN'S LEARNING

Bennett, Finn, and Cribb agree with Piaget's statement, "Play is the work of childhood." They add, "Just as lion cubs romp and play at stalking one another to build the skills they will need for survival, childhood play is how human beings ready themselves for the adult world." Play is designed to make learning fun. Trawick-Smith (2020) says with "too much adult involvement, children's activities may no longer be true play. Therefore, rolling the paint on the infant's hand or feet and pressing it on the paper is for you the adult and provides nothing for the child." Friedman, Wright, and Masterson (2021) agree: "The more that the adult directs an activity or interaction, the less likely it will be perceived as play by the child."

Sometimes well-meaning parents—and educators themselves—put pressure on teachers to send home evidence of their children's learning in the form of worksheets, coloring pages, and cute art projects. Real learning happens as children experience and experiment. Each child's learning product will be as unique as that child.

You may wonder what the parents will think if they do not receive a handprint turkey at Thanksgiving. I have had this conversation with caregivers who insisted that parents love to get the turkey handprint. The only way for caregivers to create turkey handprints with infants and toddlers is to paint the children's hands and press them onto the paper. Then the teacher goes back to add details such as eyes, feet, and wattles. This activity is not developmentally appropriate because the child has no control or opportunity for any individual expression. For preschoolers, insisting that they all make the same product in the same way (often following a teacher-created example) does not support their learning. I have found that staff are willing to find another turkey-related activity or to eliminate the project completely.

I suggest taking the children outside to experience watching leaves fall from trees or listening to the wind blow. Then, give them blank paper, paint, and paintbrushes. To elevate the experience, provide them with various materials to dip in the paint to apply to the paper, such as twigs, fallen leaves, feathers, their fingers, or sponges. The items that can be used are endless. While they explore what paint can do, you can use words such as *sticky*, *slick*, *smooth*, *goopy*, *wet*, and the names of colors. You can describe what you see them doing: "Lee, you mixed yellow and red to make orange!" "Josie, you're painting with a leaf. The leaf is spreading the blue paint on the paper." "Tyree, tell me more about your painting."

Development for children is about the learning process of the project, not the end result of the project. Making a perfect cotton-ball snowman is not as important as the children learning about snow and expressing their learning in unique ways. Friedman, Wright, and Masterson (2021) assert that "play allows children to stretch their boundaries to the fullest in their imagination, language, interaction, and self-regulation, as well as to practice their newly acquired skills."

A New Director with a Different Approach

Abbie had just started as the new program director at a center. During her first round of classroom observations, she stepped into Olivia's preschool room. Olivia was an experienced teacher who had been with the center for more than a decade.

Abbie walked over to the art center where Olivia was busy with the children doing an art project. Abbie saw that a carefully crafted snowman made of cotton balls glued onto blue paper rested in the center of the table. Each child was working on making her own version to match the teacher's example. Olivia walked around correcting the children when they started to glue a cotton ball anywhere on the paper besides in the center. She even instructed them on where to place the paper hats on their snowmen. Each snowman looked exactly like the one next to it. Even the children couldn't tell them apart when they were done.

Olivia wasn't the only teacher who was using adult-directed activities in her classroom. Abbie decided that she needed to introduce a new approach.

PROBLEM

Explorations with art materials are great for supporting creativity, fine-motor, and language development. Unfortunately, the way Olivia's activity was implemented did not nurture skills in any of those areas.

RESOLUTION

Abbie asked the licensing consultant to come in to teach the entire staff about the value of play-based learning and ways to nurture important developmental skills within the context of children's play and explorations. Abbie made it clear to the staff that she expected them to transition from adult-directed teaching to providing activities that support children's skill development, as well as promote their creativity and individuality.

She asked the staff to submit their lesson plans for review to confirm that age-appropriate activities were being planned. After giving the staff time to implement the new approach, Abbie made regular observations to provide constructive feedback and correct issues as they arose. This helped the staff to understand the expectations and trust that Abbie was not there to criticize but to support and serve as a valuable resource to help with the change.

Abbie continued to offer training for the staff to help them to provide a nurturing environment for the children. She told the staff that part of their evaluation would be based on their incorporation of hands-on, open-ended projects for the children.

CELEBRATING DIVERSITY

Early childhood classrooms are becoming more diverse in various ways—culturally, ethnically, physically, linguistically—and serve families who have a variety of family dynamics. Friedman, Wright, and Masterson advise, "A well-designed developmentally and culturally relevant curriculum avoids and counters cultural or individual bias or stereotypes and fosters a positive learning disposition in each area of the curriculum and in each child." However, diversity is not always displayed and shared within the classroom. The key to creating a center that welcomes all families is being open to learning about people—who they are, where they come from, and what is important to them. Hopefully, if a program director has been working at a center for years, the staff is trained and provided with resources to ensure that all children and their families are represented and respected within the classrooms.

Creating a Space that Celebrates Diversity

When Paris joined the center as the new program director, she decided to observe each classroom to get to know each teacher's style and approach. In Sasha's classroom, she noticed that all the photos and most of the books lacked portrayals of diverse ethnicities, cultures, and abilities. There were no children's books in the home languages of the children in the classroom. Even the dolls did not reflect the diverse community where the center was located.

Paris asked Sasha about her classroom setup. Sasha told her that she was not interested in any other cultures, and that the multiple children who were from different cultural backgrounds had to learn to adjust because they lived in the United States now. Paris thanked her for her candor, and left the room to continue her observations. It turned out that some of the other teachers held Sasha's perspective; others were afraid of offending anyone, so they did not try to incorporate diverse materials in their classrooms.

Later that day, Paris thought hard about what she had seen and heard. Her first question was whether or not the teachers who rejected the idea of inclusive practices had the ability to change. It occurred to her that these teachers simply may have not received any training on the topic.

PROBLEM

Children learn best when they feel safe and nurtured. They notice what adults say and do, and they internalize those messages. Families connect with their children's teachers and child-care center when they feel respected, heard, and welcome. Teachers can help children and their families feel accepted and part of the classroom community by intentionally including photos, books, music, and authentic items that reflect the cultures of the families.

Paris decided that, generally, Sasha and the other teachers were providing a good-quality, developmentally appropriate environment for the children. She resolved to provide training for the whole staff on implementing inclusive approaches in the classrooms. She would then give the staff time to begin making concrete changes.

RESOLUTION

It takes time to implement authentic changes in the classroom. The teachers needed help to learn to see children and families from a strengths-based perspective and to engage with them in meaningful ways. As part of the training, teachers were encouraged to invite the families to provide information and to share with their classes about their cultures. Gradually, the staff began to authentically connect with the children's families. They began to understand the richness of the children's cultures and languages and the value of exposing all the children to that diversity.

Early childhood educators should actively expose children to the various cultures of the families served in their center, as well as to cultures outside their community. Not only will this enrich the classroom environment and the children's learning, but staff will also have the opportunity to learn about various cultural customs and parenting styles, which will give them a greater understanding of the children and families they serve. One way to learn about different cultures is to invite family members to the classroom to share something about their culture and traditions. If this option is not available, then contact organizations or community leaders to come into the classroom and share with the children.

A child-care environment that conveys respect for the cultures that make up the community will display a variety of materials portrayed in authentic and nonstereotypical ways.

- Encourage staff to label items and spaces in both the children's home languages and English.
- Provide books in the children's home languages and about a variety of cultures.
- Invite families to bring photos or artifacts from home for the children to see and learn about while they are at the center.

- At circle time, invite parents, grandparents, or other family members to share fingerplays and games in their home languages or from their cultures.
- Ask family members to record themselves reading children's books or singing songs in their home languages and to share those recordings with the children.
- Encourage staff to provide materials from various cultures for the children to explore in the art centers.
- Ask families to share cooking experiences with foods from various cultures.
- In the dramatic play area, provide dress-up clothes that represent different cultures and dolls with different skin tones, hair textures, and abilities.
- Provide music from a variety of cultures for the children to dance and move to.
- Consider learning about celebrations from the different cultures in your community. If you are incorporating celebrations, you do not have to have them only when they are scheduled, especially if your program does not run year-round.
- Display photos of all the children and their families in the center.

Implementing these measures will help teachers create an environment where the students and families feel comfortable.

Friedman, Wright, and Masterson suggest, "Early childhood educators need to understand the commonalities of children's development and learning and how those commonalities take unique forms as they reflect the social and cultural frameworks in which they occur." The program director can help the staff learn to see the strengths that children and families bring to the child-care environment. "Working together, you and the family will create a shared, growing, deep understanding of their child," says Ernst (2014). For example, different cultures have different child-rearing practices. If a parent wants a practice that differs from the center's norm, the program director and teacher need to strive to understand the parent's point of view and be willing to adapt their practices if possible. This means seeking the parent's input and actively listening. If a parent speaks a language other than English, it may mean bringing in a translator. Active listening, according to Ernst, "requires that you are engaged, focused, invested in, and attending to what the other person has to say."

The director can also actively hire staff who are from a variety of cultures and backgrounds. NAEYC's *Professional Standards and Competencies for Early Childhood Educators* states, "It is important for child-care centers to employ a diverse population." Diversity within the staff of an early childhood program can go a long way toward promoting understanding.

Friedman, Wright, and Masterson assert that "social and cultural aspects are not simply ingredients of development and learning; these aspects provide the framework for all development and learning." Programs that are racially and culturally sensitive provide the support that children need to grow and mature with a sense of acceptance. Knowledge—learning about someone who differs from oneself—and exposure—getting to know someone as a human being—are the true keys to reducing all forms of prejudice. As Ernst says, "Your role, then, is to create an environment that actively seeks to empower all families based on their individual strengths and challenges."

With the program director's guidance and training, the teaching staff will provide a quality experience for the children that is both developmentally appropriate and culturally relevant. The next chapter will address some of the challenges that program directors have encountered when working with parents.

CHAPTER 8

Challenges with Parents

I was a newly hired preschool teacher, fresh out of college with a shiny new bachelor's degree and ready to change the world one child at a time. But one parent was making my life difficult. She was not happy with anything that I had planned for the children. I would talk to her daily and explain how each activity was developmentally appropriate and would support the children's skills. It did not matter what I said—she was not happy. She even told me that I did not understand child development because I did not have any children of my own. This parent challenged me in ways that I was not prepared for, but I did not get upset. At the end of the year when the child was moving up to the next class this mother's departing statement to me was, "Thank you for everything that you did for me and my child, for always taking the time to answer my questions, and for explaining why you were doing what you were doing in the classroom with the children." She had wanted to intimidate me as a young teacher, and when she was unsuccessful she showed her appreciation for the patience that I had shown her.

I have taken the patience that I learned that year into every position that I have held since. I learned that it is not enough to say that you want to provide a quality environment for children; parents need to know that you're paying the same attention to the children's developmental process. Remember: you are the expert, and the parents are often looking to you for guidance.

THE PARENT HANDBOOK

The best way to address challenges with parents is to have a well-written parent handbook. When parents enroll their children—and before the children attend—provide orientation for the families to allow them to learn how the center functions. Go over the handbook with the parents, and have them sign a statement saying that they have received and understand it.

States differ in their requirements around parent handbooks. In the states of Michigan and Washington, parent handbooks are required. However, Arizona requires parents to request a copy of the parent handbook. The parent handbook can be provided to parents as a hardcopy or electronic copy. Child-care centers in Michigan and Washington must maintain a signed statement acknowledging parents' receipt of the parent handbook; Washington also requires parents to acknowledge reviewing the handbook. There's no need to have separate acknowledgement forms for each child if siblings attend the center; one form is sufficient for the family and can be filed in one child's file. (However, to make licensing inspections easier, you may want to put a copy of the acknowledgement in each child's file or a note referring to the child's file that has the acknowledgement statement.)

Here, we'll take a look at the parent-handbook requirements for Arizona, Michigan, and Washington; familiarize yourself with the requirements for your state (Find them here: https://licensingregulations.acf.hhs.gov/). A program director can add additional information beyond that which is required; however, the director cannot omit any of the state's required content and information.

Michigan, Washington State, and Arizona all require that the parent handbook state the center's hours of operation, fee policy, child enrollment and disenrollment procedures, transportation guidelines, and discipline guidelines. The additional requirements for each state are listed below.

WASHINGTON

The state of Washington also requires that the parent handbook include the following:

- Program days, closure dates, and observed holidays
- The program philosophy
- The program's child-guidance plan and a description of the child-restraint policies as well as a statement forbidding corporal punishment
- Policies on religious and cultural activities, including how holidays will be celebrated
- Policies on water activities
- Policies and procedures on overnight care
- A description of how weapons on the premises are secured
- The sign-in and sign-out requirements

- A nondiscrimination statement
- A family engagement and partnership communication plan
- A parent or guardian permission form for photography, videotaping, or surveillance of his or her child
- Policies on alcohol, tobacco, and cannabis use and the prohibition of illegal drugs
- A list of what parents or guardians must supply for their children, such as extra clothing or diapers
- The center's expulsion policy
- Policies on off-site field trips
- The center's termination of services policy
- The center's emergency preparedness plan
- A statement outlining the staff's duty to report incidents, including *suspected* child abuse, neglect, or maltreatment
- The policy on permission for a parent or guardian's access to areas of the early learning program during business hours.
- Early learning program staff-to-child ratios
- The classroom types offered, if applicable
- Policies regarding mixed-age groups, if applicable (including when children may be in a mixed age group)
- A kindergarten transition plan, if applicable

The handbook must state how the center will handle the information required for each child's record, including:

- The importance and plan for keeping the information current
- A plan to keep the child's information confidential
- Who may legally access the child's information

The handbook must describe where the parent or guardian may find and review the early learning program's:

- Health policy
- Staff policies
- Consistent-care policy
- Menus
- Liability insurance
- Inspection reports and notices of enforcement actions, if applicable
- Other relevant program policies

If the early learning program offers any of the following, the parent handbook must also include a policy for each that applies to the program:

- Care for children with specific or special needs
- Infant and toddler care, covering:
  - Diapering
  - Feeding
  - Toilet training
  - Child sleep pattern
  - Safe sleep requirements
- Dual language learning

MICHIGAN

Michigan requires the following to be included in the parent handbook:

- Procedures for administering medication
- Holidays during which the center is open and services are provided
- The program philosophy
- Policies on food handling and feeding
- A description of the typical daily routine
- The parent-notification plan for accidents, injuries, incidents, and illnesses
- The exclusion policy for child illnesses
- A notice informing parents of the program's licensing notebook, which contains all the licensing, inspection, and special-investigation reports and related corrective action plans for the previous five years
- A notice stating that inspection reports are available on site to parents during regular business hours
- A notice informing parents that licensing-inspection reports, special-investigation reports, and corrective-action plans from at least the past three years are available on the state's child-care licensing website at www.michigan.gov/michildcare (Note: the url must be in bold print in the handbook.)

ARIZONA

In addition to the center's hours of operation, fee policy, child enrollment and disenrollment procedures, transportation guidelines, and discipline guidelines, Arizona requires the following:

- The facility's street address, city, state, zip code, mailing address, and telephone number
- Responsibilities and participation of parents in facility activities
- A general description of activities and programs
- Medication administration procedures
- A notice stating inspection reports are available on site
- Field-trip requirements and procedures
- A description of the liability insurance that is carried by the licensee and a statement that documentation of the liability insurance coverage is available for review on the facility premises
- A description of the facility's child-care services classifications
- Accident and emergency procedures
- A provision stating that the facility is regulated by the Arizona Department of Health Services, including the department's local street address, city, state, zip code, and local telephone number
- The procedures for notifying a parent at least forty-eight hours before a pesticide is applied on a facility's premises
- A statement that a parent has access to the areas on facility premises where the parent's enrolled child is receiving child-care services

The program must provide a copy of a statement of child-care services to the state licensing department every year and must provide a copy, upon request, to parents.

DISGRUNTLED PARENTS

Disgruntled parents are generally upset because they feel that they have been wronged in some way. In all circumstances, the owner and program director of the center must behave in a professional manner. As a director, your first line of defense is to listen to their concerns and apologize. Most parents want to know that you understand and are willing to listen and address their concerns. Of course, this does not mean that you must tolerate swearing and other forms of disrespect, especially in front of the children. Include a written policy in both your staff and parent handbooks addressing how the center will handle the situation. For example: parents who are swearing in the center for any reason will be asked to leave the center the first time. If the behavior happens a second time, their child will be disenrolled from the center. Some may say that this is harsh and hurts the children. I say that the center is a professional establishment and the staff must be treated with courtesy and respect. When a parent does not display that behavior, there are natural consequences as a direct result. The other children and families should not be subjected to inappropriate behavior.

Let's take a look at some common (and not-so-common) issues with parents and consider ways to handle those types of situations in a professional way.

ENROLLMENT

When they enroll their first child in child care, new parents are often not familiar with how centers function. Without previous experience, they will not always know how to navigate the routine. They typically feel stressed about returning to work and leaving their child with someone else. Whatever the parents may be experiencing, they need to know that their child is receiving quality care—that starts with developing a relationship with the program director.

In the same way that you provide new-hire orientation for staff, provide new parents with a center orientation a week before their child is scheduled to start. This is one of the best ways to communicate with them and to reassure them that their child will be safe in the nurturing environment at your center.

Maintain an open-door policy so parents can reach out to you with concerns. Take the time to go over the parent handbook in detail with them, so they are aware of how the center functions and understand the requirements and expectations of the center. Explain the services your center provides, the hours of operation, the policy on school vacation days, admission and withdrawal policies, the center's child-care philosophy, the fee schedule, the food service, and ways for the parents to be involved in the center.

During the center orientation, have the parents complete all of the necessary enrollment paperwork and provide completed physical or immunization records. This will provide you with the opportunity to review the paperwork to ensure that it is completed correctly. If anything is missing, you can require that it be provided before the child starts at the center. This process will reduce the stress of having to contact the parents after the child has started at the center for any needed paperwork. After the child has begun attending the center, parents will have a hundred and one reasons why they have not provided the information that you need to complete their child's file. I've heard everything from "I left it in the car and I will bring it in tomorrow," to "Oh, my wife has the forms," to "My husband was supposed to drop them off this morning. I'll talk to him when I get home," to "Can you give me the form again? I lost it," to "I forgot to call the doctor to get the form completed." I think I've heard everything except "My dog ate the paperwork." Getting the paperwork up front will reduce the amount of energy that you have to put into figuring out what information is needed and tracking down the parents. I realize that some centers require enrollment paperwork to be completed within sixty or ninety days of enrollment, depending on the state requirements. To make the process easy for yourself, I say forget about sixty or ninety days and require all of the information needed for enrollment *before* the child starts at the center.

TUITION PAYMENT AND COLLECTIONS

One of the most challenging areas with parents is collecting tuition payments. When a child is enrolled, clearly explain the tuition policy to the parents and have them sign a form acknowledging that you have explained the policy to them and that they agree to it. Give them a copy, and keep the original in the child's file.

Tuition payments should be consistent, and the policy should be enforced equally across the board with all families. Do not allow one family to miss several payments but disenroll the child of another family for the same issue. When parents fall behind in their tuition payments, they should receive a written notice. Children should not be told to tell their parents that they owe money. Parents should not be contacted at work in an attempt to collect tuition. Parents should not be turned away from the center without notice. And the police should not be involved in a tuition issue.

For parents who fall on hard times and are not able to pay their tuition, you can consider offering a payment-plan option. The payment plan should be described in a legal document that requires the payments over a period of no more than six months. You want to help the family but not increase their financial difficulties. The policy should state that the option is available on a case-by-case basis, and you may not wish to inform all parents of the option. After all, you are running a business and cannot afford to have the majority of the parents on a payment plan. You can also put a cap on the number of families who use this plan; once the cap is reached other families would not be able to use the payment plan.

I suggest requiring tuition payments at the beginning of each week. Collecting tuition at the end of the week makes it harder to keep the accounts current because parents will always want another day to pay their child's tuition. Don't be surprised when parents ask for a discount on their child's tuition because their child missed some days. In my opinion, child care is the only business where individuals look for a break when their child is not participating in the service that they signed up for. Centers build their budgets around the number of children enrolled. Whether or not a child actually attends, the center still must pay the same bills to operate: payroll, rent or mortgage, lights, gas, internet, cleaning fees, and other miscellaneous expenses. Holidays, vacations, staff-training days, or a child out for illness or family vacation are not reasons for a discount. The only exception to a no-discount policy would be when the center must close for multiple weeks due to disease outbreak, flooding, fire, accident, or other reason that the facility is uninhabitable, forcing the parents to find alternative care for their children. Centers should not expect or request payment under these circumstances.

PARENTAL PEER PRESSURE

Parents often feel peer pressure from other parents on many levels. For example, parents will ask about the location of a child's birthday party and even about details of the birthday gift bags and snacks. Parents will compare the child-care centers their children attend, as well as the activities that the children are involved in, such as swimming, soccer, T-ball, dance, gymnastics, foreign-language instruction, or karate. If you have not experienced parental peer pressure, just ask a first-time parent how many times they have been asked about what sports or activities their child is doing. Parents often feel that they are required to have their children involved in many activities. Don't get me wrong—there are a great deal of fun and educational activities available for young children, but if the child is not interested or the parents cannot spend quality time with their child because they are busy with activities, that is a problem. It is our responsibility as early childhood educators to help parents navigate their time management so that they are placing a higher priority on the time that they spend with their children outside of the car between activities.

Parent Bullying Another Parent

Five-year-old Alfonso told his mother that another child, five-year-old Aiden, had pushed him off the swing that afternoon. This was the second week that Aiden had injured Alfonso. While Alfonso's mother, Tamar, was listening to her son, Aiden's mother, Romi, walked into the center. Tamar confronted her and told her that Aiden had pushed Alfonso off the swing. She warned Romi that if it happened again, she was going to hurt Aiden. Romi told her to keep Alfonso away from Aiden and the problem would be solved. Tamar and Romi began to argue. When Yael, the program director, heard the loud voices in the hallway, she went out to see what was occurring. Tamar told Yael about what had happened between the two children. Romi said that Tamar was going to have a true problem if she did anything to her child.

Yael explained to Tamar that the teacher was addressing her concerns and was working with both of the boys to resolve the problem. She stated that the number of incidents between them had declined because the teacher was working with the boys to use their words to communicate with each other. She explained that parents having a shouting match at the center was not appropriate behavior. She acknowledged that Tamar was upset with the situation, but told her she could not confront Romi at the center. She warned that if it happened again, she would follow the center's policy and disenroll Alfonso. Yael said that, going forward, when Tamar had a concern, she should address it with the classroom teacher or herself.

PROBLEM

It can be upsetting for a parent to hear that their child has been hurt by another child. The teacher should have contacted Tamar and explained what had happened to Alfonso and how the situation was being addressed. This would have prevented Tamar from hearing of the incident from her child at pickup.

RESOLUTION

Yael listened and acknowledged Tamar's concerns about Alfonso being injured at the center and explained what was taking place in the classroom to resolve the situation. This communication is a vital part of the process. She also outlined the center's policy related to parents' behavior at the center and the consequences for not adhering to the policy.

Yael spoke with the teacher to make sure that she would communicate with the parents when issues occur.

CUSTODY ISSUES

Child-care centers are not the place for parents to work out their issues. Program directors must stress this when they enroll children in the program. Unless there is a court order to the contrary, each parent has equal rights when it comes to their child. If there is a court order regarding custody and visitation, the center must follow it. In that case, have each parent complete the enrollment information for the child, and treat each parent separately. This will make it easy and will keep the center out of a personal situation between the parents.

When I was a program director, a parent asked to have her children's father removed from the child-information cards because she did not want him to pick up the children in the future. Two weeks later, when the father showed up to pick up the children, I immediately phoned the mother. She said, "Thank you so much for calling. Please do not let him know anything about the request." She was afraid that he would be upset with her if he found out that she had removed him from the list of people authorized to pick the children up. She had only made that decision because she was upset with him, and she took back her request. This situation had put the center in an awkward position; center staff should not be involved in the personal disputes of parents.

I once had a conversation with a program director who was concerned because a father wanted to know what the child was learning at the center, and he was requesting to have access to his son's file, which contained the mother's information. I explained that the parent has a right to know about what his child is doing at the center and that the child's information could be shared without exposing the other parent's personal information. The director could do so while still following the custody order that was in place for the child.

Noncustodial Parent Tries to Pick Up Children

Alejandra had full custody of two-year-old Tehila and four-year-old Shira. Their father, Micky, showed up at the center and wanted to pick up the children. Micky's name was not on their information cards, but Alejandra had provided the center with copies of the custody papers and had instructed the program director that Micky was not allowed to pick the children up or have any contact with them.

When Micky showed up to the center, the assistant program director called Alejandra and let her know that he was trying to pick up Tehila and Shira. She reassured Alejandra that the children were fine and had no idea that Micky was there. The director, Gaelle, refused to release the children. Frustrated, Micky called the police. When the police officer arrived, Gaelle provided the custody documentation. After reviewing the documents, the officers escorted Micky off of the property and told him not to return to the center because the center staff had to follow the court order.

PROBLEM

If parents do not have shared custody, the center needs documentation of the custody arrangement.

RESOLUTION

Gaelle followed the correct protocol when she did not release Tehila and Shira to the noncustodial parent. Having the correct paperwork on file from the custodial parent was the only protection that the center had in this situation. Had Alejandra not provided the custody paperwork, the police may have required the center to release the children to the father.

PARENTS WHO ARE INTOXICATED OR UNDER THE INFLUENCE

There may be an occasion when a parent or legal guardian arrives at the center intoxicated or under the influence. Before this occurs, it is vital for centers to have written policies and procedures for staff members to follow. The policies should also be provided to the parents so that they will be informed as to how the center will react and resolve the situation.

Parent Is Intoxicated at Pick Up

When I was a program director for a private center, I had a parent arrive to pick up her child and it was apparent that she was intoxicated. The classroom teacher sent her assistant to my office to ask me to come down to the classroom. She did not tell me what was wrong, but upon entering the classroom, I observed the parent and immediately knew that she was intoxicated. She was laughing loudly, stumbling, and slurring her words. At that point, it did not matter whether she was intoxicated or having a bad reaction to medication—she was in no condition to operate a vehicle. I immediately asked the parent if I could speak with her in my office and she agreed. We left the child in the classroom explaining that we would return. What happened next, I would not suggest. The center did not have written policies for addressing these situations, and I was not trained on how to handle them.

Once we arrived at my office, I closed the door and explained why I had asked her to come. I did not want to approach her in an accusatory fashion, so I said that her safety and the safety of her child were my only concern. I explained that I did not feel it was safe for her to operate a vehicle in that condition. I asked if there was anyone that she could call to pick her and her child up from the center. She said no, because she was going through a divorce and did not want anyone to know that she had been drinking.

I then offered to drive her and her child home. She agreed to let me drive her home in her vehicle. I had a staff member follow us so that she could drive me back to the center. Once we arrived at her home, I informed her that this was the only time I would be driving her home. If she arrived at the center intoxicated again, I would be forced to contact the child's father or the individuals listed on the child's emergency card to pick up the child from the center, and the police would be notified if she decided to drive away from the center. The parent agreed, and she did not arrive at the center intoxicated again.

PROBLEM

I would not suggest that anyone follow the example that I have explained. I have reflected on that situation multiple times over the years and, of course, I am glad that it turned out the way it did. I also recognize that the situation could have ended badly for me on many levels. I could have had an accident, and she could have sued both me and the center. Had we had a written policy and procedures for me to follow, that would have eliminated the risk I took when I drove the parent home.

RESOLUTION

I recommend that program directors and managers have a written policy that clearly outlines the steps to be taken when and if they suspect a parent, or anyone authorized to pick up a child, is under the influence or intoxicated. Check with local law enforcement and an attorney to determine the center's legal rights and obligations as they relate to releasing children when a parent wants to leave with their child. Create a detailed policy and procedures, and provide those to the parents and staff. In this way, everyone will understand the center's written policy for releasing children and the expectations of the center. Train the staff on the center's policy so that everyone is prepared if the situation occurs. Preplanning is always the best solution when it comes to this situation. Decker and Decker (2005) advise, "Policies and procedures . . . protect the program, staff, children, and parents."

PARENTING PRACTICES

Consistency between the home and the classroom is important. Parents and teachers must understand and respect the practices in the home and in the center. Teachers must recognize parents as the child's first teachers who continue to play an intricate part in the child's development. Parents and teachers must recognize that a child's capacity for learning is not determined at birth and that there is a great deal that parents and teachers can do to enhance the child's growth and development. They have to work together to provide the best learning experience for each child.

Communication between the center and home is critical, because if the parents do not feel comfortable at the center, they will often look for another resource for child care, which could be disruptive to the child's development. When parents make a request that is not developmentally appropriate for a child, it is the teacher's responsibility to explain why the center would not be able to comply. For example, if a parent wants their child to nap for only thirty minutes so the child will sleep at home, the teacher must decide whether to honor their request or allow the child to sleep without waking them up. The American Academy of Pediatrics (AAP) (2020) says that, depending on age, young children need between ten and sixteen hours of sleep, including naps, per day. The AAP warns that depriving children of sleep can lead to irritability, difficulty concentrating, hypertension, obesity, headaches, and depression. The teacher can start by letting the parent know that sleep is an important part of the child's development: "Children who get enough sleep have a healthier immune system, and better school performance, behavior, memory, and mental health" (AAP, 2020). The teacher can also assure the parents that their child will still sleep at night after napping during the day.

Two-Year-Old Sleeping in a High Chair

Two-year-old Armani's parents asked that she be allowed to sleep in a high chair because she does not stay on her cot during nap time and might disturb the other children. They told the teacher, Senegal, that Armani often sleeps in the high chair at home.

When Armani fell asleep in her high chair after lunch, Senegal decided not to move her for fear that she would not sleep on a cot. Ivory, the program director, walked into the classroom and was surprised to see the sleeping child in the high chair. She was aware that Armani did not like to stay on her cot during nap time, but she also knew that it was not appropriate for Senegal to allow her to sleep in the high chair. Ivory did not know that the parent had approved the arrangement, but that did not matter because the center followed safe sleep practices.

PROBLEM

When parents have a request for their child that is out of the ordinary, the staff should confirm the request with the program director and obtain approval before anything is implemented.

RESOLUTION

Ivory retrained Senegal and had her sign off on the training. She was not written up but given a verbal warning. Senegal met with Armani's parents to explain the center's policy on safe sleep practices, and together they agreed to help Armani learn to stay on her cot during nap time.

Ivory added information to the parent handbook so that parents would be aware that any request that is contradictory to what the center normally does would have to be approved by the program director.

Parent Wanted to Provide Lunch for Her Daughter

Ada's mother, Karina, did not want Ada to eat the lunch provided by the center. Ada did not have allergies; this was a personal choice by the family. The first week, Ada's lunch was balanced, but the second week's lunches included candy and salty snacks. Ada's teacher, Carlisle, spoke to Karina about the type of foods she was providing, and he gave her a list of nutritious lunch items. Karina stated that she provided the foods that Ada liked to eat.

When the foods that were provided for Ada did not improve, Carlisle informed Abigail, the program director, about his concerns. Abigail spoke to Karina and explained that, because the center provides lunch for all of the children and Ada does not have allergies, they were going to have her eat the center's lunch. Karina could send extra food for Ada, but they would only give it to the child if it was healthy.

PROBLEM

The parent did not know much about healthy, nutritious foods. She had been letting her child pick what she wanted to take in her lunch. The program director must make the best decisions for the children; having this conversation with the parents is part of that. It would not have been in Ada's best interest to allow her to eat candy and salty snacks for lunch without addressing the concerns.

RESOLUTION

At first Karina was not happy with the decision, but she later told Abigail that she had learned more about nutrition from the information that Carlisle had given her. She had started providing healthy choices for Ada at home as well.

This situation demonstrates why open communication is so important. When you are able to speak with the parents about your concerns, you will develop a positive relationship. Do not be afraid to share your concerns, and be open to listening and addressing parents' concerns as well.

Child Held Hostage for Tuition

During the COVID-19 pandemic, families were not allowed to enter most child-care centers. In one instance, a parent sent a relative to pick up her child. The program director told the relative that she was going to get the child and left the relative waiting outside. The program director did not go to get the child; instead, she called the parent and informed her that she would not be releasing her child to the relative because she had an outstanding tuition balance. She said the tuition payment must be made before the child would be released. The program director had not mentioned anything to the parent at drop-off, nor had she sent a late notice to the parent.

The parent was furious with the program director for holding her child hostage for payment. She was also embarrassed because her relative was still waiting outside the center. The parent had to send the money to her relative via electronic transfer so that she could pay the program director. Then, the relative was allowed to take the child home to the family.

PROBLEM

When it comes to tuition, children should not be involved in any way. The program director must be consistent in collecting tuition and sending late-payment notifications. The parent handbook should clearly state the late-payment policy, including the policy that a child will not be admitted to the center until the tuition is paid.

RESOLUTION

The parent disenrolled her child from the center that evening. The program director was seeking payment, but because of the way she went about it, she lost future revenue.

PARENTS' FEAR OF RETALIATION

In my experience, parents have stated on many occasions that they did not want to express their concerns to a program director or teacher for fear of retaliation. They said they were afraid that their child may be treated differently by the staff or hurt in some way as a form of payback if the parent made a complaint. Open communication between parents and caregivers is so important. Parents should be able to ask questions and voice concerns without fear that something would happen to their child.

When parents express this fear to me, I explain that they should never leave their child at a center where they feel that they cannot raise a concern without the dread of retaliation. When I've asked parents what they think the staff would actually do to their child, most cannot name anything specific. Some parents fear that their child will be disenrolled if they complain or express concern about a staff member. The fear is real, and parents do not want to be the cause of their child being singled out.

Over the years, I have had several parents state that they did not speak to anyone at the center about their concerns, even when they did not feel that the staff was being appropriate with the children. There should always be open communication at the center with respect on both sides. The program director should strive to create an atmosphere of trust.

If a center will disenroll a child because the parent has a concern about the care that their child is receiving, then that is clearly not the center for that child. Center staff must intentionally help families feel comfortable and safe and must let the parents know that they welcome their concerns and appreciate their feedback.

Ironically, child-care staff may feel the same way when it comes to parents. They may feel that they cannot say anything to a parent for fear that they will disenroll their child from the center. This is why communication between the staff and the parents has to be open, honest, and respectful. The parents and staff should be on the same page when it comes to providing and receiving quality child care. Children will benefit from a harmonious relationship between the staff and the parents.

STAFF TURNOVER

Parents like consistency. When a teacher leaves their child's classroom for any reason, they and their child are affected. A family's relationship with their child's caregiver is important. Parents are often uncomfortable leaving their child with a different caregiver because they have not established a relationship with the new staff member. This lack of a relationship will cause them to discount the caregivers and their ability to provide appropriate care and supervision.

The trust that the center is providing the best care declines when there is high staff turnover. This is especially true when the center cannot keep a program director. I have spoken with many parents who describe a center as having a revolving door when it comes to program directors. To complicate matters, whenever a new program director is hired, a center may lose multiple staff members and mistakes may occur.

Generally, a group of parents will stay in the hope that the center will improve. Another group of parents will not be concerned because their child is happy at the center and that is all that matters to them. A third group of parents will be unhappy with the constant staff turnover and will actively look for a new center to take their child. They may even place their child on a waiting list for another center, and once a spot opens up, they will leave the center.

What can the director do to make parents feel better? Reduce the turnover. In my book *Build Your Dream Team* (2020), I provide ways to address and resolve issues with staff retention. When staff members decide to leave, the director should use that as an opportunity to learn. For example, consider the following:

- Review the hiring process to make sure that the correct candidates are being hired.
- Have exit conferences with staff who are leaving, and ask them to be candid with you about why they are leaving, how you can improve the center, and what they wish they had known when they were hired.
- Be willing to make changes to improve the way your center functions.

By reducing turnover and retaining the staff at the center, you are providing the children and the families with important continuity of care.

While dealing with high staff turnover, ensure that the parents are introduced to their child's new teacher and provided with information about the new person who is caring for their child. The new hire should also take the time to communicate with the parents. She should greet them by name when they arrive at the center, and introduce herself. This will assist the parents while they try to help their child acclimate to the new hire. The new hire should also make it a point to learn about each child. It is important to make a smooth transition, and communication will go a long way toward that goal. Being new to the center is not a problem, but not making the parents feel comfortable is.

When a staff person leaves, the program director should inform the parents. They should not have to ask where a caregiver is because they have not seen them for a while. You do not have to go into details about the staff member's reasons for leaving the center. Instead, simply state that the staffer does not work at the center anymore and that you wish her the best. If the staff member does not leave on good terms, there should not be any indication to the parents of the underlying reasons. You always want to promote positive energy at the center. The only exception to this is when a staff person does something inappropriate or places a child in harm's way. In that situation, the parents who are directly involved can be informed, but the general information that goes out to the remaining parents should be generic.

Whenever you face challenges with parents, remember that they want to be heard and appreciated when they have a concern. They want the program director to take their concerns seriously and not just brush them off or give them no validity. Listen and be willing to make changes, if needed.

In the next chapter, we take a look at challenging child behaviors and ways to address them when they arise at your center.

CHAPTER 9

Challenges with Children's Behavior

Challenging behavior is one of the most persistent issues that caregivers face. When children are displaying behavior that is perceived as challenging, the adults must ask ourselves why the behavior is challenging for us. Is it because we are not prepared or trained on how to handle the situation? Is the caregiver working alone and therefore unable to address the needs of the child? Could it be that the classroom is not set up to address the child's needs? Is the daily schedule not meeting the needs of the children?

Young children are made to move and explore. From the minute they figure out how to crawl or scoot, they try to reach objects and people that interest them. Toddlers have very short attention spans—no longer than a few minutes. With their new walking skills, it is hard to get them to focus on a story or any other activity for very long. Preschoolers have longer attention spans but still cannot sit still for more than fifteen or twenty minutes. Asking young children to sit through a long circle time is not developmentally appropriate. Instead of trying to force children to do what they are not developmentally ready to do, caregivers and teachers should design their schedules around what the child can do.

There are lots of other reasons why a child might engage in behavior that an adult finds challenging. Is the child new to the classroom? Could the child be hungry or tired (both of which can cause aggressive behavior)? If a child is new, help her understand how your classroom functions and consider pairing her with a buddy so she does not feel alone. If a child is tired, it is okay to let her take a nap on a cot or mat on the side of the classroom. If a child is hungry, provide a snack before lunch rather than having her wait. You will be surprised at what a difference meeting a child's needs will make in the child's temperament.

Remember that behavior is communication. Young children are just learning how to communicate their feelings and needs, and they often need help from caring adults to express themselves. If a child is exhibiting behaviors that seem challenging, consider the child's circumstances. Has there been a change in the child's family, such as a divorce, a death, the birth of a sibling, a grandparent who has moved into the home, or a family member who has become ill? Before a director or caregiver can properly address a child's behaviors, the caregiver must get to the bottom of what the behavior is communicating.

As a program director, when a staff member tells you that she is struggling with a child's behavior, that is your cue to learn more by observing in the classroom. Consider aspects such as the following:

- Classroom design:
    - Is the furniture arranged to allow easy movement from one area to another?
    - Are the learning centers clearly defined?
    - Are there adequate amounts of materials and toys?
- Daily schedule:
    - Is there a consistent daily schedule?
    - Are children being asked to sit for more than fifteen to twenty minutes at a time?
    - Do the children have opportunities to engage in activities of their own choosing?
    - Are there too many transitions from one activity to another?
- Classroom management:
    - Do the children understand the expectations in the classroom?
    - Are the expectations consistently applied?
    - Are there enough staff to maintain the adult-child ratio?
    - Are staff trained on age-appropriate discipline techniques, including redirection?
    - Do the caregivers intentionally teach the children how to interact with each other in positive ways?

In addition to the information gained from observing in the classroom, talk with the staffer about their communication with parents. Is there anything going on at home that might be affecting the child's behavior in child care? After observing, meet with the staff person to discuss what you have learned and to brainstorm together some ways to address the child's behavior and meet their needs.

Changing a child's behavior takes time; there is a rule of thumb that says it takes thirty days to learn a new behavior. When a caregiver tries a new approach, she must persist and patiently continue. We often want children to change their behavior the first time we speak to them about it, but that is an unrealistic expectation. If, after a period of trying, there is no sign of improvement, then additional help may be needed. Your observations are crucial because they are based on experience, not feelings. It may be that the child would need to be evaluated for possible special needs to see if additional services are required.

BITING

When children are biting at an early age, it is normal behavior. Young children explore with all their senses and often put things in their mouths. They are also just beginning to learn language. When a child is tired, frustrated, angry, or hungry, he may bite to express himself because he lacks the language to solve his problem in another way. Sometimes children bite simply because they are exploring what something tastes like or feels like.

If a child has bitten more than once in the classroom, the biting must be addressed. One way to do that is to understand why the child is biting. The caregiver can think about what happened when the child bit. Was he trying to keep another child from taking a toy from him? Was he frustrated because he wanted a toy that another child was playing with? Was he tired because he hadn't slept during nap time? Was he hungry because he had been too distracted to eat his snack? Has he recently had a tooth come in and is exploring what it can do?

Once the caregiver understands why the child bit, it is easier to address the reason. For example, if a child bit another child because he wanted a toy, provide multiples of the same toy so that children are not forced to wait or asked to share at an age when sharing is not something they are developmentally ready to do. If a child bit because he was hungry, make sure he eats regularly. Once the triggers have been identified and addressed, the biting should be reduced or eliminated.

Toddler Is Bitten by Another Toddler

Damian's mother, Lillian, was upset because fourteen-month-old Hunter had bitten thirteen-month-old Damian multiple times over a two-week period. After the first incident, Lillian had complained to Alaina, the toddler lead, and Nevaeh, the program director, who said they would address the situation, but the biting continued.

The plan to address the biting was to separate Hunter and Damian and have Lucy, the floater, to work in the classroom to make sure that Hunter did not bite Damian or any other children. However, the underlying issue was not addressed, and Hunter continued to bite Damian.

Lillian actually filed a complaint with the local police department because she just wanted Alaina and Nevaeh to take the issue seriously. Of course, the police department did not file a complaint on a fourteen-month-old child. Lillian did not want to disenroll Damian from the center because it was affordable and close to her work, but after her son was bitten repeatedly without any change in the behavior, Lillian was forced to disenroll him.

After Damian was disenrolled, the caregivers determined that Hunter was biting because he was having difficulty being in a group activity with other children in close proximity. When the children were all playing on the floor in the same area, Hunter would just bite the child who was closest to him, which was often Damian. Hunter was biting because his personal space was invaded and biting made the children move away from him. Once the caregivers understood the underlying reason for the behavior, Lucy made sure that Hunter had more space to himself. He no longer felt the need to bite the other children in the classroom to make his point.

PROBLEM

This situation could and should have been addressed before Damian's mother was upset to the point of feeling the need to go to the police and disenroll her child from the center.

RESOLUTION

Alaina and Nevaeh should have asked Lucy to work with Hunter to provide activities. This would help with determining what was triggering the biting so that the behavior could be addressed.

An Ongoing Biting Issue

Three-year-old Samuel was bitten four times over the course of a month by three-year-old Vince. Samuel's mother, Tessa, was upset because she felt that the preschool staff did not provide appropriate supervision in the classroom.

In the first incident, Samuel was bitten deeply into the skin on his back. Tessa said that she found out about the bite at pickup time because her son told her that Vince had bitten him, but she brushed it off thinking that it was not anything serious. At bath time that evening, she saw that the bite marks were quite deep. Samuel told her that he was sitting on the cot with his friend Vince and did not move when Vince asked him to get up. Vince got upset and bit him.

The next day Tessa asked about the bite marks, but the classroom teachers, Isabel and Rosie, did not know anything about the incident. Linda, the program director, was present in the classroom when Vince bit Samuel, because she was filling in for the lead caregiver, who was on maternity leave. She saw that Samuel had gone to Vince's cot and laid on top of Vince. Vince got upset and bit Samuel. Linda applied ice and cleaned the wound area. She said that this was the first biting incident for Vince, and she did not think that it would be a recurring problem because Samuel and Vince are good friends. Linda gave Tessa an incident report a day later because she had forgotten to complete it at the time. Tessa requested that the children be separated, but Linda told her that there was no other classroom for Samuel or Vince to be moved to.

Two days after the first incident, there was a fresh, deep bite mark on Samuel's back. None of the caregivers knew what had happened, how the bite had occurred, or when it happened. Tessa again requested Linda complete an incident report for the bite mark. The report stated that Samuel was bitten by Vince at an unknown time and there was no explanation as to how it happened.

Linda said that she was unaware of the second incident until Tessa sent a picture of the bite mark. Linda assured Tessa that she would make sure that Samuel and Vince would be monitored closely. Linda said that she made sure that Vince was always within arm's length of a caregiver. Linda said that she put Samuel and Vince in separate work groups within the classroom, but they would always find each other and play together or at least next to each other. She instructed Isabel and Rosie to supervise Samuel and Vince when they were playing together.

Vince bit Samuel a third time during the following week. Tessa said that Isabel informed her about the bite during pickup and provided an incident report. Isabel said the children were in circle time when Samuel pushed Vince and Vince got upset and bit Samuel. Isabel assured Tessa again that the two children would be monitored closely and separated, if needed, to make sure that a biting incident would not recur.

Isabel said that as soon as the bite occurred, she cleaned the wound, treated it with ice, and called Linda, who was not at the center. Linda told her to contact Tessa and explain the situation to her. Isabel contacted Tessa and explained what had happened. Linda indicated that she would call Vince's mother to seek help regarding his biting behavior in the classroom and that she had drafted an action plan listing all the measures that they would take to prevent the behavior. Isabel said that she signed the action plan and made sure that she would remain within arm's reach of Samuel and Vince when they played together.

Action Plan

- Use a flash card of a stop sign as a signal to Samuel and Vince to stop unwanted behavior
- Put Samuel and Vince into separate work groups
- Shadow Vince and keep him within five feet of a caregiver at all times

The fourth incident occurred when the children were dancing during circle time. Linda told Tessa that she was holding another child's hands, and Samuel and Vince were dancing. Samuel accidentally stepped on Vince's foot and lost his balance. Samuel grabbed onto Vince's neck, and Vince got upset and bit Samuel on the cheek. Linda informed her that they were trying to get help from a local child-care organization for Vince's biting.

PROBLEM

Linda had said that she would make sure that Samuel and Vince would be closely monitored, but that did not happen. Tessa was upset because Linda let the issue continue in the classroom, refused to separate the children, and did not require the staff to follow the action plan and supervise Vince in the classroom. After speaking to Linda, Tessa decided to disenroll Samuel from the center. She felt that there was a blatant lack of supervision because they could not prevent Vince from biting Samuel on a regular basis and had not implemented the action plan. Tessa was no longer going to allow Samuel to be injured while they worked on Vince's behavior.

RESOLUTION

Linda and her team should have included Vince's parents in developing the action plan. When a child is biting in the classroom, there must be a reason, such as an inability to use words to express frustration. The behavior will not stop until the underlying issue is addressed. Understanding what triggers the behavior and giving the child tools to help reduce his frustration can eliminate the unwanted behavior. If the child is singling out one child in the classroom, the best solution is to have them in separate areas of the classroom. If this is not possible, then a caregiver should be assigned to the child who is biting to help him when he becomes upset or frustrated.

DISCIPLINE VERSUS PUNISHMENT

Young children are just learning how to behave when they are together. It is the job of the important adults in children's lives to teach children social, emotional, and self-regulation skills. Of course, any new skill requires practice over time. Discipline teaches children these skills and corrects unwanted behavior through redirection and reteaching. Punishment, on the other hand, hurts children emotionally and/or physically, depending on the type of punishment inflicted.

Yelling at a child, putting a child in time out, threatening to call a child's parents, and other forms of punishment do not teach the child the desired behavior. I once witnessed a preschool child hit another child, then walk over and sit in the time-out chair. The child had learned that his behavior (hitting other children) would result in him being placed in time out, but he decided the punishment was worth it, so he hit the child and placed himself in time out.

I have had adults say that children should be hit and yelled at when they do something wrong. My response is to ask, "What if you were in line at the grocery store and the cashier did not like how you were loading your groceries on the conveyor belt? Would it be acceptable for the cashier to slap and yell at you?" They always say, "No, of course not." If it is not acceptable for an adult to be hit or yelled at, it is not okay to hit or yell at a child.

If a child exhibits unwanted behavior, such as throwing toys, the teacher should talk to the child and reinforce the classroom rules. She should explain that the toys could be broken or friends could be injured by thrown toys. She should also help the child find a safe activity that involves throwing within a controlled environment. If a child runs in the classroom, the teacher should also explain what could happen to her if she were running in the classroom—she could run into other children and hurt them, she could knock over another child's block tower or art exploration, or she could trip and get hurt. The teacher should arrange the classroom to reduce large open areas where a child could run and should provide opportunities outside for the children to run and release their pent-up energy. Each of these examples shows how to teach a child to behave and control their actions within the classroom.

Staff Member Hit a Child on the Hand

Lara, the lead caregiver, informed Suze, the program director, that she had observed her assistant caregiver, Robin, hit two-year-old Lynn's hand after the child threw her cup on the floor during lunch. When Lynn threw her cup, Robin hit Lynn and told her not to throw her cup anymore. Lynn cried for a second and then she was fine. Lara did not say anything to Robin when the incident occurred, but she informed Suze at the end of the day. Lara had waited because she did not want to get Robin in trouble.

Suze reviewed the classroom video and observed Lynn throwing her cup across the table. The cup did not leave the table. She saw Robin hit Lynn once on the hand. After reviewing the video, Suze contacted Lynn's mother and informed her of the incident. Suze expressed that she was sorry and that the issue was being addressed. She did not provide the staff person's name. Because it was the end of the day, Robin was not at the center, so Suze spoke with her the next morning. She asked Robin if she had hit Lynn on the hand when she threw her cup during lunch. Robin stated that she did not hit Lynn's hand; she claimed that she just held her hand and told her to stop throwing her cup.

PROBLEM

A child-care professional's first responsibility is to keep the children safe. If a staffer witnesses someone at the center being inappropriate with the children in any way, it is that staffer's responsibility to report the incident. People may think that, because there were no marks, hitting a child does not rise to the level of mandated reporting. However, if a staff person hits a child once, they may do it again. If a report is not made the first time, there will be no record of the first offense. A report has to be made immediately so that the staff person can be removed before any additional children can be harmed.

Child-care staff must understand developmentally appropriate behavior. They will never win a battle of wills with a two-year-old child. Children this age are beginning to express their opinions and still developing the language to do so. Rather than hitting a child for throwing something she does not want, it is better to redirect her. Simply set the cup on the counter and continue with lunch. The caregiver can always offer the child something to drink later on.

RESOLUTION

Lynn's mother felt that Suze was handling the situation, so she did not disenroll her child from the center. Suze terminated Robin because she touched Lynn in an inappropriate fashion and because she lied about having done so. Suze retrained her staff on recognizing child abuse and neglect and on the mandated-reporting process.

BULLIES IN THE CLASSROOM

Early childhood educators should recognize that people who are hurting tend to hurt others. Young children may bully others out of frustration that arises from low self-esteem or unaddressed emotional or developmental issues. Reaching children through early intervention programs can provide the needed resources to prevent the child from becoming a bully. If an early childhood teacher observes bullying behavior, understanding the possible reasons behind these actions will help the teacher to address the problem and possibly prevent the child from continuing to bully in the future.

Handling Bullying

Caden, the lead teacher, told Jason's mother, Reagan, that Jason was bullying another child in his class. He told Reagan that the other child's mother, Claire, had complained about the way that Jason was treating her son, Michael. Reagan then confronted Claire about what Caden had told her about Jason's behavior. Claire was upset and asked Caden why he would tell Jason's mother that she had complained about her son's behavior. He said that he wanted Reagan to know that a complaint had been made. Caden spoke with his director, Janelle, and asked what he should have done once he received the complaint. He had not received any training on how to handle parent concerns or how to deal with children who bully others.

PROBLEM

When a parent raises a concern about the behavior of another child, the staff person should not share the name of the parent who complained. The staff handbook should spell out the center's protocol for communicating with parents, and all staff members should be trained on how to handle a parent complaint.

Staff should also receive training on how to handle bullying in their classrooms. Bullies are not only hurting their victims; they are also causing problems for themselves. Bullies tend to have low self-esteem, emotional issues, or developmental issues and need help to learn positive ways to interact with other children.

RESOLUTION

Janelle met with Claire and listened to her concerns about her son being bullied and about the way Caden had handled the situation. She told Claire that the staff would be trained on how to handle these situations more effectively in the future. She also reassured Claire that her son would no longer be bullied in Caden's classroom.

Janelle asked a consultant to conduct staff training on teaching positive social skills to the children. She also held a workshop to teach parents ways to keep their children from becoming bullies, such as communicating with them about positive interactions, maintaining a positive relationship, and knowing their friends.

Reagan later apologized to Claire for confronting her. The workshop helped Reagan learn ways to work with Jason to teach him positive social skills. She also had a specialist evaluate him for other ways they could help him function successfully in the classroom.

STAFF VERBAL AND PHYSICAL ABUSE

Caregiver Pulls Child's Arm

As the program director, Cassandra, walked by the three-year-old classroom, she heard a child crying. She knew that the lead teacher, Heidi, had been having issues with the child, who was new to the center. The child cried for hours on end. Heidi's assistant teacher had been out all day, leaving Heidi working alone and trying to care for other children while also attempting to console the crying child.

A little while later, Cassandra passed the room again and heard the child still crying. She stepped into the room, and Heidi told her she had pulled the child in an aggressive manner to calm the child down. In her frustration, Heidi had acted in an inappropriate fashion that only made the child cry harder.

PROBLEM

A caregiver should not lay hands on a child. If a staff member finds themselves frustrated, before she injures a child, she should ask for assistance and know that she will receive support. The program director should have gone into the classroom immediately or sent another caregiver into the classroom when she first heard the child crying. She knew the caregiver was struggling and that the situation was compounded by the assistant caregiver's absence. Had she done so, she would have prevented the caregiver from pulling the child out of frustration.

RESOLUTION

Centers should have a written policy that addresses crying children. The policy should acknowledge the need for additional support for infants, especially when they first start attending the center and are becoming acclimated to the program. Recognize that it is natural for children to cry; that does not mean that the staff will not need an additional break from a child who is inconsolable. Having additional staff who can step in when needed will help those who may need assistance.

Staff have to be trained to ask for help before they reach the point of frustration. Before they injure a child, they know they can ask for assistance and will receive the support they need. This policy should be outlined in the staff handbook and reiterated by the program director so that staff feel comfortable and supported when they need help. During the training, provide specific examples so that staff can recognize the signs and not feel like they have to just endure the situation. The staff should also be provided with training on ways to console and comfort crying children, as well as trained on what not to do when children are crying.

Staff Calling Children Names

Victoria, the assistant program director, was informed by two staff members from the toddler classroom that lead caregiver Mackenzie spoke harshly to the children and called them names. Victoria informed Kaylee, the program director, who spoke with the staff members about what they had observed. The first assistant, Raelynn, said that she observed Mackenzie yelling and telling the children to shut up and shut their mouths and calling them jerks. The second assistant, Addison, said Mackenzie yelled at the children, telling them that they were annoying, calling them jerks, and telling them to shut up. The assistants stated that she also singled out two-year-old Lincoln in the classroom, telling him, "You're a jerk," "I don't like you," "Shut up," "Just be quiet," and "Close your mouth."

Kaylee spoke to Mackenzie, and she said that she never told Lincoln or any other child any of these things.

PROBLEM

It is never acceptable for a caregiver to call children names, demean them, or speak harshly to them. Young children are just learning social skills. It is the caregiver's role to model and teach patience, kindness, and positive conflict-resolution skills.

RESOLUTION

Mackenzie's employment at the center was terminated. Kaylee sent an email to the toddler parents informing them that their children were exposed to a staff person who was speaking inappropriately to the children in the classroom. Kaylee personally contacted Lincoln's mother, Grace, because he was directly targeted by Mackenzie. Grace felt that the center handled the situation appropriately by terminating the employee.

Threatening and Swatting Children with a Paddle

Amaya, the lead preschool teacher, had a wooden paddle hanging on the wall of her classroom. In front of the parents, she would tell the children that if they did not listen or follow directions, they would receive a swat with the paddle. Savannah's mother, Lucille, had heard Amaya's remarks, but she always thought that Amaya was joking. It was not until four-year-old Savannah came home with a bruise on her bottom and was unable to sit down because of the pain that Lucille realized that Amaya had actually paddled her child. She was enraged.

She called Amaya and expressed her concerns, and Amaya said that she had forewarned the students and parents about what would happen if they did not listen or follow directions. Amaya said she had swatted Savannah a few times over the course of two weeks and had never informed Lucille. Amaya had told the child that her parents were fine with her being paddled so there was no reason for Savannah to tell them. Savannah thought they were okay with Amaya swatting her since Lucille had only laughed when she had heard Amaya's threat.

After Lucille concluded her conversation with Amaya, she called Kennedy, the program director, and informed her about what had happened to Savannah. She said that she was disenrolling her daughter immediately.

Kennedy was shocked and immediately fired Amaya. Kennedy stated that she had never heard Amaya say that she was going to swat the children with the paddle that was in her classroom, and she made sure that the paddle was removed. She said she had thought the paddle was a wall decoration.

PROBLEM

First and foremost, it is never okay for a teacher to strike or threaten to strike a child. When Lucille heard the first threat by Amaya, she should have expressed her concern and explained that it did not matter whether she was joking or not—the statement was not appropriate.

As the program director, Kennedy should have been aware of Amaya's statements and should have ensured the children's safety in the classroom. She should have made it clear to Amaya that hitting or threatening to hit the children was unacceptable.

RESOLUTION

As a mandated reporter, Kennedy made a formal CPS complaint, which resulted in Amaya being placed on the central registry for child abuse and neglect. Kennedy retrained all the staff on their requirements as mandated reporters and on the center's discipline policy. She made it clear to them what the repercussions would be for not adhering to the policy.

We have to look at children's behavior not as being challenging but as an opportunity to make a true difference in a child's life. When caregivers take the time and invest the energy needed to guide a child through a challenging time, the child will learn that she is important, worthy of loving care, and a welcome part of the center's community.

In the next chapter, we explore staff challenges and how program directors can prepare for or prevent situations from occurring.

CHAPTER 10

Challenges with Staff

The team approach is vital to centers. As Robbins, DeCenzo, and Wolter (2019) put it, "teams typically outperform individuals when the tasks being done require multiple skills, judgment, and experience." For a team to function within the classroom, they have to be willing to see ideas from various points of view. This will allow the team to determine collectively what is in the best interest of the children, families, and ultimately the center as a whole. When the staff are not communicating or willing to see other points of view, the productivity of the team will diminish. Just remember that a group of people working together does not equate to a team. According to Northouse, "Team development is the cohesiveness of the team and the ability of group members to satisfy their own needs while working effectively with other team members."

Program directors have to collaborate with the staff to create a team environment that promotes staff working together. The first step toward this goal is making sure that everyone's voice is heard. The team members must understand that they may not all agree with all decisions, but they are in agreement with the larger goal of providing a quality program for the children and families attending the center.

Think of it this way. You are all planning a road trip, and some would like to take the scenic route, while others would like to take the fastest route. Both decisions would end with arrival at the same location, but the time of arrival would differ. Because it is a group trip, a good compromise might be to take the fastest way going and the scenic route on the return trip. The main word in this situation is *compromise*. Most people are willing to compromise if they feel that their ideas are being respected. That is what makes a successful team.

This chapter addresses actual challenges that program directors have encountered with their staff. The good news is that the majority of the challenges that program directors encounter can be resolved with clearly written policies and procedures and with open communication. Having an open-door policy as the program director provides the staff with a comfort level that will allow them to talk to you when they have concerns—before the concerns escalate.

ISSUES AROUND DISCIPLINE

When staff are frustrated because a child is not following directions, they should communicate their concerns to the program director. The staff should never feel alone in these situations, and a child should never be threatened or humiliated by the staff. When the staff have open communication with the program director, situations like the one described below will be eliminated. Staff should inform the program director when they are having a problem with a child in the classroom, before they utilize any form of discipline that is different from redirecting and talking to the child. The program director should discuss and approve the teacher's discipline plan before it is implemented.

Teacher Humiliated a Preschooler

Four-year-old George did not want to clean up his area. Doris, the new preschool teacher, was frustrated with him because he had been uncooperative for several days. She walked him down to the infant classroom, taking him past Frances, the program director, who was standing at the front desk. Frances observed them walking past her but did not question where Doris was going with George. When Doris opened the infant-classroom door, George began to cry. Doris warned, "Next time you don't listen, you will have to stay in the infant classroom." She then returned him to the classroom. She did not believe that she had done anything wrong by taking George to the infant classroom, because she had passed Frances on the way, and Frances had said nothing.

PROBLEM

Frances was not aware that Doris was having problems with getting George to cooperate. If children are having issues in the classroom, the teacher should let the program director know. The program director should then go to the classroom to help with the situation and to model appropriate supervision and redirection for the staff.

Frances had been incredibly busy with implementing a new curriculum and had not trained her new staff sufficiently on appropriate forms of discipline. She should have asked Doris where she was going with George. She needed to review the discipline policy with Doris and tell her that the staff should not remove children from the classroom as a form of discipline without speaking with the director first.

RESOLUTION

Frances met with Doris to discuss what had happened. She told Doris that shaming and embarrassing children is not the way to teach them how to behave. She worked with Doris to train her on how to redirect and speak to the children in a way that is supportive and encouraging. She told Doris that she would observe in her classroom over the next couple of days, and she asked her to focus on finding out why George was not interested in cleaning up. Was it because he wanted to complete a project or wanted to play longer?

Once Doris learned the reason behind George's behavior, she and Frances discussed ideas to encourage his cooperation. For example, if he wanted to complete a project, Doris could let him know when he would be able to finish the project. If he wanted to continue to play, Doris could give George an earlier countdown before he has to clean up. Doris felt supported in her new position and appreciated Frances taking the time to work with her on the issue.

MAINTAINING PROFESSIONALISM

The job of an early childhood caregiver is a challenging one. Early childhood staff play an important role for the children in their care. However, they are not always recognized as important educators in the children's lives during their developmental years. Children leave preschool prepared for kindergarten, and their success is due in large part to the skills they learned in their years at the child-care center. Sometimes, even the kindergarten teachers are slow to recognize early childhood educators as being an important part of the children's success. Parents often view the early childhood educators as glorified babysitters, and this view is often carried over in the way that some parents interact with the staff.

Early childhood staff are frequently underpaid and overworked, yet they stay in the field because they have a passion for working with children. They want to make a difference in a child's life. This is what brings them joy and a sense of accomplishment because they know that they are helping the children to grow and develop. This is why staff should be provided with ongoing training and supervision to ensure that they are able to implement the most current and appropriate practices in their classroom with the children. Lead caregivers are responsible for the operation of the classroom. If the lead caregiver is not up to date on developmentally appropriate practices, mistakes can be made that can possibly place the children in harm's way.

Lead Caregiver Is Not Fully Qualified

Program director Damyanti hired Chandani as an assistant caregiver in the combination preschool/pre-K classroom. When the preschool enrollment increased dramatically, Damyanti split the preschool and pre-k classrooms, resulting in the need for an additional lead caregiver. She promoted Chandani to the preschool lead-caregiver position, despite the fact that Chandani had only been working at the center for four weeks and had not completed her early childhood classes.

PROBLEM

State licensing inspections and other certification reviews include a review of the verified qualifications of all lead caregivers. If a person is in a lead caregiver position without the proper documentation of training and certification, the center will receive a citation. The caregiver also would have to be demoted or potentially terminated because she is not able to produce the required documentation of her education or experience.

When you hire a new lead teacher, you must verify that person's qualifications. Ideally, the candidate would have completed a course of study from an accredited early childhood education program and provided official transcripts before starting to work at the center. If the candidate does not have a degree or a valid (not expired) Childcare Development Associate (CDA) certification, her qualifications have to line up with the state requirements. Any continuing education units (CEUs) must be awarded through an accredited college, university, or approved online site that has the International Accreditors for Continuing Education and Training (IACET) accredited provider label or is accredited by the Distance Education Accrediting Commission (DEAC).

RESOLUTION

If a candidate has not completed a child-development program, the program director can hire her as an assistant teacher. Once she has completed her education, that person can fill a lead-teacher position when one becomes available. This situation works well; the center will not have to recruit and train a new lead teacher because a current assistant teacher meets the requirements.

If a candidate cannot complete the required courses for financial reasons or cannot produce official transcripts because they owe money to the educational organization, the center may choose to provide the needed funds. This is a business decision that should be part of the center's written policy. If you pay for one employee, you should be prepared to pay for others. If you offer assistance on a case-by-case basis, you need specific written guidelines so everyone understands how those decisions are made.

A program director must be a strong leader. Successful program directors are dependable and consistent in their leadership roles. As with any organization, the leader must be an individual trained and experienced in managing the daily operations of the overall program. As a program director and leader of a center, it is important to recognize your strengths and weaknesses. Good leadership creates a work environment that is beneficial for the center and the staff.

Some program directors resist the idea of heading a hierarchical organization. There are program directors who will not implement an organizational chart because they want everyone to feel the same at the center. They want to be just one big happy family. While that is an interesting concept, that is not how one should operate a business. There should be a clear order of command, and everyone at the center should respect the order. That in no way means that you cannot be friendly and have fun; it just means that the director and staff maintain a professional attitude and approach. A leader does not want to get to a point where she is too friendly with the staff to properly supervise. The same is true when staff are so comfortable with the management that they are not completing their work assignments. In both situations, the needs of the children and families become less of a priority. The chain of command needs to be clear and concise, because employees will appreciate program directors who provide support and guidance as well as correction when needed.

A New Owner-Director Is Threatened and Intimidated by Staff

Sharon purchased a child-care center and served as both the owner and program director. She decided to retain all of the staff, thinking that this would maintain consistency for the families and the children. She held a staff meeting and informed the staff members that the center would now teach with a Montessori-based approach.

After about a month, Sharon noticed that the staff were not implementing any of the changes that she had requested. When she asked why, they told her that they had no desire to implement the Montessori curriculum that she wanted. Not only that, but they said that she could not make them. She explained that she was the owner and they worked for her. Their reply was that if she tried to change the way that they were doing things, they would quit and take the families with them. Sharon did not want to lose the families, so she felt like she had to retain the staff even though they were being insubordinate.

When I met with Sharon as her consultant, she told me about the issues she was having. I explained that she was running a business now and that if the staff did not like the changes that she was making, she needed to make changes with the staff. She was too afraid of losing both the staff and the families.

She said that one staff member in particular had told her that she would take the families from the center. I asked her if she thought that the staff person was going to take the children to her home to care for them, or if she was planning to open her own center. Sharon said she was not sure what her intentions were. I told her that the staff person was attempting to intimidate her with threats that she could not follow through on. She was not going to take the children from the center because she did not have a place to take the children. I advised Sharon to call her bluff and make the changes that she wants at the center.

PROBLEM

The biggest obstacle that the owner-director had was herself. She had always wanted to open a Montessori center, and when the opportunity to purchase the center came around, she decided to follow her dream. She had never been a program director, and she had no managerial experience. She only had classroom experience, and she had never supervised staff. Consequently, she was having a challenging time with the staff at the center.

Before the purchase, Sharon had not researched the center. She did not know anything about the demographics of the families or the type of curriculum that had been used at the center. She was receiving pushback from the staff because she was trying to implement a curriculum they did not understand.

RESOLUTION

I advised her to start hiring new staff and to fire the ringleader. Sharon stated that she was nervous because the staff person said that she would file a complaint against the center. I told her that she could not control whether someone filed a complaint, but so long as she was maintaining compliance, she would not have anything to worry about.

She drafted a plan to train the staff on the Montessori approach and to gradually implement the new curriculum. She created a transition team made up of staff members—new and old—who were interested in Montessori. Together, they informed the families and trained the staff on the new approach.

Staff Member Took a Picture of an Upset Child

Evelin, three-year-old Charles's mother, received a phone call from Tamara, the assistant program director, informing her that Charles was upset. His teacher, Isidore, had removed him from the preschool classroom because he was throwing toys. Tamara said they had been unable to calm him down for an hour and a half. Evelin asked that, in the future, she be informed if Charles was having a tantrum because she did not want him to be upset for over an hour.

A couple of weeks later, Evelin received a message through the center's computer program from Isidore saying that Charles was upset, kicking, and screaming in the director's office. The message included a photograph of her son. Evelin called Natacha, the director, and said that Isidore should not have taken the picture of Charles.

Natacha told her that Charles was screaming when he arrived at her office because he had not wanted to leave the playground. Natacha instructed Isidore to contact Evelin and let her know that Charles was having a hard time. Isidore took the picture of Charles and uploaded it to the center's portal to show Evelin the temper tantrum that Charles was having. He decided to take the picture rather than calling Evelin because he was busy and needed to get back to the classroom. Natacha took Charles back to the preschool classroom once he calmed down.

PROBLEM

Isidore did not call Evelin to tell her about her son's behavior, nor did he speak to her when she arrived to pick up Charles from the center. He thought the photo and note in the portal was enough. Children should not be humiliated by taking pictures of their behavior. It was Natacha's responsibility to correct and address Isidore's behavior and not stand back and watch without intervening. The program director is the person in charge and should lead by example.

RESOLUTION

Because this was the second incident in which Charles was removed from the classroom, and because she felt that the staff was making fun of Charles by taking pictures of him, Evelin disenrolled him from the center.

Part of being a professional is maintaining a respectful personal distance between families and staff members while the children are attending the program. When parents and staff become too familiar with each other and form dating relationships, a number of issues can occur, such as the following:

- The individuals who are dating break up, but they still must interact because the child is attending the center.
- The child's other parent does not like the center.
- The child does not like the person whom the parent is dating.
- The child does not listen to or is disrespectful to the person whom the parent is dating.
- The parent will expect special treatment because they are dating a staff member.

The last thing a director wants is for a bad relationship to play out at the center. If you permit staff dating parents at the center, then the staff should not work in the same classroom as the child of the person that they are dating, to reduce any issues that could occur.

A center must have a written policy that clearly addresses what is or is not allowed, along with the repercussions of not following the policy. This policy should be shared with the staff and the parents so that both parties are aware of the center's stance when it comes to staff dating parents of children enrolled at the center. Of course, a program director has no control over what two consenting adults do in their free time, but the policy as it relates to the center must be clear for the protection of the center and both parties.

Staff Dating Parents

Eleven-year-old Kasim attended the child-care center's after-school program. His father, Ade, was dating a floater in the program's infant classroom, Makena.

Kasim's middle-school teacher called Ade to tell him that Kasim was not following directions at school. Ade was upset and called Makena and told her that he did not want Kasim to play at the center because of his behavior at school. When Kasim arrived at the center, Makena had him sit in the infant classroom with her instead of letting him go to the school-age classroom with the other children. She did not inform the program director, Zina, about this arrangement.

When Zina observed Kasim sitting in the infant classroom, she asked Makena why he wasn't with the after-school children. Makena explained that Ade had asked her to keep Kasim with her as punishment for his behavior at school. Zina told her that it was not acceptable for Kasim to be in the infant classroom and that Ade was not allowed to have her punish Kasim while he was at the center. Zina took Kasim to the school-age classroom where the after-school caregiver was surprised to see him. She had just thought that he was not at the center.

PROBLEM

Ade used his relationship with Makena as a route to discipline his son outside of school. This was an inappropriate response to Kasim's misbehavior, and it put Makena in an awkward position. For several reasons, Makena should not have agreed to discipline Ade's son at the program: She is not Kasim's parent. Kasim's challenging behavior occurred at school, not at the program. Neither Zina nor Kasim's after-school caregiver was aware of the situation. Makena's decision to keep Kasim in the infant classroom was not an appropriate way to discipline him.

RESOLUTION

Zina reprimanded Makena for inappropriately disciplining Kasim for an event that had not occurred at the center. She warned Makena that if anything like this occurred again, she would be terminated.

Before this incident, Zina had not been aware that Makena was dating Ade and the center did not have a policy related to staff dating the parents. After this, Zina created a policy stating that caregivers who are dating parents of children enrolled in the program must inform her, and they were not allowed to work in the same classroom as the child or to discipline the child. She had all of the staff sign the statement acknowledging the new policy.

When Ade arrived to pick up Kasim, Zina explained that his request was inappropriate and that Makena was not allowed to discipline Kasim while he was at the center because she did not work in his classroom. Zina informed him that all requests related to Kasim while he was at the center should be addressed with his after-school caregiver or herself.

The center's school-age policy requires staff to call the parents if a child who is scheduled does not arrive at the center. Zina retrained the after-school caregiver because she had not made any attempt to find out where Kasim was when he did not arrive with the other school-age children.

The early childhood profession is growing, and more men are seeking a career in caring for young children. Should males work at child-care centers? I say yes! Children should have the opportunity to interact with men as well as women in the early childhood classroom. Men often have a different approach and insight from those of women, and we are doing children a disservice when men are not recruited or encouraged to work in the early childhood field. This is especially true for children who live without a father figure in their lives. Men working within the classroom may be the only positive male role models that young children will have the opportunity to interact with on a regular basis.

How can we attract qualified men to the field? Remove the false stereotype that men working in the classroom will harm or molest the children. Remove the stereotype that women are better equipped to care for children; men are just as capable. With the proper training, which all caregivers need to be successful, men can provide appropriate care and supervision.

I once had a program director call and ask me if there were different screening procedures for hiring a male to work at the center. Once I realized that she was not joking, I told her that no, there are not different requirements for screening male candidates. All candidates and employees must be treated and screened in the same fashion.

Male Caregiver Told Not to Change Diapers

Azibo went to Latonya, the program director, to ask why Crystal, the lead caregiver in the infant classroom, would not allow him to change the children's diapers. Latonya was not aware that Crystal was not allowing him to change the children's diapers. Azibo stated that Crystal had explained that she did not believe that the parents would be comfortable with him changing their children's diapers. Azibo was upset and offended because he had worked in the infant classroom at his previous center for three years, and the parents there had never complained about the care that he had provided to their infants. Latonya told him that she would speak with Crystal about his concerns.

When Latonya spoke to Crystal about Azibo's concern, Crystal said that she would not want a male to change her child's diaper, so she was sure that the parents would not want him to change their children's diapers. Latonya explained that Azibo was to be assigned as the primary caregiver for three of the six children in the class and that he was to provide their care—including changing the children's diapers. Latonya also explained that Crystal's line of thinking was not appropriate or acceptable for the children and would not be allowed at the center.

PROBLEM

The teacher was treating the male caregiver differently from the female caregivers who worked at the center, based on her personal biases. Azibo had not provided her with any reason to think that he was not capable or trained to care for the infants. She would not have limited a female caregiver in the same fashion.

RESOLUTION

The program director should train all of the staff on the importance of treating everyone who works at the center equally. During a staff meeting, the program director should address all of the concerns that the staff may have about male caregivers, such as males should not be alone with the children, take them to the bathroom, or change the children's clothes when needed. Staff will have a better understanding if the program director provides accurate information and explains the importance of having both males and females in the classroom and in the lives of the children. Furthermore, fathers have been changing their children's diapers for centuries. No early childhood professional should be suspected of abusing the children without evidence to back up the allegations.

When you are working at a child-care center, all of your actions in the classroom are witnessed by the children. For that reason, a caregiver must display appropriate behavior at all times. When staff are under the influence, their judgment is impaired and mistakes can be made that will place the children in harm's way unnecessarily. The staff may feel that when they are on their lunch break, they can indulge, but if they are returning to work, they cannot because they will be impaired and unable to pay close attention to the children. The program director should make sure that professional behavior is clearly defined in the staff handbook, along with the consequences of not abiding by the center's policies.

Staff Member Under the Influence

Alamea, the lead preschool teacher, asked Marissa, the program director, to speak to an assistant caregiver who appeared to be intoxicated when she returned to work after lunch. The assistant caregiver, Genevieve, was slurring her speech and appeared to be under the influence. Alamea did not want her to be in the classroom with the children.

When Marissa went to the classroom, Genevieve did not appear to be herself and was not able to form a complete sentence. Marissa removed her from the classroom so that she could find out what was going on. She took Genevieve to her office where she asked her why she seemed off. Genevieve said that she had not slept well, having not fallen asleep until 3:00 a.m. Marissa sent Genevieve home early because of her behavior.

Marissa interviewed the assistant caregivers, Lydia, Magnolia, and Rylee, who had worked in the preschool classroom with Genevieve. Lydia said that Genevieve told her that she was the designated driver for her friends the night before and she had not slept. She observed Genevieve laying on the floor with the children climbing on her. She said that Genevieve was not able to control the children. She also witnessed Genevieve climbing on top of a shelving unit and sitting on it with her legs crossed.

Magnolia said Genevieve often smokes marijuana in her car in the center parking lot during lunch and returns to work smelling of marijuana. Genevieve would come back from lunch under the influence and brag about it in the classroom. Magnolia would see this behavior at least twice a week. She said she had observed Genevieve two or three weeks ago with red eyes, slurred speech, and an inability to walk straight.

Rylee, who was not in the classroom that day, said she had heard that Genevieve was smoking marijuana in the parking lot during her lunch period. She also heard that she had previously appeared under the influence, unable to focus, and had slurred speech.

Marissa asked the caregivers why they did not inform her about Genevieve appearing to be under the influence at the center. They said everyone was aware of her being under the influence at work, and they assumed that Marissa also knew.

After speaking with the staff, Marissa spoke with Genevieve. Genevieve said she had had a car accident two weeks earlier and had received a concussion. After the car accident, she was forgetful and slurring her speech. Genevieve stated that she does not drink alcohol because she is under twenty-one. She said she has smoked marijuana on her break and returned to work one time, but she has not smoked in the school parking lot. She does smoke electronic cigarettes in the center parking lot. The electronic cigarettes create smoke so someone walking by might think that she was smoking marijuana, but she was not.

PROBLEM

Staff members cannot properly care for young children when they are intoxicated. The center must have a written policy that states the ramifications of arriving to work impaired and of using alcohol or drugs at the center or during break and lunch times. Staff do not always recognize that, while their lunch and break times might not be paid for, they are still returning to work and cannot work under the influence of intoxicating substances. The policy should also outline the reporting process for suspected impairment that will place children in harm's way. All cases should be reported to the program director immediately, without exception. Unfortunately, the center did not have a written policy related to staff being under the influence at work.

RESOLUTION

Marissa suspended Genevieve for a week and informed her that what she does on her own time is her business, but she could not smoke marijuana during work hours. She stressed that she would not have anyone working at the center under the influence of any substance that would impair their ability to care for children. She warned Genevieve that if it happened again, her employment would be terminated.

Marissa completed a written policy after the incident and had each staff member sign that they had read and understood it.

The staff handbook should address the policies and procedures on how the center will provide the last paycheck for employees who decide to leave or are terminated from the center. This will provide the clarity that employees need to understand the exit process. Whenever possible, complete an exit conference with the employee so that she can provide feedback to the program director one last time before she leaves. Having a clear understanding would have prevented the following scenario from occurring.

The Police Are Called to the Center

Program director Zara fired Vaishnavi for yelling at the children in the pre-k classroom. Zara asked Vaishnavi to leave the center immediately, but Vaishnavi refused, stating that she wanted her last paycheck before she would leave. Zara was not able to provide her with her last check because the human resources department issues the checks. When she tried to explain this to Vaishnavi, Vaishnavi threatened to beat up Zara. Wakeeta, the assistant program director, could hear the verbal exchange and called the police to have Vaishnavi removed from the center.

When the police arrived, Vaishnavi was still in Zara's office demanding her paycheck. The police explained that Vaishnavi would have to leave the center and her last paycheck would be sent to her. They then escorted her out of the center. Zara was fearful that Vaishnavi would return to the center so she changed the entry code on the front door and informed all of the staff that Vaishnavi was no longer working at the center and should not be allowed in the center under any circumstances.

Zara sent out a mass email to the parents informing them that the police had been called to the center. She assured them that everything was fine and that the children were not involved. She said that if their children mentioned anything about the police being at the building, she wanted them to be aware and they could reach out if they had any questions.

PROBLEM

Working with and caring for young children can be incredibly stressful. During the interview process, Zara should have asked Vaishnavi about how she has handled frustrating situations in the classroom. She also should have followed up with Vaishnavi's references on the topic. Odds are that this was not her first time yelling at children in the classroom. How were the previous situations handled? Was she provided proper training to reduce stressful situations? Were steps put in place to let her know how she could request help if she needed it?

Additionally, the staff handbook should clearly state how staff will receive their last paychecks when they leave or their employment is terminated.

RESOLUTION

Zara informed the human resources department of Vaishnavi's firing and asked that they send her final paycheck as soon as possible. She also added a policy to the staff handbook explaining how staff will receive their last paychecks when they leave or their employment is terminated.

She met with her associate program director and lead teachers to put together ideas for trainings and other ways to support the staff's mental and emotional health. They shared their ideas with the entire staff, and then Zara and the team adjusted their plans based on feedback they received from the staff. Together, they were able to design supports to help the staff members in handling stress in healthy ways.

Owners hire program directors to ensure that the centers are operating properly. But what happens when the program director is not able to complete the task and maintain the center? The owner has to have an understanding of what is happening at the center, how the overall center is functioning, and how the center is meeting the needs of the children. I always encourage owners to obtain the training and certification they need to be able to operate the center. If an owner does not understand how a child-care center operates, and does not want to learn how to operate the center, then there should be someone else above the program director to check in and ensure that the center is functioning properly and meeting the needs of the children and staff. Had the owner of the center described in the following vignette known what was going on, the situation would not have occurred.

Owner Discovers Issues at the Center

Gaurang, the owner of a child-care center, learned that the program director, Anika, was rarely at the center and that the teachers in the toddler classrooms were regularly leaving the children alone when they took their lunch breaks and when they took a child to the bathroom. The person who informed him, Fatheha, was a former center employee. She said that, because the center was poorly run, she was afraid for the children's safety. She had voiced her concerns to Anika, but the director did nothing to improve the situation, so Fatheha had quit after working at the center for less than a month. Fatheha also warned Gaurang that if he did not address the situation that she would contact the state and file a formal complaint. Gaurang was a dentist, and his office was located in the same complex as the center. He had purchased the center the prior year and was depending on the program director to operate it. Immediately after speaking with Fatheha, he walked over to the center.

Anika was not present. When he walked into the first toddler room, he found eleven children alone. Their caregiver, Ekantika, was nowhere to be found. It was nap time and the children were lying on their cots, but several of them were awake. He then walked to a second toddler classroom where he found Chameli, the caregiver for that room. He asked where the teacher for the previous room was, and Chameli said that Ekantika had left the building to go to lunch. Before she left, she had asked Chameli to go to the other toddler classroom to check on the children every five to ten minutes. Consequently, Chameli was leaving the children in her room alone until Ekantika returned. He had Chameli combine the two toddler classrooms, even though he knew they would be out of ratio, because it was better than leaving the children alone. He then called Anika and requested that she return to the center immediately.

Before Anika returned, Gaurang walked around to observe the other classrooms. He saw a child in the infant classroom put a small plastic item into her mouth then spit it out. He told Divya, the infant caregiver, what he had seen, and she took the item from the child's hand. She said it was the cap to a glue stick and that she had no idea where it had come from. He observed a child in a walker roll herself to the diaper-changing table and grab the diapers from the shelf. The shelf also contained diaper cream, a can of air freshener, lotions, and a bottle of bleach solution that were within the child's reach. He removed the items, handed them to Divya, and told her that the items must be kept out of children's reach. Gaurang was concerned that Divya had not appeared to notice that the dangerous items were within reach of the children.

In another toddler classroom, Gaurang observed the teacher leave the children alone to take one child to the bathroom. All of the children wore diapers, but the diaper changing table was located in the bathroom. While there, she could not see the children who were left in the classroom. After speaking with the teacher, he determined that she regularly left the children unsupervised in the classroom when she took a child to the bathroom to change a diaper.

When Anika returned to the center, it was clear to him that she was not capable of operating the center properly. She seemed unconcerned about the issues that Gaurang had witnessed. When toddler teacher Ekantika returned, Gaurang fired her on the spot for leaving the children unattended.

PROBLEM

Young children should never be left unattended. Their classrooms should be safe for them, and all potentially harmful items should be stored out of the children's reach. It is the program director's responsibility to hire qualified staff and to remain on site to monitor the center's safety.

Unfortunately, the owner did not have an early childhood background, and he did not regularly check in on the center to see how it was operating.

The best way to provide appropriate care and supervision is to have a full staff of trained caregivers. In this case, the program was understaffed and poorly trained. When caregivers work alone and out of ratio, they struggle to address the children's basic needs such as feeding, diapering, holding, soothing, talking, making eye contact, engaging and supervising during tummy time, or allowing children the opportunity to independently move around. In this type of situation, infants and toddlers are often confined in high chairs, bounce seats, swings, or other equipment and, in this case, left alone. Because the program director was not present at the center, she was not supervising the staff or addressing staffing issues.

RESOLUTION

After spending the afternoon at the center and seeing that the staff were not providing a safe environment for children, Gaurang decided to close the facility. He had Anika inform all of the parents and staff.

A center should have a strict policy stating that sleeping in the classroom is forbidden under any circumstances. If staff are sleeping and a child is injured, the staff members would be directly responsible for the injury because they were not watching the children. Classroom observations and spot checking are important ways to ensure that the staff are behaving professionally. The program director would be able to see when a staff member appears to be tired and offer solutions such as an early break or lunch or a rest period. Sometimes a fifteen-minute nap is all someone needs to be productive.

Staff have to be trained that if they are tired at work, they can have a break to walk around to wake up. The center can also have a break room where coffee is available for staff who may be tired because they did not have a good night's sleep. Staff should not be put in a position of feeling that their only option is to sleep in the classroom with the children. Should a staff member see a coworker sleeping in a classroom, the staff member must report the issue to the program director so that the issue can be addressed and resolved before a child is injured.

Staff Sleeping in the Classroom

Machelle, assistant program director, observed Amari, the pre-k lead caregiver, sleeping in the classroom during the children's nap time. Amari was sitting at the table with her head down when Machelle looked into the room. When Machelle entered, Amari did not move; Machelle called Amari's name twice before she woke up and acknowledged her. Amari tried to look like she was not sleeping and began cleaning the papers that were on the table in front of her. She could not see the children that were sleeping behind where she was sitting because she had her back to the children. Machelle informed Amari that she was not allowed to sleep in the classroom, but Amari denied sleeping and said she was just resting her eyes. Machelle reminded her that she should be able to see the children at all times.

She had Amari take an early lunch break so she could rest if she needed to. While Amari was on lunch, Machelle asked the staff who frequently worked in the classroom with Amari if they had observed her sleeping. Jina, the floater, said she had seen Amari sleeping during nap time on two separate days. She said that Amari would sit at the table and write and then nod off. She knew it was wrong for Amari to sleep in the classroom even if the children were sleeping. Neema, another floater, had also once observed Amari falling asleep during nap time.

PROBLEM

Machelle was concerned because all of the center's caregivers were aware that sleeping on the job is not allowed, yet they had not informed her when they observed Amari sleeping in the classroom.

RESOLUTION

When Amari returned from lunch, Machelle gave her a two-week suspension for sleeping in the classroom and not watching the children. Machelle told Amari if she is sleepy, she should get up and walk around. She also scheduled a training for all of the staff so that they would understand that sleeping at the center is not acceptable and they are required to report staff who are sleeping on the job.

Program directors have to maintain professionalism personally and demand professionalism from the child-care staff during staff meetings. When you have staff who are frustrated during the meeting, that is a sign that they feel that they are not being heard. It is perfectly okay to be upset. However, it is not okay to be disrespectful and inappropriate, especially if children are present. A center must have policies that address staff being inappropriate and the consequences for not behaving professionally. For the program director to maintain integrity and respect during the staff meetings, these consequences must be enforced consistently. In the following scenario, you will see how the program director's lack of control causes a major problem during the staff meeting.

Staff Swearing at the Center

After a staff meeting, Zarna, the toddler assistant caregiver, called the owner of the center and informed him that three caregivers were fighting and swearing during the meeting. The program director, Samaira, was unable to control the situation, so the other staff helped to break up the fight. Zarna said that during the meeting, nine school-age children were left alone in a classroom. In addition, the staff meeting was held in a toddler classroom where three toddlers and one preschooler were present. The owner asked why the children were present during the staff meeting, and Zarna told him that the meeting started at 7:30 p.m. because Samaira said that was the only time available. Zarna was also upset because two days before, another assistant caregiver was swearing at her in the toddler classroom and threatening to fight her in front of the children. Zarna said she had asked Samaira to move her to another classroom.

The next day the center owner went to the center to address the situation. He spoke to Samaira to determine what had happened during the staff meeting and why staff were swearing and fighting at the center. Samaira said that she had tried to defuse the situation among the caregivers. One, Advika, had raised the issue that she did not feel respected by her two assistant caregivers, Urishilla and Widisha, despite the fact that Advika was the lead caregiver in the classroom. Samaira did not want to address Advika's concerns during the staff meeting; she preferred to handle the issue separately. She said that Advika, Urishilla, and Widisha were pushing and swearing at each other. Widisha did hit Urishilla during the argument, and everyone was just trying to break up the fight. Samaira ended the staff meeting and had Advika, Urishilla, and Widisha leave the center.

She confirmed that there were a total of thirteen children present at the center during the staff meeting, including the younger ones who were in the room. She said the older children were in another room watching a movie; the caregivers took turns checking on them during the staff meeting. All of the children could hear the arguing and swearing.

She admitted that the meeting time was not ideal, but she did not have a better time to conduct staff meetings because the center remained open until midnight. Samaira said that she was having a lot of issues at the center with the different personalities. She was moving Zarna to a different classroom because she was not working well with the other teacher in the toddler classroom.

PROBLEM

Because of the time of the meeting, the center could not provide appropriate care and supervision for children during a staff meeting. Staff meetings should be conducted when the children are not present or during a time that would not take caregivers' attention away from the children. If the center is open late, the staff meeting could be conducted on a Saturday morning or afternoon. Staff should be paid for attending the staff meeting.

Caregivers should never swear or fight in front of the children.

RESOLUTION

Samaira terminated the employment of Advika, Urishilla, and Widisha for their unacceptable behavior.

Because the center is open extended hours, she decided to be more creative when scheduling the staff meetings. She thought about separating the staff and having two separate meetings, one with the assistants and one with the lead caregivers. She did end up having two meetings, but decided to hold one with the infant and toddler staff and one with the preschool and pre-k staff.

Child-care centers must have written policies and procedures that are reviewed frequently and updated when needed. Staff meetings should include a mini-review of the center's policies and procedures so staff will remember what is required of them. For example, the director can have a staff member explain a policy to the group. This will help the director determine the level of understanding that the staff have related to that policy and will give the staff an opportunity to discuss the policy so that everyone is on the same page. If staff are not clear on the policy, that would be the time to train the staff to clear up any confusion.

After policy reviews and updates, all the staff should sign off to acknowledge that they have been trained on the policies. This documentation is important when staff try to say that they were not informed about the center's policies as a way to deflect their responsibility. When this happens, you can refer them to the signed document and then hold them accountable for their actions.

Directors, too, must follow and enforce the policies and procedures, or the staff will not see the need to follow them and will not respect the director's authority. Directors must lead by example and enforce the policies and procedures fairly and equally with all staff.

In the last chapter, we discuss outdoor play. The majority of states have regulations that require child-care centers to take the children outside daily except in inclement weather. Even with these rules in place, there are still teachers who do not take the children outside and parents who do not want their children to go outside. Following are ways to make outside experiences enjoyable and valuable for students and staff, and ideas for sharing that value with parents.

CHAPTER 11

Outdoor Play

Outdoor play is as important as the play that happens in the classroom. "This means that outdoor play must be as carefully planned, resourced, and supported as indoor play and wherever possible be available to the children on a continuous basis," say Duncan and Lockwood (2008). Maxim (1992) agrees: "Outdoor time is an important part of the curriculum and requires planning; it is not simply a time for children to release pent-up energy." But often, little planning is applied to creating a learning environment outdoors for the children.

I have observed staff within the classroom interacting with the children in appropriate ways, but the minute they take the children out on the playground, they stand or sit and just look at the children with no direct interactions. Of course, when the staff are not as committed to the children's activities when they are outside, accidents can occur. Most states require child-care centers to take the children outside daily (except in inclement weather), but teachers and parents often resist the idea. My guess is that they do not see the importance of outdoor play. This chapter is designed to change that viewpoint and to encourage program directors to promote outdoor activities for the children. As Duncan and Lockwood say, "Good quality play opportunities should be provided outdoors as well as indoors."

DAILY OUTDOOR PLAY

With proper training, Cohen and Waite-Stupiansky (2020) say, "teachers quickly realize how motivating and exciting it is for children to learn outdoors, which makes teaching more enjoyable and effective." Providing the necessary training helps the staff to understand the benefits of outdoor play for children as well as how to transform the outside into a developmental experience for the children. "Access to outdoor provision, which offers children the same play opportunities as they have indoors, is what all settings should aspire to," advise Duncan and Lockwood. When children have enriched outside experiences with free exploration, they will have opportunities to expand their growth and development. According to Duncan and Lockwood, "The outdoors provides an environment different to indoors where they can experience the elements and engage and experiment with the natural world to experience textures, smells, sounds, shapes, and gradients, which cannot be offered indoors." Children should have outdoor experiences daily, so long as there is not inclement weather.

Many states have rules related to daily outdoor play for children attending child-care centers.

For example, early learning providers in Washington must have programs and daily schedules that include active outdoor time. Infants and toddlers must have twenty minutes (less if the infants cannot tolerate it) of outdoor play time for every three hours of programming. Preschool-age and older children must have thirty minutes of active outdoor time for every three hours of programming. In addition, programs that operate more than six hours a day must provide ninety minutes of active play for preschool age and up, or sixty minutes of active play for infants and toddlers (thirty minutes of which may be moderate to vigorous indoor activities).

White and Coleman (2000) recognize that "the education of young children does not end in the classroom. Playgrounds also provide opportunities to support and expand children's understanding of their world."

Children Not Taken Outside Each Day

Two-year-old Logan's mother, Morgan, complained that the children in the toddler classroom were not taken outside daily. She had provided the center with boots and gloves for Logan, and she noticed that the boots were not being used. She questioned his teacher Mary, who said that she had not taken the children outside and would not be taking the children outside until a new child in the classroom adjusted. Morgan did not like Mary's response, so she contacted the center's regional manager and complained about the children not going outside.

Alexander, the district manager, went to the center and spoke to Mary, as well as to Laren, the infant lead caregiver; Trinity, the preschool lead caregiver; Sierra, the pre-k lead caregiver; and Emerson, the program director. Alexander was shocked by the staff's responses.

Mary explained that she did not take the children outside because she had a new child in the classroom who was constantly crying. She had not taken the children outside for the past month. Before the new child started, she said she took the children outside three or four times a week depending on the weather. She admitted that she did not take them out daily before the new child arrived.

Laren said she did not take the children outside daily and never had since she started working at the center a year earlier. She said Emerson did not instruct her to take the children outside daily.

Trinity stated that she regularly takes the children outside, but if the children were not dressed for the weather, she would leave them inside with her assistant or in another classroom if their numbers were low. Sierra stated that she takes the children outside daily unless there is inclement weather such as heavy rain, thunder, lightning, wind chill, or high heat index. She takes them outside in the morning and in the afternoon.

Emerson stated that the center's policy requires that the children go outside daily. She was not sure why the children were not taken outside daily, but she admitted that she did not monitor the classrooms to ensure that they were going outside. She had no reason to think that the staff were not taking the children outside.

PROBLEM

This situation demonstrated that the program director did not have open communication with the staff or the parents because the parent did not express her concerns to Emerson, and Mary did not inform Emerson about the parent's concerns. If either the parent or the staff member had an established relationship with the director, the situation could have been resolved by Emerson without Alexander.

Children need to be outside where they can run, jump, climb, explore, and experience nature. Staff cannot use new children in the classroom as an excuse for not taking the class outside. Emerson should have monitored the classroom to ensure that the staff were taking the children outside daily. It is not enough to assume that the staff are completing the activities, even if she trusts the staff. It is always best to verify. If the program director does not have the time to follow up on each classroom, then they should make sure that the staff are incorporating outside activities into their weekly lesson plans to remind the staff of the requirement.

RESOLUTION

Because Mary and Laren were not taking the children outside daily, they were reprimanded, retrained on the center's outdoor-play policy, and required to sign an acknowledgement statement. Alexander placed Emerson on increased monitoring, meaning that Emerson was required to complete increased onsite inspections with coaching for six months. Alexander also changed the outdoor schedule, which stated that the infants would go outside whenever possible, to state that each child in the infant classroom would go outside once a day either in the morning or afternoon. The infants would not have to go outside as a group, but each child should be taken outside each day.

PARENT RESISTANCE TO OUTDOOR PLAY

For a variety of reasons, parents may object to staff taking the children outside. They may think that the weather is too chilly, too hot, or too wet for outdoor play. Some may think that the cold or rain will make their child sick, which is a myth. Of course, the child was outside before arriving at the center.

The Norwegian adage is true: "There's no bad weather, only bad clothing." Rachel Larimore, author of *Preschool Beyond Walls* (2019) advises:

> [G]enerally speaking, clothing is appropriate if it keeps you dry, helps you maintain a comfortable body temperature, helps protect the skin against sun damage, and keeps out any wind. Appropriate clothing can get dirty. It also allows you enough freedom of movement to run, jump, bend, and so on. Appropriate footwear will keep your feet comfortable and dry . . .

Other parents may think that outdoor time interferes with children's learning. Of course, that is not true. Children are made to move. In their book *Move to Learn*, Joye Newman and Miriam Feinberg (2015) advise that "movement experiences buil[d] a foundation for the development of sensory, visual, and perceptual motor skills, allowing children to concentrate on learning." In fact, researchers have found that children focus better after outdoor play. Claire McCarthy (2020), senior editor at Harvard Health Publishing, lists six reasons children should play outside, including the positive effect on *executive function*, which she defines as "skills that help us plan, prioritize, troubleshoot, negotiate, and multitask."

Help parents understand that their children should go outside daily. Explain that outside time is an extension of the classroom where children have opportunities to develop their social, emotional, and language skills, as well as physical abilities.

Parent Does Not Want Child to Play Outside

Dawn arrived at the preschool classroom to pick up Raffaele, and the knees of his pants were dirty. She complained that she did not want him to go outside again because she was taking him to a play date after school and, now, she had to take him home first to change his clothes. Baptiste, the preschool teacher, stated that he was sorry that she would be inconvenienced and if it would help, she was welcome to leave additional clothes at the center that Raffaele could change into after playing outside. Dawn refused to leave extra clothes because she did not want him to go outside. Baptiste explained that keeping Raffaele inside was not an option because all of the children were taken outside twice a day, once in the morning and once in the afternoon, as part of their daily routine.

Dawn was not happy with Baptiste's response. She left the classroom and went to the program director's office, where she explained her concerns about Raffaele's dirty knees and reiterated her request that he no longer go outside. Erick, the program director, explained that Raffaele really enjoys digging outside, which is how his knees were getting dirty. He stated that it would not be fair to Raffaele to ask him to stop an activity that he truly loves. Dawn said she was going to call in a complaint to the state because she did not want Raffaele to go outside. Erick provided Dawn with the phone number for Alim, the center's licensing consultant.

Once Dawn left the center, Erick emailed Alim and informed him about the situation and wrote that Dawn might file a complaint against the center. Dawn did call Alim and expressed her concern with the center's refusal to honor her request. Alim was aware of the situation, so he listened and explained that the center was following the state licensing requirements by taking the children outside. Alim told Dawn that the center would be in violation if they did not take the children outside each day. He also informed her that if she were to enroll Raffaele in any other center in the state, her son would still be required to go outside daily. Alim apologized but said he was not going to be able to help her because the center was following the rules that were put in place to provide a developmentally appropriate learning experience for the children. Dawn disenrolled Raffaele from the center because the center would not honor her request.

PROBLEM

The outdoor policy should be included in the parent handbook that is provided when they enroll a child in a program. Additionally, a center should require each child to have an extra change of clothes at the center in case he has an accident or his clothes get wet or dirty. This would help the parents to understand that their child may get dirty while playing outside.

RESOLUTION

Erick's email to Alim was a smart decision. It is a good idea to inform your licensing consultant when you think that a complaint will be made against the center. That way, the consultant has both sides of the story and can explain the rules to the parents when necessary. This creates a partnership between the program director and the consultant.

SUPERVISION OUTDOORS

Many teachers can be found standing around on the playground, not engaging with the children. Often, the reasons are that the director does not require staff to address outdoor play in their weekly lesson plans and the curriculum used may not address outdoor play. Staff may use outdoor time as a break from the day, not paying attention to the children in the same way that they do within the classroom. Consequently, children can be injured on the playground. The best way to reduce accidents is by checking the area, watching the children, and planning outdoor activities.

Blind Spots Outside

Some preschool children had discovered an area behind a shed near the playground. There, they found a bucket and, for whatever reason, were urinating in it. This went on for weeks before a child went home smelling of urine. When the parent questioned her child, the child explained about the bucket behind the shed and said that the bucket had spilled by accident. When the parent asked the teacher, she had no idea that the children had been going behind the shed and urinating in a bucket.

PROBLEM

A blind spot is any area where the staff are unable to see the children from every vantage point. Having blind spots is not a safe situation for children. If staff cannot see the children, they are not able to provide appropriate care and supervision. Staff should check for blind spots by walking around the play area and the adjacent areas, observing them from different vantage points. Remember that children will crawl into small spaces to hide, so staff should check in the play structures, behind buildings, and anywhere else a child could squeeze into.

RESOLUTION

The teacher informed the director of the situation. The program director had a handyman build a fence so that the children could not access the area near the shed.

Many early childhood programs feature large play structures on the playgrounds. While these may attract families, they leave little room for engagement or creativity on the part of the child or staff. When I see a large playscape I also tend to see staff standing around or sitting on benches on the side of the playground not engaging with the children. In most of these cases where there is a large playscape, the teachers are not utilizing the outdoor space as an extension of the classroom.

If a center does include a large play structure, it should be checked and inspected regularly, even if the state only requires the play equipment to be inspected once. All equipment, after years or months of use, will need repair, and the need for repair is not always visible by the undiscerning eye. Have the structure inspected by a certified playground inspector. (See the appendix for resources related to playground and center safety.) White and Coleman (2000) state, "as in the classroom, playground learning centers that support active play (e.g., climbing, swinging, running, riding) should be grouped together and separated from less active play areas (e.g., gardening, sandbox, reading, nature study)."

Playgrounds that include natural elements, such as logs, trees, stones, grass over hills for the children to crawl on, stumps, and gardens (flowers, vegetables, or fruit) offer many more ways for children to explore, investigate, imagine, and challenge themselves. It is easy to create art and music and dramatic play (including imaginary cooking) areas outdoors. Keep in mind that whatever type of playground material you decide to incorporate outside for the children, it should be checked daily to make sure that the area is still safe for the children. For example, I was once at a center where I noticed several squirrels on the playground, which backs up to the local park. I saw that a bag of dry corn had been left out on the playground under a table. The squirrels had torn the bag open, but the staff had not noticed. Over the course of the day, many squirrels had converged on to the playground, posing a possible risk to any child who wandered too close. When I pointed this out to the staff, they discarded the bag and tossed what little corn remained over the fence.

PLAYGROUND TRANSITIONS

Of course, sometimes children will become so engrossed in their play outside that they do not hear a teacher asking them to line up, or they will hide to avoid going back indoors. Staff must be especially careful to match children's names and faces as they transition to the classroom.

Two Preschool Children Left on the Playground

Eliana, the program director, was called down to the toddler classroom by Bella, the toddler assistant caregiver, because a child had hit his head while coming in from outside and needed an ice pack. While Eliana was in the toddler classroom, Beverly, the toddler lead caregiver, told her that she had looked outside a few minutes earlier and had seen a child named Mason from the preschool classroom standing alone on the playground. She had sent Bella outside to get him and bring him into the toddler classroom until they could get a preschool teacher to come get him.

Just about then, Mila, the lead caregiver from the preschool classroom, came to pick up the stray preschooler. She said that another child from the preschool room, Noah, was also missing and had been left outside. Mila went out to the playground to look for him and found him sitting in the play structure tower. She brought him inside.

Eliana was upset and confused as to how two children from the same classroom were left outside alone on the playground. Eliana then questioned all of the staff involved before contacting the parents. Bella explained that the toddler and preschool classes had been on the playground together. The toddler class had exited the playground first and had been inside for about ten minutes before Beverly told her that she saw a preschooler outside alone. Bella said that when she brought Mason in, he seemed a bit confused as he did not know where his friends and teachers were. Beverly called Mila to tell her that Mason had been left outside and that she needed to come to their classroom to get him.

Mila said that she had been distracted because a child had bumped his head right as all of the children were heading inside, and she had failed to do a proper name-to-face check at the door to the playground. She said that when they got all the children back into the preschool room, she began the name-to-face check and realized that two children, Mason and Noah, were missing. She left her assistant with the class and headed to the toddler classroom to retrieve Mason, and then went outside to bring Noah in. Noah was not crying and did not appear upset. She stated that Mason and Noah must have left the line when the rest of their classmates were walking back inside.

PROBLEM

Name-to-face checks must be completed anytime children are moved from one room to another or back and forth from the building to the playground.

RESOLUTION

Eliana changed the policy because, previously, the staff was required to complete the name-to-face checks, but they were not required to check off the children's names on the attendance sheets. She retrained the staff on the center's supervision policy and on properly completing the name-to-face sheets. She called Mason's and Noah's parents to inform them that their children had been left outside alone for a brief period of time. Both parents were happy to hear that the staff were being retrained, and they felt confident that the situation would not occur again.

To prevent children from being left outside, the program director can stage mock incidents of missing children to give the staff practice in what to do. Testing the staff will help them to recognize the seriousness of the situation. The director can also do random checks to see whether staff have an accurate count of the children who are present. The staff should know how many children they have in their classrooms at all times. If the staff are not aware of the number of children that are present, or if their name-to-face sheets are not accurate, they would need retraining. The key is to ensure that all staff are responsible for the children.

If a caregiver has the misfortune of actually misplacing a child, the caregiver should acknowledge her mistake and take the necessary steps to ensure it does not occur again. When a child is misplaced, it is never the fault of the child. The caregiver is responsible for the child's safety. If the caregiver is not willing or able to accept responsibility, they should not be working with children.

Time spent outdoors is valuable learning time. Staff should engage with the children and provide an extension from the classroom with activities outside. They should include outdoor activities on their lesson plans that they submit to the program director for review. The outdoor play area should be safe and the activities should be appropriate for the children. The program director should observe the staff outside on the playground to ensure that the staff are engaging with the children.

Appendix: Online Resources

Child Development and Developmentally Appropriate Practice

Center on the Developing Child at Harvard University: https://developingchild.harvard.edu/

Center on the Social and Emotional Foundations for Early Learning: http://csefel.vanderbilt.edu/

Child Development: https://www.naeyc.org/resources/position-statements/dap/principles

Developmentally Appropriate Practice: https://www.naeyc.org/resources/topics/dap

Zero to Three: https://www.zerotothree.org/

Head Start

Early Childhood Learning and Knowledge Center: https://eclkc.ohs.acf.hhs.gov/

Licensing and Support

Child Care Aware of America: https://www.childcareaware.org/about/child-care-aware-of-america/

National Database of Child Care Licensing Regulations: https://licensingregulations.acf.hhs.gov/

Programs that Support Early Learning: https://www.ed.gov/early-learning/programs

Playground Safety

Find a Playground Inspector in Your State: https://www.playgroundsafety.org/certified/school

Public Playground Safety Handbook: https://www.cpsc.gov/s3fs-public/325.pdf

Safer Playgrounds, Safer Play for Kids: https://www.cpsc.gov/safety-education/safety-guides/kids-and-babies/safer-playgrounds-safer-play-kids

Poison Safety

Kids and Babies: https://www.cpsc.gov/Safety-Education/Kids-and-Babies

Safe Sleep Practices

Cribs: https://www.cpsc.gov/safety-education/safety-guides/kids-and-babies/cribs

Safe Sleep for Babies: https://www.cdc.gov/vitalsigns/safesleep/

Special Education/Exceptional Children

Division for Early Childhood of the Council for Exceptional Children: https://www.dec-sped.org/

Teacher Training and Professional Development

The Care Courses School Inc.: https://www.carecourses.com/PublicPages/Home.aspx

Child Care Training Information by Location: https://www.carecourses.com/PublicPages/StateInformation.aspx

ChildCare Education Institute: https://www.cceionline.com/child-care-staff-training/

Council for Professional Recognition Child Development Associate (CDA): https://www.cdacouncil.org/en/ed Web: https://home.edweb.net/

North American Reggio Emilia Alliance: https://www.reggioalliance.org/

T.E.A.C.H. Early Childhood: https://www.teachecnationalcenter.org/teach-early-childhood/

Teaching Our Youngest: https://www2.ed.gov/teachers/how/early/teachingouryoungest/teachingouryoungest.pdf

World Forum Foundation: https://worldforumfoundation.org/about-us/

References and Recommended Reading

Administration for Children and Families, US Department of Health and Human Services. n.d. National Database of Child Care Licensing Regulations. https://licensingregulations.acf.hhs.gov/

American Academy of Pediatrics. 2020. "Healthy Sleep Habits: How Many Hours Does Your Child Need?" HealthyChildren.org. https://www.healthychildren.org/English/healthy-living/sleep/Pages/healthy-sleep-habits-how-many-hours-does-your-child-need.aspx

American Journal of Play. 2020. "Play as a Basic Pathway to the Self: An Interview with Thomas S. Henricks." American Journal of Play 7(3): 271–297. https://www.journalofplay.org/sites/www.journalofplay.org/files/pdf-articles/7-3-interview-play-as-a-basic-pathway--to-the-self.pdf

Arizona Department of Health Services, Bureau of Child Care Licensing. 2019. *Arizona Administrative Code and Arizona Revised Statutes for Child Care Facilities*. Phoenix, AZ: Author. https://www.azdhs.gov/documents/director/administrative-counsel-rules/rules/sps/bccl-facility-rules.pdf

Bennett, William J., Chester E. Finn, Jr., and John T. E. Cribb, Jr. 1999. *The Educated Child: A Parent's Guide from Preschool through Eighth Grade*. New York: The Free Press.

Bond, Thomasa. 2020. *Build Your Dream Team*: How to Recruit, Train, and Retain Early Childhood Staff. Lewisville, NC: Gryphon House.

Bond, Thomasa. 2021. *Dr. Thomasa Bond* (blog). https://www.drthomasa.com/

Boyd, Brenda J., and B. Kay Pasley. 1989. "Role Stress as a Contributor to Burnout in Child Care Professionals." *Child and Youth Care Quarterly* 18(4): 243–258.

Centers for Disease Control and Prevention. 2021a. "Child Abuse and Neglect Prevention." Violence Prevention, Centers for Disease Control and Prevention. https://www.cdc.gov/violenceprevention/childabuseandneglect/index.html

Centers for Disease Control and Prevention. 2021b. "What to Do If an Infant or Child Is Mistakenly Fed Another Woman's Expressed Breast Milk." Breastfeeding, Centers for Disease Control and Prevention. https://www.cdc.gov/breastfeeding/recommendations/other_mothers_milk.htm

Chambers, Harry E. 2001. *Finding, Hiring, and Keeping Peak Performers: Every Manager's Guide.* Cambridge, MA: Perseus.

Chawla, Sarita, and John Renesch, eds. 2006. *Learning Organizations: Developing Cultures for Tomorrow's Workplace.* Portland, OR: Productivity Press.

Ciulla, Joanne B, ed. 2014. *Ethics: The Heart of Leadership.* Westport, CT: Praeger.

Cohen, E. Lynn, and Sandra Waite-Stupiansky, eds. 2017. *Theories of Early Childhood Education: Developmental, Behaviorist, and Critical.* New York: Routledge.

Cohen, E. Lynn, and Sandra Waite-Stupiansky, eds. 2020. *STEM in Early Childhood Education: How Science, Technology, Engineering, and Mathematics Strengthen Learning.* New York: Routledge.

Cooper, Dominic, Ivan T. Robertson, and Gordon Tinline. 2003. *Recruitment and Selection: A Framework for Success.* London, UK: Cengage.

Decker, Celia A., and John R. Decker. 2005. *Planning and Administering Early Childhood Programs.* 8th ed. Upper Saddle River, NJ: Pearson Merrill.

Duncan, Jacqueline, and Madelaine Lockwood. 2008. *Learning through Play: A Work-Based Approach for the Early Years Professional.* New York, NY: Continuum International.

Ernst, Johnna D. 2014. *The Welcoming Classroom: Building Strong Home-to-School Connections for Early Learning.* Lewisville, NC: Gryphon House.

Friedman, Susan, Brian L. Wright, and Marie L. Masterson, eds. 2021. *Developmentally Appropriate Practice in Early Childhood Programs: Serving Children from Birth Through Age 8.* 4th ed. Washington, DC: National Association for the Education of Young Children.

Gini, Al, and Ronald M. Green. 2014. "Moral Leadership and Business Ethics." In *Ethics, the Heart of Leadership*. Westport, CT: Praeger

Hart, Susan. 2011. *The Impact of Attachment: Developmental Neuroaffective Psychology*. The Norton Series on Interpersonal Neurobiology. New York: W. W. Norton and Company.

Heidemann, Sandra, and Deborah Hewitt. 2010. *Play: The Pathway from Theory to Practice*. 2nd ed. St. Paul, MN: Redleaf.

Kemple, Kristen. 2017. *Planning for Play: Strategies for Guiding Preschool Learning*. Lewisville, NC: Gryphon House.

Larimore, Rachel A. 2019. *Preschool Beyond Walls*: Blending Early Childhood Education and Nature-Based Learning. Lewisville, NC: Gryphon House.

Machado, Jeanne. M. 2007. *Early Childhood Experiences in Language Arts: Early Literacy*. 8th ed. Clifton Park, NY: Thomson Delmar Learning.

Marquardt, Michael J. 2011. *Building the Learning Organization: Achieving Strategic Advantage through a Commitment to Learning*. Boston, MA: Nicholas Brealey.

Maxim, George W. 1992. *The Very Young: Guiding Children from Infancy through the Early Years*. 4th ed. New York: Macmillan.

Mayo Clinic. 2021. "Nutrition for Kids: Guidelines for a Healthy Diet." Healthy Lifestyle, Children's Health, Mayo Clinic. https://www.mayoclinic.org/healthy-lifestyle/childrens-health/in-depth/nutrition-for-kids/art-20049335

McCarthy, Claire. 2020. "6 Reasons Children Need to Play Outside." *Harvard Health Blog*. https://www.health.harvard.edu/blog/6-reasons-children-need-to-play-outside-2018052213880

Michigan Department of Health and Human Services. 2021. "Children's Protective Services." Michigan Department of Health and Human Services. https://www.michigan.gov/mdhhs/0,5885,7-339-73971_7119_50648---,00.html

Mississippi State Department of Health, Child Care Facilities Licensure Division. 2019. *Regulations Governing Licensure of Child Care Facilities*. Jackson, MS: Author. https://msdh.ms.gov/msdhsite/_static/resources/78.pdf

Morrison, George S. 2008. *Fundamentals of Early Childhood Education*. 5th ed. Upper Saddle River, NJ: Pearson.

National Association for the Education of Young Children. 2019. *Professional Standards and Competencies for Early Childhood Educators*. Position statement. Washington, DC: National Association for the Education of Young Children.

National Association for Education of Young Children. 2021. *Developmentally Appropriate Practice.* Position statement. https://www.naeyc.org/sites/default/files/globally-shared/downloads/PDFs/resources/position-statements/dap-statement_0.pdf

Nemours KidsHealth. 2019. "Sleep and Your 1- to 2-Year-Old." Parents, Nemours KidsHealth. https://kidshealth.org/en/parents/sleep12yr.html

Newman, Joye, and Miriam Feinberg. 2015. *Move to Learn: Integrating Movement into the Early Childhood Curriculum.* Lewisville, NC: Gryphon House.

Northouse, Peter G. 2021. *Introduction to Leadership: Concept and Practice.* 5th ed. Thousand Oaks, CA: SAGE.

Osland, Joyce S., and Marlene E. Turner. 2010. *The Organizational Behavior Reader.* 9th ed. Upper Saddle River, NJ: Pearson.

Pyle, Angela, Martin Pyle, Jessica Prioletta, and Betül Alaca. 2020. "Portrayals of Play-Based Learning: Misalignments among Public Discourse, Classroom Realities, and Research." *American Journal of Play* 13(1): 53–86.

Reno, Hilde, Janet Stutzman, and Judy Zimmerman. 2008. *Handbook for Early Childhood Administrators: Directing with a Mission.* Boston, MA: Pearson.

Robbins, Stephen P., David A. DeCenzo, and Robert M. Wolter. 2019. *Supervision Today!* 9th ed. New York: Pearson.

Sergiovanni, Thomas. J. 2007. *Rethinking Leadership: A Collection of Articles.* Thousand Oaks, CA: SAGE.

Shoemaker, Cynthia. 1999. *Leadership and Management of Programs for Young Children.* 2nd ed. Upper Saddle River, NJ: Pearson.

Stanford Children's Health. 2021. "Nursemaid's Elbow in Children." Stanford Children's Health. https://www.stanfordchildrens.org/en/topic/default?id=nursemaids-elbow-90-P02772

State of Alaska Department of Health and Social Services, Division of Public Assistance, Child Care Program Office. 2020. *Child Care Licensing Policies and Procedures Manual.* Anchorage, AK: Author. https://dhss.alaska.gov/dpa/Documents/dpa/programs/ccare/Documents/Manuals-Brochures/Child-Care-Licensing-Policy-and-Procedure-Manual.pdf

State of Michigan, Bureau of Community and Health Systems, Child Care Licensing Division, Licensing and Regulatory Affairs (LARA). 2019. *Licensing Rules for Child Care Centers.* Lansing, MI: Author. https://www.michigan.gov/documents/lara/BCAL_PUB_8_3_16_523999_7.pdf

State of Montana, Department of Public Health and Human Services, Licensure Bureau—Child Care Licensing. 2018. *Licensing Requirements for Child Care Centers*. Helena, MT: Author. https://dphhs.mt.gov/assets/ecfsd/childcarelicensing/LicensingRequirementsforChildCareCenters.pdf

Trawick-Smith, Jeffrey. 2020. *Young Children's Play: Development, Disabilities, and Diversity*. New York: Routledge.

US Department of Agriculture. 2013. "Nutrition Standards for CACFP Meals and Snacks." Child and Adult Care Food Program, USDA. https://www.fns.usda.gov/cacfp/meals-and-snacks

US Department of Agriculture. 2021. "Feeding the Future with Healthy School Lunches." National School Lunch Program, USDA. https://www.fns.usda.gov/nslp

Wah, Alejandra. 2020. "Cognitive Processes Underlying Play and Pretend Play: A Comparative Cross-Species Study on Degrees of Memory, Perception, Imagination, and Consciousness." *American Journal of Play* 12(2): 156–177.

Waite-Stupiansky, Sandra. 2017. "Jean Piaget's Constructivist Theory of Learning." In *Theories of Early Childhood: Developmental, Behaviorist, and Critical*. New York: Routledge.

Washington Administrative Code (WAC). 2021. Chapter 110-300 WAC Foundational Quality Standards for Early Learning Programs. http://app.leg.wa.gov/WAC/default.aspx?cite=110-300

Weiser, Margaret G. 1991. *Infant/Toddler Care and Education*. 2nd ed. Upper Saddle River, NJ: Pearson Merrill.

White, C. Stephen, and Mick Coleman. 2000. *Early Childhood Education: Building a Philosophy for Teaching*. Upper Saddle River, N. J: Pearson.

Index

A

Abandonment, 46
Accreditation, 2
Adult-to-child ratios, 36, 91–97
  challenging behaviors, 158
  issues related to, 95–97
Alaska
  adult-to-child ratios, 93
  licensing requirements, 25
  requirements for program directors, 12–14
Alcohol. *See* Intoxication
American Academy of Pediatrics, 150
Arizona Department of Health Services, 93
Arizona
  adult-to-child ratios, 92
  licensing requirements, 25, 26–28
  parent handbook requirements, 140, 143
  requirements for program directors, 12–14
  square footage requirements, 91–92
Assessment, 8

B

Background checks, 30–31
Being open to growth and change, 8–9
Being supportive, 6–7
Benefits and incentives, 15–16
Best practices, 126–130
Biting, 159–162
Blind spots, 60, 102, 107, 192–193
Blocks/construction center
  infant room, 99
  preschool classroom, 105
  toddler room, 100
Boiler, furnace, water-heater inspection records, 25
Books/language/literacy center
  infant room, 98
  preschool classroom, 104
  toddler room, 100
Budgeting, 2, 15
Building and equipment, vi, 2
  leaking roof, 35–36
  maintenance and safety, 33–44

no heat, 38–39
playground injury, 40–42
rodents on the playground, 39–40
transportation, 42–44
water not working, 36–37
Bullying
by parents, 146–147
in the classroom, 164–165
Business models, vi, 9–11
chain centers, 9–10, 15-18
corporate centers, 10–11, 15–18, 88–89
franchise centers, 10, 15–16, 18, 89
government-funded child care, 11, 15–16, 18, 89
privately owned centers, 11, 15–16, 18, 88

C

Categorizing information, 8
Celebrating diversity, 134–137
Centers for Disease Control and Prevention, 45, 50
Chain centers, 9–10
hiring for, 15
policies and procedures, 17–18
training, 16
Challenges
biting, 159–162
bullies, 164–165
discipline issues, 1
discipline vs. punishment, 162–164
staff verbal and physical abuse, 165–168
with children's behavior, vi–vii, 157–168
with parents, vi–vii, 139–155
with staff, vi–vii, 169–186
Change
weighing the costs and benefits, 8
Child abuse and neglect, 45–48, 165–168
Child custody issues, 147–148
Child development associate credential, 12–13, 15–16
Child protective services, 45, 47–48
Childcare Development Associate certification, 172
Children with special needs
online resources, 198
policies and procedures, 22
Children's behavior
biting, 159–162
bullies, 164–165
challenges, vi–vii, 157–168
discipline issues, 1
discipline vs. punishment, 162–164
staff verbal and physical abuse, 165–168
Child-use spaces, 26
Choking hazards, 34
Class pets, 27
Classroom arrangement and management, vi, 91–113
adult-to-child ratios, 91–97
approved capacity, 91–97
celebrating diversity, 134–137
challenging behaviors, 158
daily schedule, 109–113
design and set-up, 97–108
discipline issues, 108
infant and toddler classrooms, 97–102
preschool classroom, 103–107
sample problems, 93, 96–97, 108, 112–113
Compromise, 169
Computer center
preschool classroom, 106
Construction play, 122
Continuing education units, 12, 15, 172
Corporate centers, 10–11
hiring for, 15
policies and procedures, 17–18
training, 16
policy for interacting with the media, 88–89
Council for Early Childhood Professional Recognition, 13

COVID-19
  confusion about drop-off procedures, 62–63
  families not allowed in centers, 152
Creative/art center
  infant room, 99
  preschool classroom, 105
  toddler room, 101
Creativity
  open-ended products, 132–133
  play and, 124
Cribs, 198
Criminal background checks, 14–15
Critical thinking skills, 131
Custodial care, 118

D

Daily schedule, 109
  challenging behaviors, 158
  sample for preschool, 109–110
  sample for toddlers, 109
  transitions, 110–113
  visual, 110
Deciding what children should learn, 131–134
Demeaning children, 166–167, 170–171
Developmentally appropriate practices, vi, 10, 121–137
  best practices, 126–130
  celebrating diversity, 134–137
  deciding what children should learn, 131–134
  importance of play, 122–125
  online resources, 197
  role of the teacher, 125–126
Discipline issues, 1, 73–79
  classroom setup and, 108
  issues around, 170–171
  not following policy, 5–6
  policies and procedures, 24, 28
  vs. punishment, 162–164
Distance Education Accrediting Commission, 172
Diversity. *See* Celebrating diversity
Documentation
  licensing, 25–27
  transportation, 42–43
Dramatic play center
  infant room, 99
  preschool classroom, 106
  toddler room, 101
Drug use
  by parents, 148–149
  by staff, 178–180
Dual-language learners, 134–137

E

Early childhood education certificate, 13
Electrical outlets, 33
Emergency and evacuation plans, 26
Emotional development. *See* Social/emotional development
Enrollment issues, 144–145
Environmental health inspection records, 25
Environmental problems, 85–87
Equipment and materials lists, 25
  infant room, 98–99
  preschool classroom, 104–107
  toddler room, 100–101
Evacuation drills, 90
Exceptional children. *See* Children with special needs
Executive function, 190

F

Failure to protect, 46
Fear of retaliation, 153
Fee policies, 24, 26
Feedback for staff, 4
Field trips
  keeping track of children, 71–72
  scheduling, 1

Fine motor center
  infant room, 99
  toddler room, 101
Fine motor skills
  play and, 121, 123
Fire safety, 90
  drills, 90
  inspection records, 25
  inspections, 34–35
Food service
  allergies, 50–51
  policy, 24
  program plan, 26
Franchise centers, 10
  hiring for, 15–16
  policies and procedures, 18
  policy for interacting with the media, 89
  training, 16

G

Games with rules, 122
Good faith, 47
Government-funded child care, 11
  hiring for, 15
  policies and procedures, 18
  policy for interacting with the media, 89
  training, 16
Gross motor center
  infant room, 99
  preschool classroom, 106
  toddler room, 101
Gross motor skills
  play and, 121, 124

H

Head Start, v, 11, 197
Health, vi, 45–90
  child abuse and neglect, 45–48
  discipline, 73–79
  fire safety, 90
  hygiene, 57–59
  interacting with the media, 88–89
  management of injuries and emergencies, 82–85
  mandated reporting, 47–48
  medication administration and care of sick children, 79–82
  nutrition and food handling, 48–54
  sleep, 54–57
  supervision of children, 59–73
  surveillance of environmental problems, 85–88
Hiring, 1, 14–16
Hot-glue guns, 85–87
Hygiene, 57–59

I

Imagination
  play and, 124
Improper supervision
  by a parent or caretaker, 46
  by center staff, 59–73
Infants
  caring for, 115–120
  emotional development, 118–119
  equipment and materials list, 98–99
  language development, 120
  outdoor play, 188
  physical development, 119
  primary caregivers, 115–117
  room setup, 97–98, 102
  supporting curiosity, 131
Injuries and emergencies, 82–85
Insubordination, 173–174
Interacting with the media, 88–89
International Accreditors of Continuing Education and Training, 172
Interpersonal skills, 3–4
Intoxication
  parents, 148–150
  staff, 178–180

L

Language development, 120
  play and, 122–123
Lead caregivers, 171–173
  not fully qualified, 172–173
Lead hazard risk assessment records, 25
Learning organization, 8
Lesson plans
  reviewing, 2
Licensing and Regulatory Affairs for the State of Michigan, 93
Licensing, v–vi, 23–31
  documentation, 24–27
  for program directors, 12–13
  maintaining compliance, 2
  online resources, 198
  policies and practices, 27–28
  sample problems, 29–31
  state policy changes, 29–31
  typical state policy requirements, 23–28
Literacy skills, 124
Lockwood, M., 187–188

M

Maintaining professionalism, 171–186
Mandated reporter responsibility, 47–48
Manipulatives/math center
  preschool classroom, 107
  toddler room, 100
Marketing, 2
Math skills
  play and, 124
Mayo Clinic, 48
Meals
  cooking and serving, 2
  open plan, 111
  when parents send junk food, 151–152
Medication
  administration, 79–82
  policy, 24
Memory skills
  play and, 122
Menu planning, 2
  policies and procedures, 27
Michigan
  adult-to-child ratios, 93
  Department of Health and Human Services, 46
  fire drills, 90
  licensing requirements, 25, 27, 29
  licensing rules, 132
  parent handbook requirements, 140, 142
  square footage requirements, 92
  state requirements for program directors, 12–14
  tornado drills, 90
Micromanagement vs. hands-on modeling, 4–6
Mississippi Department of Health and Human Services, 93
Mississippi
  adult-to-child ratios
  Department of Health and Human Services, 13
  fire drills, 90
  first-aid certification required, 82
  state requirements for program directors, 12–14
Modeling, 4–6
Montana
  adult-to-child ratios, 93
  state requirements for program directors, 12–14
Montessori Accreditation Commission, 13
Montessori approach, 131
Montessori credential, 12–14
Move to Learn (Newman & Feinberg), 190
Music center
  infant room, 98
  preschool classroom, 104
  toddler room, 100

N

Name-to-face checks, 60–61
National Association for the Education of Young Children, 15, 97, 110, 121, 123, 136
National Child Abuse Hotline, 47
National Database of Child-Care Licensing Regulations, 12–13, 198
Nemours KidsHealth, 54
Nursemaid's elbow, 84–85
Nutrition and food handling, 48–54
Nutrition plans, 26

O

Object play, 122
Observation, v, 1, 131
    challenging behaviors, 158
Occupational therapists
    working with, 2
Open-door policy, 1, 3, 6–7, 144
Open-ended products, 132–133
Open-ended questions, 127, 131
Outdoor play, vii, 187–194
    age-appropriate equipment, 87–88
    child left alone on the playground, 66–67
    daily, 187–189
    injury, 40–42
    online resources, 198
    parent resistance to, 189–191
    playground transitions, 192–194
    rodents, 39–40
    supervision, 191–192

P

Paddling, 167–168
Parent handbooks, 17, 20–22, 140–142
    children with special needs, 21–22
    state requirements, 140–143
Parents
    challenges with, vi–vii, 139–155
    communicating about an injury, 83–84
    custody issues, 147–148
    daily communication with, 116–117
    disgruntled, 143–144
    enrollment, 144–145
    failure to pick up their child, 73
    fear of retaliation, 153
    informing of a formula mix-up, 50–51
    informing of a playground injury, 40–42
    informing of problems at the center, 35–40
    intoxicated or under the influence, 148–150
    obtaining permission to give meds, 80
    parenting practices, 150–151
    peer pressure, 146–147
    raising concerns about child's treatment, 75–79
    resistance to outdoor play, 189–192
    staff turnover, 153–155
    tuition payment and collections, 145
Paying bills, 1
Payment plan options, 145
Payroll, 2
Pedagogy, vi, 121
Peer pressure
    parental, 146–147
People skills. *See* Interpersonal skills
Pets. *See* Class pets
Physical abuse. *See* Child abuse
Physical development, 119
Planning for Play (Kemple), 122
Play, 121–125
Play facilitators, 127
Play partners, 127
Playground. *See* Outdoor play
Playground safety inspection records, 25
Poison safety
    online resources, 198
Policies and procedures, 17–20
    discipline, 24
    exclusion for child illness, 24
    fees, 24
    food-service, 24

inspections, 24
licensing, 26–28
medication, 24
on handling children who are ill, 81–82
open-door, 1, 3, 6–7
transportation, 24
volunteers, 19–20
written, 186
Positive reinforcement, 28
Potty accidents, 58–59
Preschool Beyond Walls (Larimore), 190
Preschool
attention spans, 157
classroom setup, 103, 107
curriculum, 131
equipment and materials list, 104–107
outdoor play, 188
sample daily schedule, 109–110
Pretend play, 122
Primary caregivers, 115–117
daily communication with parents, 116–117
sample problem, 117
Privately owned centers, 11
hiring for, 15–16
policy for interacting with the media, 88
politics and procedures, 18
training, 16
Proactive vs. reactive, vii
Problem solving, 121–122
Professional development
online resources, 198–199
Professional Standards and Competencies for Early Childhood Educators (NAEYC), 110, 123, 136
Program director
business models, 9–11
hands-on role model, 4–6
hiring and training staff, 1, 14–17
interacting with the media, 88–89
interpersonal skills, 3–4
open to growth and change, 8–9
parent handbook, 20–22
policies and procedures, 17–20
qualifications records, 25
qualifications, vi
qualities of, 2–3
required information, vi
role of, vi, 1–22
sample problems, 5–8, 22
state requirements for, 12–14
supportive, 6–8
Program plans, 25

R

Redirection, 28
Reggio Emilia approach, 131
Required inspection policy, 24
Rough-and-tumble play, 122

S

Safety, vi
building and equipment, 33–44
child abuse and neglect, 45–48
discipline, 73–79
fire safety, 90
health and, 45–90
hygiene, 57–59
interacting with the media, 88–89
management of injuries and emergencies, 82–85
mandated reporting, 47–48
medication administration and care of sick children, 79–82
nutrition and food handling, 48–54
sleep, 54–57
supervision of children, 59–73
surveillance of environmental problems, 85–88
online resources, 198
Sample problems
addressing policy changes, 29

age-appropriate playground equipment, 87–88
blind spots outside, 192–193
caregiver aggression, 75–79
caregiver hit a child on the hand, 5–6
caregiver pulled a child's arm, 165–166
caregivers hitting children, 74–75, 77–79
center over capacity at licensing inspection, 30
change in maximum group size, 94
child has nursemaid's elbow, 84–85
child held down on his cot, 56
child held hostage for tuition, 152
child hits head, 83–84
child injured in unapproved area, 70–71
child left alone at reception desk, 63–64
child left alone in the parking lot, 64–65
child left alone on the playground, 66–67
child left behind at pick-up time, 96–97
child left classroom and did not return, 68–69
child left in lobby, 59–61
child left unsupervised during drop-off, 62–63
child misplaced on field trip, 71–72
child sleeping in a swing, 56–57
child swallowed a bead, 102–103
children left on playground, 193–194
children not taken outside each day, 188–189
children placed in harm's way, 69–70
children with special needs, 22
communication issues, 118–119
creating a space that celebrates diversity, 134–135
disqualifying background checks, 30–31
handling bullying, 164–165
hot-glue-gun injury, 85–87
incorrect dosage administered, 81
keeping food from toddlers, 52
lead caregiver is not fully qualified, 172–173
leaking roof, 35–36
licensing consultant visits, 129–130
male caregiver told not to change diapers, 177–178
new director with a different approach, 133–134
new owner-director is threatened and intimidated by staff, 173–174
no heat, 38–39
noncustodial parent tries to pick up children, 148
ongoing biting issue, 160–162
owner discovers issues at center, 181–183
parent bullying another parent, 146–147
parent concerned that child is playing to much, 124–125
parent does not want child to play outside, 190–192
parent is intoxicated at pick up, 149–150
parent wanted to provide lunch, 151–152
parents fail to pick up their child, 73
playground injury, 40–42
police called to the center, 180–181
potty accident, 58–59
primary caregiver is concerned about a child, 117
reading an inappropriate book to the children, 130
rodents on the playground, 39–40
sanitary issues, 52–54
staff calling children names, 166–167
staff dating parents, 175–177
staff member hit a child on the hand, 163–164
staff member posts video of children fighting, 89
staff member took picture of upset child, 174–175
staff member under the influence, 178–180
staff sleeping in the classroom, 126, 183–184
staff swearing, 184–185
teacher gives OTC medication without parental permission, 80

teacher humiliated a preschooler, 170–171
threatening and swatting children with a paddle, 167–168
toddler falls asleep before lunch, 55
toddler is bitten, 159–160
toddler left outside on the playground, 112–113
toddler sleeping in a high chair, 150–151
too many hats, 7–8
transition turned hostage situation, 67–68
water not working, 36–37
wide open spaces, 108
worksheets, 7
wrong bottle of breast milk, 49–50
wrong bottle of formula, 50–51
Sanitary issues, 52–54
Scaffolding, 125
School success, 122
Science center
preschool classroom, 104
toddler room, 100
Self-regulation, 122
Sensory center
infant room, 99
preschool classroom, 104
toddler room, 100
Sexual abuse, 46
Sick children
caring for, 1, 79–82
exclusion policy, 24
Sleep, 54–57
online safe sleep resources, 198
parenting practices, 150–151
staff sleeping at center, 183–184
Social media, 88–89
Social workers
working with, 2
Social/emotional development, 118–119
play and, 122–123
Sociodramatic play, 122
Space heaters, 38
Special education. *See* Children with special needs
Specialists
supervising, 2
Speech pathologists
working with, 2
Staff handbooks, 17
Staff
addressing concerns of, 2, 3
aggression, 75–77
benefits and incentives, 15–16
building trust with, vi, 2–3
challenges with, vi–vii, 169–186
conducting meetings with, 2
creating work schedules, 30
dating parents, 175–177
evaluating, 1
files, 25
grounds for termination, 16–17
hiring and training, 1, 14–17
hitting children, 74–75, 77–79
intimidating and threating new owner-director, 173–174
issues around discipline, 170–171
maintaining professionalism, 171–186
member under the influence, 178–180
rewarding, reprimanding, and terminating, 2
sleeping in the center, 183–184
swearing, 184–185
taking pictures of upset children, 174–175
turnover, 153–155
verbal and physical abuse, 165–168
Stanford Children's Health, 84
State of Alaska Department of Health and Human Services, 93
State of Montana Department of Public Health, 93
State policy changes, 29–31
State policy requirements, 23–28
documentation, 24–27
for program directors, 12–14
policies and practices, 27–28

Supervising children, 46, 59–73, 191–193
Symbolic thinking, 121–122

T

Teacher
  online resources, 198–199
  role of, 125–126
  training, 16
Team building, 169
Termination, 16
Toddlers
  emotional development, 118–119
  equipment and materials list, 100–101
  language development, 120
  outdoor play, 188
  physical development, 119
  primary caregivers, 115–117
  room setup, 97–98, 102
  sample daily schedule, 109
  short attention span, 157
  supporting curiosity, 131
Tornado drills, 90
Transitions, 110–113
  playground, 193–195
Transportation, 42–44
  checklist, 42–43
  policy, 24
Tuition payment and collections, 145
Tummy time, 119

U

U.S. Department of Agriculture
  Child and Adult Care Food Program standards, 49
  National School Lunch and School Breakfast Program standards, 49
U.S. Department of Education, 11

V

Visual schedules, 110
Volunteers, 19–20
  supervised vs. unsupervised, 19
  supervising and screening, 2

W

Washington Administrative Code, 93
Washington
  nutrition requirements, 49
  parent handbook requirements, 140–142
  outdoor play requirements, 188
  state requirements for program directors, 12–14
Worksheets, 7, 132–133

Y

Yelling, 162